AMERICAN POETRY
SINCE 1970:
UP LATE

AMERICAN POETRY SINCE 1970: UP LATE

SELECTED AND WITH AN INTRODUCTION
BY
Andrei Codrescu

Four Walls Eight Windows, New York

First edition published by:

Four Walls Eight Windows
Post Office Box 548
Village Station
New York, New York 10014

Library of Congress Cataloging-in-Publication data

American poetry since 1970.

    1. American poetry—20th century.   I. Codrescu,
Andrei, 1946–
PS615.A426 1987   811'.54'08   87-12028
ISBN 0-941423-03-4
ISBN 0-941423-04-2 (pbk.)

Composition by Commercial Typographers of Connecticut
Designed by Hannah Lerner
Printed in U.S.A.

First printing November 1987
Second printing January 1988

ACKNOWLEDGMENTS

Grateful acknowledgment is made to the following for permission to reprint material copyrighted or controlled by them:

KAY BOYLE for "Poets," as originally printed in THIS IS NOT A LETTER, published by SUN & MOON, Los Angeles, © 1985 by Kay Boyle. Reprinted by permission of the author.

THE TED BERRIGAN ESTATE and BLUE WIND PRESS for "Lady," "Frank O'Hara," "People Who Died," "Today's News," "How to Get To Canada," "Things to Do in Providence," "Cranston Near the City Line," "Whitman in Black," "Last Poem," "People of the Future," as originally printed in SO GOING AROUND CITIES: NEW AND SELECTED POEMS 1958–1979, published by BLUE WIND PRESS, Berkeley, © 1980 & 1986. By permission of the estate and of the publisher.

MAUREEN OWEN for "African Sunday," "Novembers or straight life," from ZOMBIE NOTES, © 1985, SUN BOOKS, New York. By permission of the author.
MAUREEN OWEN and KULCHUR PRESS for ' "Some Days," Dorothy Parker said, "it's better than digging ditches," ' "for Emily Dickinson," "Three Mile Island," from HEARTS IN SPACE, © 1980, KULCHUR PRESS, New York. By permission of the author and publisher.

JOHN GODFREY and Z PRESS for "Errant," "Reveille," from WHERE THE WEATHER SUITS MY CLOTHES, © 1984, Z PRESS, Calais, Vermont. By permission of author and publisher.

ED SANDERS and P.C.C. BOOKS for "Yiddish Speaking Socialists of the Lower East Side," "The Five Feet" from HYMN TO MAPLE SYRUP & OTHER POEMS, © 1985, P.C.C. BOOKS, Woodstock, New York. By permission of author and publisher.

PHILIP LAMANTIA and CITY LIGHTS BOOKS for "Wilderness Sacred Wilderness," "Irrational," "Surrealism in the Middle Ages," "Violet Star," from MEADOWLARK WEST and BECOMING VISIBLE, © 1986 and 1981, CITY LIGHTS BOOKS, San Francisco. By permission of author and publisher.

ALICE NOTLEY AND KULCHUR PRESS for "Flowers of the Foothills & Mountain Valleys," "Poem," "Poem," "World's Bliss," from WALTZING

CONTENTS

KAY BOYLE

Poets

Poets, minor or major, should arrange to remain
   slender,
Cling to their skeletons, not batten
On provender, not fatten the lean spirit
In its isolated cell, its solitary chains.
The taut paunch ballooning in its network of veins
Explodes from the cummerbund. The hardening artery
    of neck
Cannot be masked by turtle-throated cashmere or
   foulard of mottled silk.

Poets, poets, use rags instead; use rags and consider
That Poe did not lie in the morgue swathed
Beyond recognition in fat. Consider on this late March
Afternoon, with violet and crocus outside, fragile as
   glass,
That the music of Marianne Moore's small polished
   bones

Was not muffled, the score not lost between thighs as
   thick as bass-fiddles
Or cat-gut muted by dropsy. Baudelaire did not throttle
   on corpulence,
Rimbaud not strangle on his own grease. In the
   unleafed trees, as I write,
Birds flicker, lighter than lace. They are the lean spirit,
Beaks asking for crumbs, their voices like reeds.

William Carlos Williams sat close, close to the table
  always, always,
Close to the typewriter keys, his body not held at bay
  by a drawbridge of flesh
Under his doctor's dress, no gangway to lower, letting
  the sauces,
The starches, the strong liquor, enter and exit
With bugles blowing. Over and over he was struck thin
By the mallet of beauty, the switchblade of sorrow,
  died slim as a gondola,
Died curved like the fine neck of a swan.

These were not gagged, strangled, outdone by the
  presence
Of banquet selves. They knew words make their way
  through navel and pore,
More weightless as thistle, as dandelion drift,
  unencumbered.
Death happens to fatten on poets' glutted hearts.
  ("Dylan!"
Death calls, and the poet scrambles drunk and alone to
  what were once swift, bony feet,
Casting a monstrous shadow of gargantuan flesh before
  he crashes.)

Poets, remember your skeletons. In youth or dotage,
  remain as light as ashes.

*

UP LATE: AN INTRODUCTION
by *Andrei Codrescu*

The 1960 Grove Press anthology of "New American Poetry" (later enlarged somewhat and retitled "The Postmoderns") has been one of the most influential books in the history of American poetry. It introduced the Beat Poets, the Black Mountain Poets and the first generation of New York School Poets into a scene dominated mostly by academics. In the 1950s and well into the 1960s the term "academic" meant a poet liked by professors. Some of these poets became professors themselves—uneasily. A "respectable" poet was an odd notion, and the early poet-professors drank themselves to death trying to be both. The conventional history of modern American poetry, which the 1960 anthology debunked, simply recounted the academic careers of poets shrivelling under the "anxiety of influence." The poet-professors never went away, but became rather professor-poets, capable both of explicating themselves and of maintaining the conventional view against the mounting evidence. The latest such tale, "A History of Modern Poetry" (Harvard, 1987) by David Perkins, John P. Marquand Professor of English and American Literature at Harvard University, is dedicated to the proposition that poetry, like all things, has been getting worse since the days of the gods, in this case Ezra Pound and T.S. Eliot but mostly Eliot. This isn't hard to prove if one follows the conventional path carved by academic consensus in the past forty years. It is a path that leads from Eliot to his conservative epigones of the New Criticism, who included John Crowe Ransom, Allen Tate and Cleanth Brooks, the author with Robert Penn Warren of a student bible on the appreciation of poetry. From there the road goes to a drunken village of poet-professors of the 50s inhabited by folks like Ted Roethke, Robert Lowell, John Berryman, Sylvia Plath and Adrienne Rich (in her pre-feminist phase), and then it becomes a series of footpaths, the most promising of which leads to a campfire tended by the neo-primitivists Robert Bly, Gary Snyder and James Wright. Another path leads from Auden to John Ashbery and James Merrill, two poets far enough apart and sufficiently difficult to provide a thousand graduate students with raw career material. It's a neat picture. The only thing about it is that it's all wrong, ignoring as it does the other facts of the American poetry scene: hundreds of poets who feel no anxiety about T.S. Eliot or sympathy for him, the explosion of Surrealism, politics, song and performance in the past twenty years, the wealth of experiment that seriously challenges all current critical assumptions, and last but not least, the genuine popularity of poetry in an age said to have no "culture." Dr. Perkins must have stepped very lightly indeed to have noticed none of it. As Anselm Hollo writes in a poem called "The Musicians": "You missed them. They didn't miss you."

"New American Poetry" offered a different reading of the history of American poetry, one that proceeded from Whitman through Pound into the future. It also exploded many of the formal conventions that make a reading such as Dr. Perkins' possible. Being alive, most American poets in the 60s and the 70s took their license to write for granted. What is astonishing is that now, 27 years after the Grove book, the academics are back in the saddle, and that their influence through graduate writing programs, continues to spread. Certain raids on that pioneering anthology were necessary, and one finds quite a few of those poets incorporated in the canon, but in such a way as to minimize the overall meaning. That meaning, quite simply, was that one's contemporaneity is a given, and that if one is alive one has to get on with it. The point was the *making*. "You just go on your nerve," said Frank O'Hara. "If someone's chasing you down the street with a knife you just run, you don't turn around and shout, 'Give it up! I was a track star for Mineola Prep.' " And others had a score to settle. For Amiri Baraka, "The black artist's role in America is to aid in the destruction of America as he knows it." Which is a kind of re-making, an opening. Certainly not a closure.

The difficulty of making an anti-academic anthology of contemporary poetry was already evident in "New American Poetry," and had been problematic even before that, beginning with Pound's own collection of Objectivist poets. Many American poets, since Whitman, thought it necessary to write long poems because America is big. Pound's "Cantos" were never finished. William Carlos Williams tried to write *the* American poem, a long series of works that endlessly link the "things" of the continent in the measured pace of his "variable foot." Geography was also the question for Charles Olson. "I take SPACE to be the central fact of man born in America, from Folsom cave to now," is how he begins "Call Me Ishmael." Allen Ginsberg's HOWL is immense and should not be excerpted. Robert Duncan talks about the "open field." The same sense of breadth, only vertically in time, pertains to the "ethnopoetics" of Jerome Rothenberg who attempts to establish the continuity of Indian oral poetries with literary modernism. The "language poets" find language itself territorial. The effort to say something in the vastness of America seeks resolution in the long poem, whether composed of fragments or continuous speech. By their nature, anthologies lend themselves to formal miniatures, to sonnets, to small lyrics. An academic contemporary of "New American Poetry," "New Poets from England and America," edited by Donald Hall and Louis Simpson, is a "proper" anthology. It presents closed poems. The alternative anthology is rife with fragments and selections from longer works, it anthologizes the unanthologizable, it is almost an anti-anthology.

In the 1970s the clear distinctions of the year 1960 dissolved. The confusion of political radicalism with esthetic radicalism began to destroy the sophisticated polemics within American poetry. The classic anthology of this epoch is Paul Carroll's "Young American Poets" (Follett 1969). Carroll's anthology was the first to fail in a way that has since become excruciatingly familiar: it was conciliatory instead of partisan. Carroll put side by side young New York School Poets with neo-academics. Ted Berrigan and W. S. Merwin. Clark Coolidge and James Wright. Each poet had a large photograph accompanying the text. It was this photograph, more than anything else, that told the story. The soon-to-appear *American Poetry Review* serialized Carroll's anthology in this essential regard. Every poet, big or small, whether represented by one or twenty poems, has his or her photograph above the poems. Even if one were to disregard for a moment the ugly parody of the idea of newspaper that A.P.R. is (i.e., it has no news), the conceit is perfectly contemporary. The picture is the message because all pictures are equal, therefore all poets, new or old, are equal. Carroll's anthology celebrated the death of the word and gave the green light to "poets" rather than poetry. We are all poets, it said, we should stick together. The plumbers do. We should have a union. A false community was thus born in the early 1970s.

In the mid-1970s, the National Endowment for the Arts got into the picture in a big way. Avowedly apolitical, the NEA is anything but. Grant-givers are, like professors, people with a formal sense. During the same period, universities and colleges began to hire poets with academic degrees. The professor-poet became commonplace. The mandarinization of American poetry was rapid. All issues have ceased: in their place we have the photograph, the grant and the degree. This is not a case of letting "a thousand flowers bloom," nor does it signal the victory of the "academics" over the "new American poets." The distinctions between neo-academics of the 1980s and outsider poets are blurred. Every anthology after Carroll's fared a little worse: all esthetic criteria became appeals to quantitative "fairness." Editing by resume became the norm. Things have come to such a pass that the latest dishing of the kind from Morrow, a hefty 784 pages, is stocked entirely with young professors who have gone to the same schools, keeping up the class spirit with the conventional shorthand of the Workshop. The editing criterion is *sociological*. The average American poet herein, the jacket tells us, is married, has two children, has received a National Endowment for the Arts or a Guggenheim grant, and teaches in a college where he edits a small magazine.

But the past two decades have also been the most exciting years in American poetry. We have seen the emergence of black, feminist, gay and ethnic poetries. Activist poetry has been central to the philosophy of these groups and the enormous changes they have made in America. Poetic experiment flourished. Poets began collaborating with sound, and also with music and other arts. Thousands of translations from many languages appeared. Poetry was introduced to children in schools at all levels. The 1970s also brought about the prominence of the poetry reading. Until late in the 1950s, poetry readings were extremely awkward affairs. The explosion of poetry readings, and now poetry "performances," has created a new genre: poetry made to be read aloud. On any given night in San Francisco, New York, and other cities, there are four or five readings being given simultaneously in different places. Each has an audience. Blockbuster poetry readings for political or environmental causes have drawn thousands of people. The readings have provided poets with communities. But here too, fine distinctions seemed to disappear in the general chorus of goodwill generated by undiscriminating audiences. For all that, it is not very difficult to ignore the blurring of distinctions, and still speak of adversary American poetries. The status quo, while not "academic" in the old, formal sense, is still the dead weight we must struggle with. This time it is its informality that grates, because unlike the stiffer-lipped academia of the 1950s, the new establishment affects a phony ease. William Carlos Williams has been put to uses he would have never dreamt of, and has, in a sense, taken Eliot's place as the god of the workshop. In the process he has been transformed into a kind of country rube, the author of "no ideas but in things," and some poem about a red wheelbarrow. The difficult critic of culture has all but disappeared under these "things."

The true poets are operating today in a field larger than the narrows of academic or political succession. What is at stake is a certain sense of the world against a modest professionalism. The paradox of the current American poetry scene is that the undereducated hold the mainstream, while the sophisticated poets work in relative obscurity. Today's outsiders are, for the most part, within the radical mainstream of American poetry that stretches from Whitman and Dickinson through Pound and

Stein, but with the added influences of dada, Surrealism, painting, political activism, drugs and rock'n roll.

Anthologies have not reflected the enormous experimental strength of contemporary poetry. Perhaps it hasn't been possible, given the vast numbers of poets working now. The real activity has taken place in literary magazines, beginning with the great mimeos of the late 1960s, "Fuck You: A Magazine of the Arts," edited by Ed Sanders, "C," edited by Ted Berrigan, "The World," edited by Anne Waldman, on through the mid-70s with "Blue Wind," edited by George Mattingly, "Toothpaste," edited by Alan Kornblum, "Strange Faeces," by Opal L. Nations, "Big Sky," by Bill Berkson. These were magazines important to me, but there were dozens of others. They each could have produced their own anthologies. The thick university quarterlies held no fascination for working poets in the last two decades. A different world was being made by mimeo and quick offset. In the 1980s an upgrading of technology has, paradoxically, restricted the freedom of the page. Many experimental magazines now favor the prose paragraph over the exploded page. The emergence of the prose paragraph as a favorite poetic form for experimental poets in the 1980s follows directly from a continuing preoccupation with the long poem, but it is also a symptom of an inward time attempting to recoup its critical *density*. Many of the poets here work also in the shorter lyric, but as in the Grove book, one will find an extraordinary number of fragments. Important book-length poems by Clark Coolidge, Bernadette Mayer, Anne Waldman, Alice Notley, Fanny Howe, Lewis Warsh and Charles Bernstein could not be excerpted at all.

The poets presented here are various. They include mostly experimental writers born since 1945, with significant exceptions. The exceptions are poets whose continuing influence makes them less "historical" than their contemporaries. They are markers, generational bridges, lighthouses. They have been appropriated for use by this generation. There are second and third generation New York School Poets here, California Zen Surrealists, performance and "new wave" poets, erotic lyricists and "language" poets, in short, all that is new now.

Aside from the many connections among these various workers, certain (risky) generalizations can be made. Visual art has been a particular influence on many New York poets who have been closely connected to painters. Japanese and Chinese poetry, as well as Zen Buddhism, have influenced the West Coast poets. French Surrealism has been important. The questions raised by the image are everywhere. This generation has experienced a crisis of the imagination brought about by our image-clogged *fin-de-siècle*. It has become increasingly difficult to distinguish reality from the illusions of commodity culture. Our problem has been the need to redefine imagination in order to make it more real, less "imaginary." Andy Warhol was important to us because he stopped the production of images. It was sufficient to take them out of context. It's been our generational lot to sift through the debris of industreality to force reality through the cracks. "Romanticism" is no more accessible to us than true wilderness to the city dweller. We live in a defoliated world: dimming the lights is no solution. It falls to us to rethink our *place* in a world that is dis-placed, electronic, simultaneous, imaginary. New American Poetry, since Whitman, has been at odds with official culture over the facts of America. But even more than our predecessors, we have had to make an effort *not to imagine*, to abstain from images in order to get hold of the facts. At the same time there is little warmth in facts—hence the need to sing, to share, to affirm. We had to save the lyric because we had to celebrate *against* the evidence. The making of community against anti-social technology is the chief object of the poetry gathered here. Popular culture as it appears in these poems has been deconstructed for communal use. List-making, from Ted Berrigan's "Things to Do in Providence" to Trinidad's litany of best-selling girl groups from the fifties is an incantation against the organized forgetting of capitalism. The purging of the commodity church is an agonizing process and it is not ironic, though it is often hilarious. Demystifying in order to believe is steady work. Sometimes black, most often purgative, humor is one of the ritual constants of this generation, whose poetic physiognomy is shaped by an erotic and sometimes unstoppably gruesome laughter.

Our poetries may differ but they owe much to what William
Carlos Williams called "the beauties of travel": "The beauties of
travel are due to/ the strange hours we keep to see them." In the
sense that the nocturnal is open, dangerous and unpredictable,
while the diurnal is practical and planned, one might call the
poets here Romantics. This could be the case, if it were possible.
Many are "romantic," to be sure, but not in a literary sense. The
majority are anti-literary, as avantgardists have always been. This
is, however, an avantgarde without a single program, in a country
where the term "avantgarde" never even took root, having been
supplanted by the more academic and ambiguous "modernism."
There have been clashes of ideas, mainly about the role of
"language" vis-à-vis "experience." The "new romantics," (Darrell
Gray, Tom Clark, the editor) have clashed with the "language
poets," (Ron Silliman, Barrett Watten, Charles Bernstein) over this
issue, but this has not been a replay of the battle between the New
Critics and the New American poets in reverse. At issue was the
language poets' claim that language be included in the range of
experience, alongside "real" life. Since all the works included here
are verbal constructs, the argument is temporarily abolished.
Both factions are well represented here, with their poems (or
texts) intact. Whatever the differences, we have all stayed up late
in the particular faith of New American Poetry.

New Orleans, April 16, 1987

AMERICAN POETRY
SINCE 1970:
UP LATE

TED BERRIGAN

Lady

Nancy, Jimmy, Larry, Frank, & Berdie
George & Bill
        Dagwood Bumstead
                Donna, Joe, & Phil
Making shapes this place
          so rightly ours
              to fill
as we wish,
      & Andy's flowers too, do.

      I've been sitting, looking
thinking sounds of pictures
          names
            of you
        ———

of how I smile now
      &
      Let It Be.
        ———

& now I think to add
      "steel teeth"
           "sucking cigarette"
   "A photograph of Bad."
      Everything you are gone slightly mad.
    America.

      *

Frank O'Hara

Winter in the country, Southampton, pale horse
as the soot rises, then settles, over the pictures
The birds that were singing this morning have shut up
I thought I saw a couple, kissing, but Larry said no
It's a strange bird. He should know. & I think now
"Grandmother divided by monkey equals outer space." Ron
put me in that picture. In another picture, a good-
looking poet is thinking it over; nevertheless, he will
never speak of that it. But, his face is open, his eyes
are clear, and, leaning lightly on an elbow, fist below
his ear, he will never be less than perfectly frank,
listening, completely interested in whatever there may
be to hear. Attentive to me alone here. Between friends,
nothing would seem stranger to me than true intimacy.
What seems genuine, truly real, is thinking of you, how
that makes me feel. You are dead. And you'll never
write again about the country, that's true.
But the people in the sky really love
to have dinner & to take a walk with you.

*

People Who Died

Pat Dugan . . . . my grandfather . . . . throat cancer . . . . 1947.

Ed Berrigan . . . . my dad . . . heart attack . . . . 1958.

Dickie Budlong . . . my best friend Brucie's big brother, when
    we were

                five to eight . . . . killed in Korea, 1953.

Red O'Sullivan . . . hockey star & cross-country runner
                    who sat at my lunch table
                        in High School . . . car crash . . . 1954.

Jimmy "Wah" Tiernan . . . . my friend, in High School,
            Football & Hockey All-State . . . car crash . . . 1959.

Cisco Houston . . . . . . died of cancer . . . . . . 1961.

Freddy Herko, dancer . . . jumped out of a Greenwhich Village
                                        window in 1963.

Anne Kepler . . . my girl . . . killed by smoke-poisoning while
    playing
                the flute at the Yonkers Children's Hospital
                during a fire set by a 16 year old arsonist . . . 1965.

Frank . . . . Frank O'Hara . . . . hit by a car on Fire Island, 1966.

Woody Guthrie . . . . dead of Huntington's Chorea in 1968.

Neal . . . Neal Cassady . . . died of exposure, sleeping all night
                in the rain by the RR tracks of Mexico . . . 1969.

Franny Winston . . . just a girl . . . totalled her car on the
    Detroit-
                        Ann Arbor Freeway, returning
                        from the dentist . . . Sept. 1969.

Jack . . . Jack Kerouac . . . died of drink & angry sicknesses . . .
    in 1969.

My friends whose deaths have slowed my heart stay with me
    now.

*

Today's News

My body heavy with poverty (starch)
It uses up my sexual energy
    constantly, &
I feel constantly crowded

On the other hand, *One*
Day In The Afternoon of
    The World
Pervaded my life with a
    heavy grace
             today

I'll never smile again

Bad Teeth

But
I'm dancing with tears in my eyes
(I can't help myself!) Tom
writes he loves Alice's sonnets,
    takes four, I'd love

to be more attentive to her, more
    here.
The situation having become intolerable
the only alternatives are:
    Murder & Suicide.

They are too dumb! So, one
becomes a goof. Raindrops
start falling on my roof. I say
Hooray! Then I say, I'm going out

At the drugstore I say, Gimme some pills!
    Charge 'em! They say
Sure. I say See you later.

Read the paper. Talk to Alice.
She laughs to hear
        Hokusai had 947 changes of address
In his life. Ha-ha. Plus everything
        else in the world
going on here.

✳

How to Get to Canada

borrow 50 from George
Spend 2 for *Tarantula*
    and 4 for a little Horse
    and 5 for two meals
    and 1 or 2 for King-size Chesterfields
    and 2.50 to ride the bus
    and 2 more for taxicabs
    & 1 for tips & 25 cents for 1 more
    bus . . . . buy a ticket
    for 31. Check your bag, free.
    Steal *Night Song, & Prison Letters
    From A Soledad Brother.* Wait . . . . . . Fly:
    15 cents is plenty to keep you in the sky.

✳

Love

Missing you

in Air Canda

✳

Things to Do in Providence

                Crash
Take Valium   Sleep
        Dream &,
                    forget it.
                _____

Wake up new & strange
                displaced,
                    at home.
        Read The Providence Evening Bulletin
                    No one you knew
                                got married
                                had children
                                got divorced
                                died
            got born
                    tho many familiar names flicker &
                    disappear.
                _____

    Sit
                watch TV
                                    draw blanks
            swallow
                pepsi
                meatballs
                . . .
                    give yourself the needle:
        "Shit! There's gotta be something
                    to do
                        here!"

JOURNEY TO SHILOH:
        Seven young men on horses, leaving Texas.
        They've got to do what's right! So, after
        a long trip, they'll fight for the South in the War.

No war in Texas, but they've heard about it,
      & they want
to fight for their country. Have some adventures
      & make
their folks proud! Two hours later all are dead;
one by one they died, stupidly, & they never did
      find out why!
There were no niggers in South Texas! Only
      the leader,
with one arm shot off, survives to head back to Texas:
all his friends behind him, dead. What will happen?

———————

Watching him, I cry big tears. His friends
were beautiful, with boyish American good manners,
           cowboys!

———————

Telephone New York: "hello!"
                     "Hello! I'm drunk! &
                     I have no clothes on!"
      "My goodness," I say.
                     "See you tomorrow."

———————

Wide awake all night reading: *The Life of Turner*
             ("He first saw the light in Maiden Lane")
             A.C. Becker: Wholesale Jewels
                            Catalogue 1912
            The Book of Marvels, 1934:
                         The year I was born.
No mention of my birth in here.   Hmmm.
                  Saturday The Rabbi Stayed Home
                  (that way he got to solve the murder)
                     LIFE on the moon   by LIFE Magazine.

———————

My mother wakes up, 4 a.m.: Someone to talk with!

Over coffee we chat, two grownups
I have two children, I'm an adult now, too.   .

Now we are two people talking who have known each other
a long time,
Like Edwin & Rudy. Our talk is a great pleasure: my mother
a spunky woman. Her name was Peggy Dugan when she was
young.
Now, 61 years old, she blushes to tell me I was conceived
before the wedding! "I've always been embarrassed about
telling you
til now," she says. "I didn't know what you might think!"
"I think it's really sweet," I say. "It means I'm really
a love child." She too was conceived before her mother's
wedding,
I know. We talk, daylight comes, & the Providence Morning
Journal.
My mother leaves for work. I'm still here.

———

Put out the cat

                              Take in the clothes
                                   off of the line
        Take a walk,
                   buy cigarettes

———

two teen-agers whistle
        as I walk up

                    They say: "Only your hairdresser
                        knows for sure!"
          Then they say,
                "ulp!"
        because I am closer to them.
    They see I am not hippie kid, frail like Mick Jagger,
but some horrible 35 year old big guy!

              The neighborhood I live in is mine!

"How'd you like a broken head, kid?"
                    I say fiercely.

(but I am laughing & they are not one bit scared.)

So, I go home.

Alice Clifford waits me. Soon she'll die
at the Greenwood Nursing Home; my mother's
mother, 79 years & 7 months old.
> But first, a nap, til my mother comes home
> from work, with the car.

The heart stops briefly when someone dies,
a quick pain as you hear the news, & someone passes
from your outside life to inside. Slowly the heart adjusts
to its new weight, & slowly everything continues, sanely.

Living's a pleasure:
> I'd like to take the whole trip
> despite the possible indignities of growing old,
moving, to die in poverty, among strangers:
> > that can't be helped.

So, everything, now
> is just all right.   I'm with you.
> No more last night.

Friday's great

10 o'clock morning sun is shining!

I can hear today's key sounds fading softly

& almost see opening sleep's epic novels.

*

Cranston Near the City Line

One clear glass slipper; a slender blue single-rose vase;
one chipped glass Scottie; an eggshell teacup & saucer, tiny,
fragile, but with sturdy handle; a gazelle? the lightest pink
    flowers
on the teacup, a gold circle, a line really on the saucer; gold
line curving down the handle; glass doors on the cabinet which
    sat
on the floor & was not too much taller than I; lace doilies? on
the shelves; me serious on the floor, no brother, shiny floor or
shining floor between the flat maroon rug & the glass doors of
    the cabinet:

I never told anyone what I knew. Which was that it wasn't
for anyone else what it was for me.

The piano was black. My eyes were brown. I had rosy
cheeks, every sonofabitch in the world said. I never saw them.

My father came cutting around the corner of the A&P
& diagonally across the lot in a beeline toward our front
    sidewalk
& the front porch (& the downstairs door); and I could see him,
    his
long legs, quick steps, nervous, purposeful, coming & passing,
    combing
his hair, one two three quick wrist flicks that meant
    "worrying" &
    "quickly!"

There were lilacs in the back yard, & dandelions in the lot.
There was a fence.

Pat Dugan used to swing through that lot, on Saturdays, not too
  tall,
in his brown suit or blue one, white shirt, no tie, soft brown
  men's
slippers on his feet, & Grampa! I'd yell & run to meet him &
"Hi! Grampa," I'd say & he'd swing my arm and be singing his
  funny
  song:

"She told me that she loved me, but

  that was yesterday. She told me

that she loved me, & then

  she went away!"
  _____

I didn't know it must have been a sad song, for somebody!
He was so jaunty, light in his eyes and laugh lines around
them, it was his happy song, happy with me, it was 1942 or 4,
and he was 53.

                              *

Whitman in Black

For my sins I live in the city of New York
Whitman's city lived in in Melville's senses, urban inferno
Where love can stay for only a minute
Then has to go, to get some work done
Here the detective and the small-time criminal are one
& tho the cases get solved the machine continues to run
Big Town will wear you down
But it's only here you can turn around 360 degrees
And everything is clear from here at the center
To every point along the circle of horizon
Here you can see for miles & miles & miles
Be born again daily, die nightly for a change of style
Hear clearly here; see with affection; bleakly cultivate
    compassion
Whitman's walk unchanged after its fashion.

*

Last Poem

Before I began life this time
I took a crash course in counter-intelligence
Once here I signed in, see name below, and added
Some words remembered from an earlier time,
"The intention of the organism is to survive."
My earliest, & happiest, memories pre-date WWII,
They involve a glass slipper & a helpless blue rose
In a slender blue single-rose vase: Mine
Was a story without a plot. The days of my years
Folded into one another, an easy fit, in which
I made money & spent it, learned to dance & forgot, gave
Blood, regained my poise, & verbalized myself a place
In Society. 101 St. Mark's Place, apt. 12A, NYC 10009
New York. Friends appeared & disappeared, or wigged out,
Or stayed; inspiring strangers sadly died; everyone
I ever knew aged tremendously, except me. I remained
Somewhere between 2 and 9 years old. But frequent
Reification of my own experiences delivered to me
Several new vocabularies, I loved that almost most of all.
I once had the honor of meeting Beckett & I dug him.
The pills kept me going, until now. Love, & work,
Were my great happinesses, that other people die the source
Of my great, terrible, & inarticulate one grief. In my time
I grew tall & huge of frame, obviously possessed
Of a disconnected head, I had a perfect heart. The end
Came quickly & completely without pain, one quiet night as I
Was sitting, writing, next to you in bed, words chosen
    randomly
From a tired brain, it, like them, suitable, & fitting.
Let none regret my end who called me friend.

*

People of the Future

People of the future
while you are reading these poems, remember
you didn't write them,
I did.

*

MAUREEN OWEN

African Sunday

Fuck I want to be bound by devotion!   Tortured
by passion!
            just like the ad says   for d h Lawrence's
Sons and Lovers   in today's Sunday Times   instead I'm
here with you   listening to a voice   from 1523 say
"wisdom is the thing that makes knowledge work"   & a
herd of zebras blows back   & forth on the line   A sheet
of wild ungulates   munching their way over the Serengeti
to us   shins in the dust   of those belts razed
by the sun   hooves in our buttercups   Everything
is energy   When she said   "Men take everything   little
by little   they take the power   the dream the hope
the house   & the car"   she meant energy   & how in her
dream it came back to her   She hummed her own notes.
she felt her body astonishingly vague   the wave
nature of electrons   taking over   Toes teeth
skin lost borders   merged like 5 o'clock traffic   This
is what happened to St. Teresa   when she went flying.
Once after class   I asked my deepest Jesuit   if he
thought she actually did fly   that is to say   go to
the window   & lift off into the night airs   His head
yanked up   flurries of test papers   shifting   "Of Course"
he huffed   "Of Course she flew!"

＊

"Some days," Dorothy Parker said, "it's better than digging ditches."

for Rebecca Brown

The United States is giving the Suez Canal back to Panama
    it seems like only yesterday Tyrone Power was
building it   against all odds . . . . I thought
at dinner   When B said suddenly   "I hate my
    forehead!"
We all looked closer.   But no   it was a perfectly normal
forehead.   When Nijinsky died they cut open his feet
to see the magical bone structure   birdlike
though towards the last   he thought he was a horse
his legs under the loose   material   alluding
to a headlong gallop   away   from inner states of terror.
Jane Bowles in Paris   writing   "Dear Bupple
    . . ."   Telling
him   Alice Toklas admires your book tremendously   &
Eudora Welty came over to dinner   and is a great admirer
of yours. . .   As for her own work   Eudora had returned
the copy   unable to finish it   and a friend in the hotel
a charming   brilliant girl called Natika   didn't
like it either really   The days go by   they give us
    more
and more   and more to loose.   You loose!   This is not
    always
a tragedy.   Beyond a certain point   it is impossible
to live at face value   in the end it will be the length
of our extravagance   that allows us to imitate   at last
the masculine impatience!   The sea wedged like the chunk
    of
some jewel between the shore and the horizon.
Remember!   It was only the low houses that
made the men on horseback seem so
    important!   Without
passport, papers, or luggage   Refusing to turn back at
the border   we will merely say to the guards   "Let us
    Pass."

Greta Garbo made only 27 movies during her entire lifetime.
Beatrix Potter hated children.
Hawthorne wrote in his notebook: "Herman Melville's linen
is none too clean."
Or as She said   in a precocious letter shortly after the 2nd
     novel
"And to think of the Grande Affaire I gave up for it!   Lawdy!

*

For Emily (Dickinson)

The girl   working the xerox in the stationery store
has a "thing"   for one of the customers   "I'm in love!"
she blurts to complete strangers buying stamp pad ink.
"Am I shaking!   Last week when he came in   I
stapled my thumb."   It's not just a shift in season
but a hormone that sets the trees off too   from plain
green they go   cheeks flushed   & dropping
everything!
Like the baby bashing through them   hooting   "More!"
&   the radio   announcing   "It's a Sealy Posturepedic
     morning!"
the landscape's gone silly   with abundance of motif   where
the tossed baby   Plunks   into the damp pyramid   &
is gone   from the base a small scuffed shoe
chanting   "Leafs!   Leafs!"   Here
is all the drama of the emperor's flight!   Imperial
dragon robes swept up   porcelains scattered
& the eerie glazed stillness   the soft mist Thudding
where the stately picnic   had been.
Is it a theory of numbers   or just   Quantity
that lifts us   up from under the armpits   with Fred
Astaire singing   in grand finale crescendo   "It
doesn't matter where you get it   as long as you got it!"
          O furious Excesses!

She set her tough skiff   straightaway
into the sea   for love of danger!
        tho all the birds have lost   their cover
                & You   O Bald October
                        I knew you   when you
                        still had hair!

*

Novembers or Straight Life

It's guys   like Emerson   that always fuck it up
Who from his journals—marked for later use in
Social Aims   under "Manners" wrote

> My prayer to women would be, when the bell rings,
> when visitors arrive, sit like statues.

Impossible!   to give passionate head   after   reading
        that!
Impossible   to blow you   under propelling tables!   our
beers whitecapping   on the nap   Oblivious!   of swizzle
sticks   & Cinzano ashtrays embedding   in our backs!
While the Pope hits a new low   & the Professor   who is so
brief   as to be left with nothing more to say   has rectified
this once again   by repeating everything three times . . . . . even
a tree surgeon will bend over the fence   asking   "Is your
husband home?   Is your husband home?   Is your husband
home?"   as though you didn't hear him   instead of simply
choosing not to answer.   How To Talk To Assholes   was a
possible title I was considering   in honor of the doctor
studied my severely swollen thumb   & inquired   as to
        whether
any strenuous exercise had   been taken of late   "perhaps
        yanking
a fitted bedsheet over a mattress?"   he postulated . . . .
        "Is this a town?"   I asked
        "Yes," said Uncle Alfred,   "This is Raven Brook,
        and here is Jake waiting for us."

*

Three Mile Island

"Just stay inside," said His Luminescence,
the Governor, "and shut your doors and
windows."

Don't drink the beer that's brewed in Pennsylvania. O Rolling
Rock   Goodbye!
Don't sip the milk   eat the yogurt   Spread the butter
pet the calves!   Pick the purple flowering raspberry   Wild
Geranium   sweet joe-pye-weed   pasture rose   in the
meadows on the farms   of Harrisburg.   You can't
see it   hear it   smell it   taste it   & Federal
Officials & Engineers   assure us   the   "danger is
down"   But don't roast the pork!   Sauté the peppers
steam the asparagus   bake the potatoes   shuck the
corn!   No strawberries   & no peaches!   from those
shores of the Susquehanna.
We had power say the townsfolk!   pop-up toasters   magic
hair dryers!   micro ovens!   electric blankets   automatic
knife sharpeners   4-way gadgets!   &   Lights   that
we could burn & burn!
Now citizens are gathering   like clouds   on the horizon
of the ground.   Bullfrogs pausing in the puddles.   Cows
are acting strange.   & through flamingo dawns are falling
gamma rays so sifting down the alley   past the high school
Radiation's lurking!
        & we can't drink the beer   that's brewed in Pennsylvania!
        O Rolling Rock!   Goodbye!

(*Rolling Rock* is a kind of beer that's brewed and bottled in a little town,
Latrobe, PA.)

❋

JOHN GODFREY

Errant

Denzel Brush zipped up his periscope and treed the bartender
with his Delphic glower. Few sacraments hissed so lovely on the
spitted broil, and the peat-like smoke from his pipe cast our bulg-
ing eyeballs on the barometer, and some of us who are attracted to
bar-anything wander over, and fall into his grasp. Now we are as
depressed as the huge vulva of mist that mounts the Empire State
Building and lowers until it hurts. If you are so charmed, would
you either remove your clothes or not bathe in the punch. Words
come to insults regarding maternity, paternity, manliness, articu-
lation, and virile equipment of the adversary. I ask who *he* is
without feeling the fear, of him, in my radio.

It's the cold of rain in my shirt that sobers me, the streetlights
doubled by terry-lined curbs. Runoff bubbling under hubcaps
highlights the hush, the walker unattended by marvelous piano
theory. (So help me, Alban Berg is the man in the moon.) One
young man has had the presence of mind to play garbage can
timbales in the crop of drops. Even if the moon weren't new (Berg),
it would not tonight caress this old face (Rosemary Clooney). I
insert myself into that part of the building set aside for the front
door, and I blow. The bricks do not fall down. I make sure that last
taxi docks at the red light, and then there's my key.

*

Reveille

Under mercury light the little pup strives. A sinister shadow ducks under the curb—I must describe it all over again, it confuses acquiescence into fertility. How it speeds up the sky and prolongs the night. It is false. It is brilliance in miniature and alludes to her face.

Miles of cruciform sidewalk. Enticed by magazines that are really radios, odd couples nag each other as one strays to a window and one to a cellar. They are expansive because they are small. A tall boy is the man, a short woman is the girl, alarm and its buffer. Both need more than enthusiasm. How mental is your queen when disturbance is the rule! A thousand such couples wave in inert profusion at one figure across the street. I imagine their kiss, I project passion into strange fittings to make it confess a hymn that is my song after all.

I simmer in the half-light of a stoop, raising beers under a pompadour on the first brisk night, pressure more potent than any barometer can read. To see your hand to the tramp of feet is a way to measure strangers. To feel your hair on my finger accidentally is common sense, a way of leading you to me as the watch moves. We return to our bed through the bakery smells of daybreak, sky palling, empty of jets. The schedule is suspended, then resumes like gray dead hands in the east, and I want you never to die.

✻

ED SANDERS

Yiddish Speaking Socialists of
The Lower East Side

They came when the Czar banned the Yiddish
          theater in 1882
They came when the iron-tipped Cossack's whip
            flicked in the face of their mother
They came when their parents were cheated out of
          their farms in Vilna
They came to escape the peasants at Easter, hacking
          with scythes and knives
They came when the Revolution of 1905 was crushed
They came when the soldiers broke up their socialist
          presses in Crakow
They fled from Siberia, dungeons and work camps,
          for printing leaflets and fliers—

      pamphlets and poems and leaflets and fliers
      to spread in the workshops
      spread in the streets
      spread in the factories

      in the spirit the era had spawned
      the spirit the era had spawned

          "In di gasn
              tsu di masn
          Into the streets
              to the masses"

They came to Antwerp and then to London
                and then to Ludlow Street
            to make a New World
            inside the New World
            at century's turn—
            The Yiddish speaking socialists
            of the Lower East Side

Some remembered
        with pangs and tears
                the beautiful rural life
                        wrested away

Mushroom hunting in the dampened woods
Bundles of grain in the carts
Market day in the shtetl

Some strained their eyes
for the gold-paved streets of the West
just to be greeted by one of those
"incomprehensible economic collapses"
that New York gives to its poor

The East Side
        had been slums
                since the overcrowding
                        after the War of 1812—

but the tenement rents of 1903
            were higher than
                    nearby "better" places

2/3's of them owned by speculators
getting 15 to 30% (or more)

so that a family of ten
            was jammed
                    in a two room flat

                plus boarders!

till a leafleteer
                in desperation
                                lay aside his ink
To open a curbside store
                with a gutter plank
                                and 3 brown bales of rag

Or they carried the cribs
                to the hallway
                                to set up a sweatshop—
They were not alone

From thousands of windows
                came the clackety-clacks
                                of foot-treadled sewing machines

and the drum-like sounds
                of long bladed scissors
                                chewing on oaken boards

and the lungs turned gray
                with tidbits of tweed
and the red hot irons
on the tops of the coal stoves
to smoothe out the bundles of cloth

and the sweet gulps of air
                on Cherry Street
walking out kinks of the legs at dusk
from a day at the torturing treadle.

A rose curled around the mallet of pov.
The Lower East Side
was the strongest socialist zone
                in the United States

for the first twenty years
of this century.

It was a
        wild world of words

and everywhere
        the song
                of the wild lecture

arose above a wild lectern—
Scott Nearing
                at the Rand School of Social Science
Morris Hillquit
                at the Workmen's Circle
Emma Goldman
                at the Educational Alliance
Eugene Debs
                coming in from Terre Haute
                        to Webster Hall

And political discussions
        on the summertime roofs
                in Yiddish, Russian, Polish & English—

        wild world of words

Labor Day parades from East Broadway
to Union Square
Cousins on the floor
        from fleeing Siberia
                after the Revolution of 1905

Union meetings at the Labor Lyceum on E. 4th—
                Flashes of the Ideal
                        in murk
                                in muck
                                        in mire

Talking all night at the Cafe Royale
at 12th and 2nd Avenue

after the Yiddish plays at
the Kessler or Tomashevski Theaters

Garment worker rallies at Cooper Union

Joining the Women's Trade Union League
Fighting for the shorter work week
6 and 1/2 days to six, and then
to 44 hours, on the way to 40

Flashes of the Ideal
in murk
in muck
in mire

In di gasn
tsu di masn

To make a New World
inside the New World
at century's turn
the Yiddish speaking socialists
of the Lower East Side.

For twenty years the East Side socialists grew.
They filled the arenas
and packed the streets

though those who stand
in the bowl of shrieks
know how the bowl
stands silent
so often

when the votes are
counted.

There was a party in the streets
The Lower East Side had never seen
the night in 1914 that Meyer London,
whose father had worked in an anarchist print shop,
was elected to Congress

They danced and sang
through Rutgers Square past the Daily Forward
till the sun blushed the color of communes
above the docks.

Meyer London served for three terms
until the Democrats and Republicans in
the State Assembly
gerrymandered his district.

In 1917 the Socialist Party of N.Y.C.
sent ten assemblymen to Albany
and seven to the N.Y.C. board of aldermen
and even elected a municipal judge

while Morris Hillquit
pulled 22% of the vote for mayor—

It looked like the Socialist surge
might move as a spill of thrills
out through the state

                    In di gasn
                        tsu di masn

to make a New World
inside the New World
                at century's turn
the Yiddish speaking socialists
                        of the Lower East Side

And then, in the spring of 1917
                    the U.S. Congress
                            voted for war

The Socialists
        met in St. Louis
                that same April

& issued
        what was known as
                the St. Louis Resolution—

"We call upon the
                workers of all countries

to refuse support
                to their governments
                        in their wars."

Some were sympathetic
                to the strong socialist and
                        union movements in Germany

in a struggle
                against
                        Czarist barbarism—

others felt it
        was just a distracting disturbance
                        between Russian
                                & German militaries.

The Lower East Side was split.
                The pressure to support
                        their new country

was great—not that pogroms
       by the Brooklyn Bridge were feared
    though the death-tined rioting peasant's rake
         was not that far
            in the past.

The Wilson administration
        generated war hysteria

Scott Nearing, Eugene Debs
        went to jail

the government threatened
the mailing rights of the Jewish Daily Forward
and other socialist papers
opposing the war.

And then it
    was different
after the armistice

There was hideous inflation
and F.O.B.
      Fear of Bolsheviks—

and many, mayhemic forces
were set against the
Lower East Side socialist zone.

The anti-red hysteria was nationwide
The Wobblies were crushed
The strikers of Seattle crushed
The Palmer Raids
Federal troops used to club down
              honest dispute
Emma Goldman deported
Five Socialists expelled from the
           N.Y. Legislature

and the Socialist Victor Berger
banned from his seat in the Congress.

There was a split in
the Socialist Party in 1919

& the birth of the Communist Party.

You think there was factionalism
in the 1960s—
The factions of 1920 hissed
like 35,000 ganders
                in an amanita valley—

and a Democratic Socialist
in the '20's and '30's
was wedged in pain among
the sharp tongued Moscow leftists
and sharp tongued bitter-shitter rightists.

Oh they failed
to spread the East Side zone
into a broader country
of psychopathic landboomers
& smug townies
who thought they could hog
the keys to the sky

There was the fact that
a climate of lectures and rallies
can aid in the first rough forward step,
                but rarely the second—

They knew with all the hurt of their years
how the socialist fervor fell—
and the failure of those
                who had seen the socialist dawn
to break it from sea from sea.

Most of them fled the rubbly slums,
and tens of thousands more,
for few there are
who joy
to live in dirt

They joked how the ships
brought the greenhorns to Rutgers Square
as the moving vans
took the radicals to the Bronx

> For most
> the game
> was to get OUT
>
> but for some
> like Congressman London
> the East Side
> was the
>   world
> in which to stay
>
> He was there all his life
> till killed by a car
> as he crossed 2nd Avenue—
> Shelley had Keats in his pocket
> London had Chekhov.

Oh they failed
but I can hear their ghosts
walk down the cobbles
outside the St. Mark's church

the poets, the strikers, the printers,
the firebrands, the leafleteers—
comrades when the world had its glow—

with a passion for Justice
        that never fades away
though heartbreak
        to know
                that they had failed

to make a New World
inside the New World
at century's turn
They were the Yiddish speaking socialists
of the Lower East Side.

In researching "Yiddish Speaking Socialists of the Lower East Side,"
the books below supplied much useful and thrilling information:

The House on Henry Street, Lillian Wald
Memoirs of a Revolutionary, Eva Broido
World of Our Fathers, Irving Howe
How the Other Half Lives, Jacob Riis
*Labor & Farmer Parties in the
        United States*, Nathan Fine
Born One Year Before the 20th Century, Minnie Fisher

✳

The Five Feet

You can always fight the foulest grief
with drinks and thrills
You can channelize your septum
with thousand dollar bills

But you better get obsessed again
on the Change Wheel's rungs
or they'll let the tumors grow
in the hummingbird's lungs

You've got to have five feet
to skitter down the road

One foot in the grave
One foot in the glitter
One foot in the gutter
One foot in the glory
One foot near the Grail

Lawrence said to build a Boat of Death
upon that main
Well, you'd better patch the leaky Boat of Life
call it Paradise Plain

There's nothing wrong with writing lines of verse
on a foam-flecked oar
Even if we cannot join Matisse
through Plato's door

You've got to have five feet
to skitter down the road

One foot in the grave
One foot in the glitter
One foot in the gutter
One foot in the glory
One foot near the Grail

✻

PHILIP LAMANTIA

Wilderness
Sacred Wilderness

It's cozy to be a poet in a bed, on a copse, knoll, in a room
It's terrible to be a poet dragons around to bite off your wings
    and
  dream of the Standing One
as Nietzsche turns into Victor Emmanuel Re di Italia
Helen Ennoia looks up into the eternal pools of the eyes of
    Simon
  Magus
and all the botched lies of mythic ties kick open the corpse
  a bag of museum dust
               manikin
in the manner of Simon Rodia, Buffalo Bill, like P.T. Barnum
  like
  Alka Seltzer
        goes against it
burnt pork eaters
El Dorado is the flashback to pancake mornings 'home is where
    you
  hang yourself'
        signed Bill
The games of golf on the misogynist wastes
centuries multiply metaphysical field notes
There's the sleep of Ra in the West
a blurred photo of purple and lumens
on a windy hilltop in the manner of Man Ray

luminous sky my own poetry chimes at the horrid hour of
hideous
  chimes
Poe's Appalachia in the far western sea where the forest saves
    us
  the forest hides us telepathenes in a circle of friends
salacious hour of shadows regions of the undead
hangnails of the Gilak an infinite crystalline substance spun all
    the
  traditions
moored in nine powers the gurgling carburctors
the video cassettes the people are coming we're at
the communion on the mountaintop it's true but
the wheel turns the beaver chews the pole holding up the world
It's coming back home like a dream-memoir at the death of day
  in the poetical pastiche framing a mask of postcard view
    from
  the dawn of Ra
it's the moment of Maldoror
the collage objects of the end days conjunct the plutonic week a
  roadshow of nineteenth-century bison
as the Buffalo Bill Follies autodestruct by 1916

*

Irrational

    On a hill in Frisco
    the gothic spread of the mantle
    Pelican fragments
    through the black port
    of a species speaking stones

It will be another earth, parallel earth, in ancient states of
  becoming—igneous, mineral boiling seas of other earthen
  worlds

But this one, once called 'the new world' is again the old world
    of
  ancient earth, all the more living from the neural feet of
    vision,
  Vesta the giver of forms

The return of the ancient earth is America in the gothic art of
its
  name, *Armorica—Hy-Brazil*—ancient Americas rising like
  hieratic
  light in Thomas Cole's Hudson River painting

as in the Hopi cosmos and the alchemical visitation
the earth within the crust we tend
to the sidereal maps of its seas, luminous shell over the sun
belt
    of sky
  for those who fly to the sun
This old earth this old America is beginning to smoke the
    krita-yugic
  paradise, the Age of Gold

As poetry is wedded to silence
the last word heard is the gold of silence the ancient earth is
        weaving
    the humanisphere is turning
    landing dead on arrival
    the seances of poets Poe Blake Whitman
    Emily Dickinson Samuel Greenberg
                Jones Very above all

*

Violet Star

1

While I continue to rave
over the dissimilar modes
molding
excessively finite
transmutable
at the coming of serpentine volition
son of the daughters of sleep
the absolute at every street corner with a braided cap
the hair-lined tongue
disagreeably spills *the indeterminate* over the mirror
of the world

The avalanche of anti-gravity machines
a tight rein to these vehicles
sometimes seen with the word "seer" spelled
backwards
the fire-coated heroic
dances over the sparkling ruins
bird beaks
luminously
at the grating of historical jungles
the cities continually sink into mirages
the oil of tombs and frontal lobotomies "treasures" of
the ruling classes
the evening salvo of "the serpentine flag"
my last glimpse into the card of *The Exploding Tower*
galvanic
to the ignition of the levitated glance

2

The truth is to see the mounted zephyr mutilate itself
    in a bowl of chick peas
The pastors of iniquity dance
on the night before crumbling cement in the beeswax
    of torment
the moment to transpire cities
What if the road is dizzy from the clashing tubs?
Alcohol venison sunlight like a steel fist
floodgates will open
invisible powers through the cataclysm at hand

a necklace of human heads
the sibilant voices cracked on a rock of *techne*
The cars fold obsidian men into the stale marshes
The open almond of rust invents the glare of high
    noon
Beware the teeth of numbers
but the lunar feel of steel going limp
another world
flight of the tamarind trees in the Mozartian sky
the shrouded catastrophes staring from the monoliths
the way the curve of planets escapes into view
beyond all the blind revelations
the fortunate thunder writes out the changes on the
    headdress of cured feathers
opening the old Amerindian tonic
the timeless in time and the regional compass

*

Surrealism in the Middle Ages

I'm eight years older than Artaud when he died
For thirty years I've looked on the world he said consolidated in
    1946
It's still consolidated, but denser. 'Enough, you charlatan, you
    hangnail
  vampire, the phantom above all
only the phantom, I don't want any doppelgängers in my
    stadium'
The mountain ridge extends the eating and the metabolic
    metaphors
  why not rhyme?
obscene photographs are burning like lava from Mount Rainier
'Surrealist? . . . Man, we don't like those labels, yeh don't have
    to label
  poetry . . . it *is*, man . . .'
Me, I'm preromantic. I'd as lief roll up a leaf to Lady Day as
    anybody
the blessed clichés in sight of the tower
'a': the winter scape ghost eggs in the pan
the material image static on the Ohio River
the breasts of mounds nearing prison
pit of the world cycle sudden illumination
the coiled dream door
hungry snow cycling the land of earth's horizon
an afternoon with Osiris in the *stellae*, scorpion at hand
Masterless, the enigmas seep out of the air
on a roundout without memoirs
to red ribbons the wind-scrivener wheels to ancient storms
medusae in an optic dance
metallic blue hats across the bar
loup-garous back from the tropics
Scott Joplin's ragtime and a faraway land to the Natchez Trace
murder as only euro-americans can sing it

a slice of wigeon's tail against the timbers waiting at the bend
   of the river
great flyway of ineffable seasons
Mississippi echoic spangle there's the sea it can only be the
   Columbia
   or the Klamath
loon loon I see the pelican clear
Violent Ocean (another name) Pacific never

pulverable dunes of the Least Sandpiper

*

ALICE NOTLEY

Flowers of the Foothills
& Mountain Valleys

Compassion is pungent
& sharply aromatic. Small
yellow heads in late summer.
Love & hatred are
delicate & fragrant.
Around a yellow disc.
Glory is found along the shores
intoning "I change but in death."
Sincerity has delicate &
feathery leaves. Dignity is
fragrant & looks like a little
brown nail. The leaves
of hidden worth are deeply cut;
a 19th century American
artist & inventor. Sir
Thomas Campion blooms in July
pinkly with notched petals. The
clearest of gins taste of
bluish protection, lovely
Mary & little Jesus found
refuge, in Egypt, in gin.
Hid from sight in
the bark of the cinnamon tree
a light flashes on & off,
dazzles, whistles. Remembrance
is the most fragrant, love is
the most dark pink, courage
is grey-green growing wild.

*

Poem

I believe the yellow flowers think with me
& that Charles Olson's arms are all around
"You can't say that can you Alice?" Bernadette
Her voice in on it too, all the way from
New Hampshire, farther than cloud and cloud
It's going to rain on us when that branch there
Stops rustling. Have a last sip of my Calistoga, Sweets.
The first drop, the shade darker. "When
It starts to rain Mom I'm still gonna go to Merrit's
With my big coat on and play in the rain."
The tree just changed colors! it's glowing
A light chartreusely—it's all for Charles though
The earth slopes kindly down around me as if
To say the closure will be a little, just a little, like this.

*

Poem

A clitoris is a kind of brain
That woman stroking hers in *Hustler*
is thinking: I wonder, are there
misprints in the Manhattan Telephone Directory?

*

World's Bliss

The men & women sang & played
they sleep by singing, what
shall I say of the most
poignant on earth the most glamorous
loneliest sought after people

those poets wholly beautiful
desolate aureate, death is a
powerful instinctive emotion—
but who would be released from
a silver skeleton? gems
& drinking cups—This
skull is Helen—who would not
be released from the
Book of Knowledge? Why
should a maiden lie on a moor
for seven nights & a day? And
he is a maiden, he is & she
on the grass the flower the spray
where they lie eating primroses
grown crazy with sorrow & all
the beauties of old—oh each poet's a
beautiful human girl who must die.

*

After Tsang Chih

I was brought up in a small town in the Mohave Desert.
The boys wouldn't touch me who was dying to be touched,
        because I was too quote
Smart. Which the truck-drivers didn't think as they
        looked and waved
On their way through town, on the way to my World.

*

Backyard

The cat's eye marble is green.
One sandal. Shade. If I were a
girl from the Sagamon River, or if
I am. I then turned to the page
called Free. The wind in my
hair & the church in my head
& the reticence of. No I
haven't been waiting. Expression
of engineer of an intimate clime
It must still be love which I
talk. But you see. Shaky as
pale lavender ones. High talk to cure
an old tired fear. There's an
old plastic coffee cup in the
forest of the lemon tree. But
what I mean is. White
oleanders in the sky attached to
leaves. If you love me, all
of nature, let the wind blow.

＊

The Night Sits in This Chair

The night sits in this chair
on lengthening stripes stalking
themselves like raining
over a sea, and the brunette
outside sweeps with her hair
pavement that's staying dark.
Love's in session. When my face
comes back I sip more of the wine.

＊

In Ancient December

in the ideal American
Willie Nelson, poet laureate
hapless which one
his silvery voice floated down
& pitiless King
& cold cold Persephone sobbed
& a dancing carrot
. . . She told me you were good,
you were gonna do just fine. There's several ways to
use your pants. But only one sure way down. To go to
bed & dream of apartment in flames, rather, small fires,
here & there, & tall & slender at the door? Could I
lead her out without them? Could she leave without
everyone as I never have in any dream ever? I can't
keep my eyes open here. For example if Old Diane as
Eurydice. Who knocked a pervert downstairs when she was
forty; has a blind old boyfriend now whose whore old
girlfriend broke her nose; her son works for the Mafia.
A survivor is a woman who teaches you everything strangely
after some years of knowing, in a sudden and flash you
barely notice, while I'm learning it too listening washing
a dish & wondering why I learn from the one who returned
from her & which of us two will sing a song of it? And
she doesn't even need it. Does she listen to, to
Vic Damone? Maybe. Who's her favorite singer, Ted?
Perry Como, followed closely by Mario Lanza & Frank Sinatra.
Though probably she thinks her son had a beautiful voice
never did nothing with it. Oh God I still can't wake up.
Connie Francis. Get the humor of that? That's Diane. If
I can wake on up:

The song called "Get Away"

Never leave you
Never leave here

Get away by
Telephone, by starpoint by access

Never leave story
Never leave breaking
Get away by chair
By bend
By River mine

Never never leave you
Or kind of thing
Or talking to
It being later now
And never leave you. . . .

Can you worship loss? I can't remember it. I forgot to
sing it off from happening I had to arrange the flowers,
thousands everywhere, & thinly & it being purple I forgot
to see it ten thousand times. She forgot to. She
forgot to too. She would have forgotten anyway. She
didn't forget at any rate, she didn't anything. I didn't
either. I woke up I woke up again & I can't remember I
guess that's just it, but I didn't forget to sing this
time, but I forget what I'm singing. What am I singing?
Singing singing? What am I singing?

✶

I the People

I the people
to the things that are were &
     come to be.
We were once what we know
     when we

make love When we go away
   from each other because
we have been created
   at 10th & A, in winter &
of trees & of the history of houses
   we hope we are
notes of the musical scale of
   heaven—I the
people so repetitious, & my
   vision of
to hold the neighbors loose-
   ly here in
light of gel, my gel, my vision
   come out of
my eyes to hold you sur-
   round you in
gold & you don't know it
   ever. Everyone
we the people having our
   visions of
gold & silver & silken liquid
   light flowed
from our eyes & caressing
   all around all the
walls. I am a late Pre-
   in this dawn of

                        We the people
to the things that are & were
   & come to be
Once what we knew was only
   and numbers became
It is numbers & gold & at 10th
   & A you don't
have to know it ever. Opening
   words that show

Opening words that show that we
   were once
the first to recognize
   the immortality of numbered
bodies. And we are the masters
   of hearing & saying
at the double edge of body &
   breath
We the lovers & the eyes
All over, inside her
   when the wedding
is over, & the Park "lies cold &
   lifeless"
I the people, whatever is said
   by the first
one along, Angel-Agate. I wear
   your colors
I hear what we say & what
   we say . . . (and I
the people am still parted in
   two & would cry)

*

MICHAEL BROWNSTEIN

Declaration of Independence

When, in the midst of the thriving alien
Corn of congratulation for clever auspices
To spray out cruel politics like little birds
Set in rows, knocking them and breaking
The backs, just to suck out blood
Of complacency and dumb wistful resignation
Whose dumpy quality is force-fed inward
Against the natural flow of their actual
Energies all their lives, doubly dizzy
From wheezing through nostrils of boredom
On a vacation isle they fought for frantically
Only to ruin and poison artificially
With plastic clicking hands holding mule-like
Pills of false and clotted rest, *then* I
Get up much earlier than the rest, and smoke
Under creaking trees shocked by ice,
Lace of sunlight, glittering fir and snow,
Hours eating from this planet's tasty
Dwindling peace of mind.

*

Triplets

Exaggerated lives, phony body postures, overblown gestures
Flashy plastic clothes, subliminal packaging, no architecture
Cosmetic patina covering the face, neck and hands

Averted glances, city block survival, celery stalks at midnight
Dogshit, stunted sycamores, unisex block and tackle
Inverted weather front, stagnant airshaft, walleyed abdication

Politics, art, artificial beef and monster injected chicken
Aerosol junkies spray themselves illusory jellied youth product
Trash 14th St., vinyl nazi Madison, Plymouth Rock retirement
    village

Sensory deprivation, smokescreen social causes, "What about
    me?"
Lowest common denominator, subway to nowhere, quaint
    souvlaki
People turning into pullets, distributor caps, jackhammers

*

For Them

For them the Arctic is the image, a touch of eternity
The perpetual coming on of Winter
The milk's been in the icebox for three weeks now
It still *looks* white but it tastes kind of grey
Drifting away here on the Alex Quinn Show
"Librium 25 mg. has usually been found to provide
Dependable control of severe anxiety, affording
Basic Support as an adjunct to counsel and reassurance."
Polyrhythmically metamorphosed illuminated ceilings.
I stare up at the ceiling and easily can see
There's gonna be a rumble up in Paradise tonite.
But I no longer believe the story that is commonly told.
The story goes that I stood up among them in the endless
American meeting hall and yelled, "You goddamn idiots!
Why don't you just shape up!"
Then my heart grew huge and started beating madly
My eyes wildly spilled out onto the street

And I became one of them. Yes, I became that which
I most did not wish to become.
For during their stages of development
All things appear under forms
Opposite to those that they finally present.
This is an ancient doctrine.
I am thirty-one years old.
The newspapers tell me there's a revival of Charles Ives
Going on now, and I have to laugh:
What about the immense SMILE button, pal,
Whose rusty pin jabbed into your heart adds its color to your
    fate?
How's it feel to survive on a diet of newsprint and chickenshit?
They must be drugging 'em like pillars of salt up in Paradise
    tonite.
Paradise, whose baggy white clouds and thin green sky
The newspapers utterly fail to notice. Silly newspapers.
And the lingering image of the soft bowling-green Connecticut
    garden
That spawned Charles Ives
In a summertime in which many flowers bloom
Is actually the exact mirror image of the Arctic
Where the taxis are waiting in their long white room.
They start up all over again every morning
Without a single word . . . Except that it says here
An Army spokesman could not respond tonite
About reported plans to manufacture "ton quantities"
Of VX, an odorless, colorless compound
That attacks the nervous system
When inhaled or absorbed through the skin.
A quart jar of VX allegedly contains
"Several million lethal doses," the aide said.
The heart swoons while the head just fades away.
And if, as Goethe said, architecture is frozen music
Then it sounds today as if a pack of rats
Is slowly being tortured to death.
Let me make this as clear as possible:

The metal door downstairs slams and the building vibrates
With the sound of the one subway going by
And the sound of the other subway being built . . .
Yes, a new subway is being built for them.
It will take nineteen years and cost 4 billion dollars
And by the time it opens all of them will be gone,
All for whom it's being built will have vanished from the
    streets forever.
They will have surfaced by then somewhere deep inside the
    Arctic Circle
Carrying with them an entirely different, new set of needs
Primary among which will be the overwhelming need for a nice
    hot drink
And a fire, and a friend.

*

Floating

A cloud was hidden by the sun as she steeped tea drank under an opening in the window and stepped out onto the lawn off the bare wood-plank porch. She wore old red jersey over a hard happy body, and stared down the slope before the house, a Japanese text and prints under her left arm in the curve above her hip. A small flag from the old Republic of China was her only ornament, and it was sewn near the top of her jersey at about the collarbone. She was a lover of Asian artifacts, cultures, and the varied ways of life. But it was a serene, uncomplicated love, and nothing much was needed to make her forget it. Releasing her hold on these interests was like pushing over a Ming vase filled with warm milk in a mound of dark summer topsoil. The vase rolled a little and came to rest, blue and vermilion porcelain part-designs showing through the green bunches of leaves, with a touch of hot chocolate brown, the earth, underneath. With her Hasselblad she would take a few color slides of this release from preoccupation and, after they were developed, project them onto one of the cool white plaster walls inside her house. Whenever anyone asked me about her, I would always say she lived "further down the road."

*

JOANNE KYGER

from "All This Everyday"

When I used to focus on the worries, everybody
      was ahead of me, I was the bottom
    of the totem pole,
     a largely spread squat animal.

How about a quick massage now, he said to me.
I don't think it's cool, I replied.
Oh, said he, after a pause, I should have waited
     for *you* to ask *me*.

The waves came in closer and closer.

When I fall into the gap of suspicion I am no longer here.

In this world that has got closed over by houses
     and networks, I fly out
from under the belly. Life's dizzy crown
of whirling lights, circles this head. Pure
with wonder, hot
with wonder. The streets become golden. All
size increases, the colors glow, we are in myth.

We are in easy understanding.
Scarcely talking, thoughts pass between us.
       It is memory. As I search to find
this day's sweet drifting. The fog out to sea, the wind.

———

Still
    our breath our sun
  our moon, our stars, our space
 our water that flows
out the mountain, our ocean, our roads, our paths
    and into this year and into the next
    into the warm grey day, the damp smells rising
  up out of the earth.
     See, we can learn to move gracefully
    through this past learning
   This is a dream about 2 sources
    of lineage and language
     about strength and ease
  green tips that are fingers
 pointing to the sky.
    In the sun in the mist
  on the hill across
      I remember spring now in summer
   in sun petals
    the quick grass springs back, a vehicle
 for what passes through
Not for identity of I's and sorrows
  Struck by humility total of truth
 Listening to separate existence of worlds
  since I was born
    To look at the substance
  of what passes by the eyes
      sparkling
  in pages of notes of music
  and remain in memory as renewal,
 as voices from out on the water
 as craft
that carries this   voyager   forward. Back
 out of time, is this moment
  when I write to you
   these notes of myself

      *

Not Yet

Not tomorrow night
but the night after
    tomorrow
Not tomorrow
    but the night after
    tomorrow
Then the moon will be full
Then the moon will be full

———————

It's been a long time

NOTES FROM THE REVOLUTION

During the beat of this story you may find other beats. I mean
a beat. I mean Cantus, I mean Firm us, I mean paper, I mean in
the Kingdom which is coming, which is here in discovery.

It is also Om Shri Maitreya, you don't go across my vibes,
but with them, losing the pronoun. It is Thy, it is Three,
it is I, it is me.

Machines are *metal*, they serve us, we take care of them. This
is to me, and this is to you. You say you to me, and I say you
to you. Some machines are very delicate, they are precise, they
are not big metal stampers. She made enough poetry to keep
her company.

My Vibes. You intercepted my vibes. The long shadows,
the long shadows, the long shadows. My sweet little tone,
my sweet little tone is my arm.

On what Only: The song that girl sang the song that girl sang

———————

News bulletin from Keith Lampe

Soon

Little Neural Annie was fined $65 in the Oakland
Traffic Court this season for "driving while in
a state of samadhi." California secular law requires
that all drivers of motor vehicles remain firmly seated
within their bodies while the vehicle is in motion.
This applies to both greater vehicles and lesser
vehicles.

_____

No one was watching the tortillas.
You were.
That my new name. No One.
That's my new name. No One.

Now this tiny pause from my bursting brain
I am Beautiful. This is my name.

See I am It. I am getting It.
I am the big rolling, breathing, sliding
sighing, lifting.
Ground!

_____

A small field of tall golden headed grass, heavy with seed
    at the top
Why did I travel so far away from you who wishes to be
    snug in her home
The grotesqueness of this California woman who wishes
    to take off her clothes but instead displays herself in
    provocative attitudes
Wrapping my shawl about my waist I went into sparkling water
    on shale reef.
    I am not empty
Small sea anemones show their pink and blue insides.
Everything I walk on is alive

There is something in me which is not open
        it does not wish to live
          it is dying
But then in the sun, looking out to sea,
        center upon center unfold, lotus petals,
the boundless wave of bliss

           *

September

The grasses are light brown
and the ocean comes in
long shimmering lines
under the fleet from last night
which dozes now in the early morning

Here and there horses graze
    on somebody's acreage

        Strangely, it was not my desire

that bade me speak in church to be released
    but memory of the way it used to be in
careless and exotic play

    when characters were promises
  then recognitions. The world of transformation
is real and not real but trusting.

        Enough of these lessons? I mean
didactic phrases to take you in and out of
love's mysterious bonds?

      Well I myself am not myself.

and which power of survival I speak
for is not made of houses.

It is inner luxury, of golden figures
that breathe like mountains do
and whose skin is made dusky by stars.

*

And with March a Decade in Bolinas

Just sitting around smoking, drinking and telling stories,
the news, making plans, analyzing, approaching the cessation
of personality, the single personality understands its demise.
Experience of the simultaneity of all human beings on this
planet,
alive when you are live. This seemingly inexhaustible
sophistication of awareness becomes relentless and horrible,
trapped. How am I ever going to learn enough to get out.

The beautiful soft and lingering props of the Pacific here.

The back door bangs
So we've made a place to live
here in the greened out 70's
Trying to talk in the tremulous
morality of the present
Great Breath, I give you, Great Breath!

*

Destruction

First of all do you remember the way a bear goes through
a cabin when nobody is home? He goes through
the front door. I mean he really goes *through* it. Then
he takes the cupboard off the wall and eats a can of lard.

He eats all the apples, limes, dates, bottled decaffeinated
coffee, and 35 pounds of granola. The asparagus soup cans
fall to the floor. Yum! He chomps up Norwegian crackers
stashed for the winter. And the bouillon, salt, pepper,
paprika, garlic, onions, potatoes.

He rips the Green Tara
poster from the wall.   Tries the Coleman Mustard, spills
the ink, tracks in the flour.   Goes up stairs and takes
a shit.   Rips open the water bed, eats the incense and
drinks the perfume.   Knocks over the Japanese tansu
and the Persian miniature of a man on horseback watching
a woman bathing.

Knocks *Shelter, Whole Earth Catalogue,*
Planet Drum, Northern Mists, Truck Tracks, and
Women's Sports into the oozing water bed mess.

He goes
down stairs and out the back wall.   He keeps on going
for a long way and finds a good cave to sleep it all off.
Luckily he ate the whole medicine cabinet, including stash
of LSD, Peyote, Psilocybin, Amanita, Benzedrine, Valium
and aspirin.

*

ANSELM HOLLO

manifest destiny

to arrive in front of large video screen,
in pleasantly air-conditioned home with big duck pond in back,
some nice soft drinks by elbow, some good american snacks
    as well,
at least four hundred grand in the bank, & that's for checking,
an undisclosed amount in investments, & a copacetic evening
watching the latest military *techné*
wipe out poverty everywhere in the world
in its most obvious form, the poor

*

no complaints

six for robert grenier

high plains drifting

on the high plains,
when we meet
the inspector
we say, "buenas tardes, inspectór"

on the phone

"when do you go to bed?"
she asked me.

"when do you go to tibet?"
was what i heard.

"never," was my reply. "i've never
felt like going there."

---

there was some panic on the plane

people were screaming let me off let me off

then one man with an english accent stood up & said

no complaints

---

good
        to do the little
physical
            things
in the lonely place
sung by
        the ancients
                            we swim to meet

---

too little & too late

too brittle & too fated

we are but rabbits that pass at dusk

---

parenthesis

the part in her hair had a little bend

                        at the end

❋

behaviorally

it is possible to state
the case for pigeons
as sensibly-behaving
organisms

& against poets
as schizophrenic
humanoids

poets
emit verbal responses
i.e. write verses
that produce
few pellets of food

& even fewer
food surrogates
such as money or fame

thus b.f. skinner has said
without meaning offense   he said
that poets are not
sensible

*

the terrorist smiles

opens small notebook
has another drink
& writes:

no way the feeling
however new

will work in old form
however despised or desired

the higher the technological level
the more denatured the consciousness
used to it

& the more destructive
the collapse of both

may the finite
human carriage enter
good delight

by means of an effective
dialect that confounds
the single-minded
lovers of multiplication

*

lecture

for Hans Breder

the *meta-social*
takes us
all the way forward
to *dada & gaga*
mama & soma

the only active
schools of american poetry

unless one considers
the *dominant* school
of *coma*
anything but the *robot* manifestation

of prevailing system of *exploitation*

*

t.v. (1)

"for he is ishi   the last of his tribe"

"couldn't help noticing your aftershave"

the brain which takes that in its stride

is yours & mine   & it is late

*

t.v. (2)

funny
nazis!

twenty-five years
pass.

then,
more funny nazis!

*

the language

the language
comes loose in the head

the lights in the driveway
signal my neighbors' coming & going

it always is 2 a.m.,
as i am

& yet, in the woods there are marvelous places
my daughters go there, every day
bringing home armfuls of mint
& their own fragrant faces

to counter the general grayness & sense of mala suerte
graven on those worn by the males in this tribe

who persist in confronting, confronting
horns lowered
facing the emptiness to be populated with foes

hannes, i love you
you are my son.
we are the boys.
we are the men.
we do learn to live with the fact
of the language, thus confronting us
with division, which is the nature of all

that moves, is born,
& leads a life,
& gives it on.

*

big dog

i bring you
this head,
full of breath-
takingly beautiful
images of yourself

& put it in
your lap.

now i breathe
more quietly.

now you pat me.

now i sigh.

in a moment or two
i'll get up and
be a man again.

*

if

if your child tastes salty
go see the doctor

if the bed breaks
fix it

if your name is
wyot ordung

you wrote script
of "robot monster"
world's most inept movie

go see the monster

if you like gospel bluegrass
let me just say that simple
piety
    no matter how pretty
never quite made it

if you think my poems
make "an unpretentious
friend
    easy to live with
day after day"

you must be wyot ordung
using a pseudonym:

come see the monster

            *

anthropology

"The culture of a people
is an ensemble of texts
which the Anthropologist
strains to read"

over the shoulders of those to whom they properly belong

"The essay, whether of thirty pages
or three hundred, has seemed
the natural genre in which to present
cultural interpretations"

and the theories sustaining your jobs   you jokers.

*

aubade

night's ride's over

sun up   radio on

airedale wanda trots by window

time to see
what's there,
not forgetting what won't be

(the what
includes all whos)

so, coffee, here i come

here i come, dear shoes

*

BERNADETTE MAYER

A Woman I Mix Men Up. . .

A woman I mix men up
In my dreams & other ways, I wonder
If this is the same as knowing
What is & is not socialism, a man I'm sure

Does the same thing, mixing up
The mother for the lover or
Vice versa not to mention the mighty
Homosexual mix-ups which happen
Just as much, oh god whoever

He or she might be, I ask you
Why is David Lewis or Lewis Ed?
Why Anne Catherine or Catherine Ted?
Because I am not or don't want to be sure
I raise these questions to the heavens
Wherein I might, as proposed by a child
Sit on a cloud risking falling through
Should the child know a cloud is not solid
& should she bring no parachute, I feel

The risk's as great in loving as it is
In voting & you my lover's meeting even in
Dreams this other woman or man of your own sex
Seems like the newspapers, all too predictable
What types in what outfits'll appear
Doing what in what postures, suits & poses, to remake

The world is something not enough people dream of, one
Shouldnt use the word dream & one shouldnt use
The words should and shouldnt, cast off the book & find
No expectations, understanding liberalism's not
The same as conservatism or (god forbid) mysticism, there is
Morning and there is midday and there is night, there are
Phases of this one moon factually attached to the earth

Scatter the dictionaries, they dont
Tell the truth yet, I mix up words with truth
And abstraction with presence, who cares
Without a form who I am, I know I will timely die
But you two, God and this his image the junky bomb
Live forever to destroy the eternal the immortal
In what they used to call Man, now not.

*

The Tragic Condition
of the Statue of Liberty

A collaboration with Emma Lazarus

Give me your tired, your poor,
Your huddled masses yearning to breathe free,
The wretched refuse of your teeming shore.
Send these, the homeless, tempest-tost to me,
I lift my lamp beside the golden door!
Give me your gentrificatees of the Lower East Side
    including all the well-heeled young Europeans
    who'll take apartments without leases
Give me your landlords, give me your cooperators
Give me the guys who sell the food and the computers
    to the public schools in District One
Give me the IRS-FBI-CIA men who dont take election day off

Give me the certain members of the school board & give me
    the district superintendent
Give me all the greedy members of both american & foreign
    capitalist religious sects
Give me the parents of the punk people
Give me the guy who puts those stickers in the Rice Krispies
Give me the doctor who thinks his time is more valuable
    than mine and my daughter's & the time of all the other
    non-doctors in this world
Give me the mayor, his mansion, and the president & his white
    house
Give me the cops who laugh and sneer at meetings where
    they demonstrate the new uses of mace and robots instead
    of the old murder against people who are being evicted
Give me the landlord's sleazy lawyers and the deal-making
    judges
    in housing court & give me the landlord's arsonist
Give me the known & unknown big important rich guys who
    now bank on our quaint neighborhood
Give me, forgive me, the writers who have already or want to
    write bestsellers in this country
Together we will go to restore Ellis Island, ravaged for years
    by wind, weather and vandals
I was surprised and saddened when I heard that
the Statue of Liberty
    was in such a serious state of disrepair & I want to help
This is the most generous contribution I can afford.

*

Laundry & School Epigrams

For all of us
There is clothing
We have to wear it
Even if it is not cold.

Oh Kore is the covering of nakedness
To be forever the chore of women?

Unnumbered goddesses
That I or he can invoke,
Who shall take the responsibility
For the laundry totally
In this century?

Clothing is scattered
All about the house.
Who'll gather it all up
And separate the dirty from the clean,
Then do the washing?

We wash and hang up
The clothing to dry.
Do you think men
Wish this laundry
To be forever wet?

Did you know that in school
They still say stay in line
Don't talk and
Boys on this side
Girls on the other
Isn't that nice
For prison, get ready!

Put your children
In the public schools, friends.
They'll get a chance to meet
The female police
& eat Chicken McNuggets.

✳

Eve of Easter

Milton, who made his illiterate daughters
Read to him in five languages
Till they heard the news he would marry again
And said they would rather hear he was dead
Milton who turns even Paradise Lost
Into an autobiography, I have three
Babies tonight, all three are sleeping:
Rachel the great great great granddaughter
Of Herman Melville is asleep on the bed
Sophia and Marie are sleeping
Sophia namesake of the wives
Of Lewis Freedson the scholar and Nathaniel Hawthorne
Marie my mother's oldest name, these three girls
Resting in the dark, I made the lucent dark
I stole images from Milton to cure opacous gloom
To render the room an orb beneath this raucous
Moon of March, eclipsed only in daylight
Heavy breathing baby bodies
Daughters and descendants in the presence of
The great ones, Milton and Melville and Hawthorne,
        everyone is speaking
At once, I only looked at them all blended
Each half Semitic, of a race always at war
The rest of their inherited grace
From among Nordics, Germans and English,
        writers at peace
Rushing warring Jews into democracy when actually
Peace is at the window begging entrance
With the hordes in the midst of air
Too cold for this time of year,
Eve of Easter and the shocking resurrection idea
Some one baby stirs now, hungry for an egg
It's the Melville baby, going to make a fuss
The Melville one's sucking her fingers for solace

She makes a squealing noise
Hawthorne baby's still deeply asleep
The one like my mother's out like a light
The Melville one though the smallest wants the most
Because she doesn't really live here
Hawthorne will want to be nursed when she gets up
Melville sucked a bit and dozed back off
Now Hawthorne is moving around, she's the most hungry
Yet perhaps the most seduced by darkness in the room
I can hear Hawthorne, I know she's awake now
But will she stir, disturbing the placid sleep
Of Melville and insisting on waking us all
Meanwhile the rest of the people of Lenox
Drive up and down the street
Now Hawthorne wants to eat
They all see the light by which I write, Hawthorne sighs
The house is quiet, I hear Melville's toy
I've never changed the diaper of a boy
I think I'll go get Hawthorne and nurse her for the pleasure
Of cutting through darkness before her measured noise
Stimulates the boys, I'll cook a fish
Retain poise in the presence
Of heady descendants, stone-willed their fathers
Look at me and drink ink
I return a look to all the daughters and I wink
Eve of Easter, I've inherited this
Peaceful sleep of the children of men
Rachel, Sophia, Marie and again me
Bernadette, all heart I live, all head, all eye, all ear
I lost the prejudice of paradise
And wound up caring for the babies of these guys

*

Essay

I guess it's too late to live on the farm
I guess it's too late to move to a farm
I guess it's too late to start farming
I guess it's too late to begin farming
I guess we'll never have a farm
I guess we're too old to do farming
I guess we couldn't afford to buy a farm anyway
I guess we're not suited to being farmers
I guess we'll never have a farm now
I guess farming is not in the cards now
I guess Lewis wouldn't make a good farmer
I guess I can't expect we'll ever have a farm now
I guess I have to give up all my dreams of being a farmer
I guess I'll never be a farmer now
We couldn't get a farm anyway though Allen Ginsberg got one
    late in life
Maybe someday I'll have a big garden
I guess farming is really out
Feeding the pigs and the chickens, walking between miles of
    rows of crops
I guess farming is just too difficult
We'll never have a farm
Too much work and still to be poets
Who are the farmer poets
Was there ever a poet who had a self-sufficient farm
Flannery O'Connor raised peacocks
And Wendell Berry has a farm
Faulkner may have farmed little
And Robert Frost had farmland
And someone told me Samuel Beckett farmed
Very few poets are real farmers
If William Carlos Williams could be a doctor and Charlie
    Vermont too,

Why not a poet who was also a farmer
Of course there was Brook Farm
And Virgil raised bees
Perhaps some poets of the past were overseers of farmers
I guess poets tend to live more momentarily
Than life on a farm would allow
You could never leave the farm to give a reading
Or go to a lecture by Emerson in Concord
I don't want to be a farmer but my mother was right
I should never have tried to rise out of the proletariat
Unless I can convince myself as Satan argues with Eve
That we are among a proletariat of poets of all the classes
Each ill-paid and surviving on nothing
Or on as little as one needs to survive
Steadfast as any farmer and fixed as the stars
Tenants of a vision we rent out endlessly

*

Warren Phinney

A little boy on August first night
Got into the colors possible in the light
Of this universe & of his cock
We spoke the words the little boy
My little boy like in the liturgy & in the litany,
Thee, more august that is magnificent
Than any of the daily concerns, his soft skin.
And losing my judgment I forgot about his Volkswagen
Which was needed in the morning to carry his father
And his mother to work, it was not his car
But the drive wasnt far and before you left
After the phone calls were answered
From friends to find you there was time
For another mention of the Russian Revolution

Then I wound up with my feet at the head of the bed
Knowing hippily about our stars, your guitar
& the meeting from which we fled, the proper porcupines
Having eaten enough of your parents' car's gaslines
To give us time to make the little more love
We'd dreamed of before the tow truck came.

٭

Sonnet: Kamikaze

Dawn & night of fighting, lovers like actual wars
And as gentle men might be gentle, so they are not.
Jeans we all wear independent of our mutual sexes
Some lipsticked & rouged & eye-linered, some not.
I dont want to meet him, he does not prepare the food;
Also I am old. He the same age, younger, awaits my death.
A scholar, he doesnt count the births or clothes;
A scholar too, I keep track of the ages of the clothing.
Love seems to die for him with love's attention;
No point in thought or fight with dyed-in-wool women.

If we cant get along then who the fuck can?
I will not run or go forward American, divine wind.
A person, I must insist on a heartless agreeing;
A person too, he must agree some love can be.

٭

It Was Miss Scarlet
With the Candlestick
in the Billiard Room

As there are taped sororal presents & psychological reversals
    in the radio/film/video/photography/painting/dance/
    non-poetry dream-world sphere
So you didnt bother to introduce me to your confrere
Who has pretty blonde hair & was working there

Now I am making love in a hotel with _____
But the door's open & woman-haters come in, eagles

I've got my period on the sightless precipice
You act like fucking Tarzan on, leaping from the lobby
To a tree over what's invisible (though I showed you)
To thee who often scorns being agile

Since nobody can come with grace in this situation
I go out to get something to eat & have an orgasm
While waiting for a barbecued food I cant mention
Then I cash a check for eleven thousand fifty-five dollars
Gotta get a new zipper for my designer jeans

And you, not you, smeared with menstrual blood
Leave some on display like a fucking wedding sheet
In a glass golden cigarette case on the street
Snow White! The forest's on the side of the city!
Plus we see Peggy.

✳

Booze Turns Men Into Women

A sip of Coors makes children be
Nuclear power plant contractors
Wild Turkey turns men into deer
Molson's Canadian Beer makes
All the people fear laundromats
Stolichnaya turns women into Rolling Rocks
Men turn women into oatmeal stout
Jack Daniel's turns men into Queen Anne's lace
Triple Sec turns men into margaritas
Der Budweiser juven often undoes mein leben
Grand Marnier turns women into
ancient mariners
Creme de Cassis creates
Child toxic waste entrepreneurs
Watney's weakens warriors
A taste of jeniver turned Beatrice into a t-square
Martell's makes men Mooseheads
Heinekens dimwit God couscous miracle elf
Gins turn men into safety pins
Chivas Regal makes men sewing needles
Blackeyed Susans turn men into Jack Daniels
Women wake from highballs as walnuts
Cocktails alienate communalists and
A glass of Schaeffer'll
Make your kid a general

*

The Complete
Introductory Lectures
on Poetry

for Ted Berrigan

It was when the words on the covers of books,
Titles as true as false leaves led me to believe
In inviting the ultimate speculation of love—
That I could learn all of the subject—
That I first began to entertain what is sublime

Like a moth I thought by reading JOKES AND
THEIR RELATION TO THE UNCONSCIOUS or BEYOND
THE PLEASURE PRINCIPLE or EAT THE WEEDS or
THE ORIGIN OF THE SPECIES or even a book on
COUP D'ETATS or THE PROBLEM OF ANXIETY I
Could accomplish the knowledge the titles implied

Science that there is often more
In the notes on the back of a discarded envelope,
Grammar in the shadows slanted on the wall
Of the too bright night to verify the city light

And then awakening, babies, to turn and make notes
On the dream's public epigrams and one's own
Weaknesses, self that's prone to epigrammatic ridicule

And to meditate on fears of all the animal dangers
Plus memories of reptilian appellations for all
Our stages of learning to swim at a past day camp

It is to think this or that might include all
Or enough to entertain all those who already know
That in this century of private apartments
Though knowledge might be coveted hardly anything
Is shared except penurious poetry, she or he
Who still tends to titles as if all of us
Are reading a new book called THE NEW LIFE.

❊

ANDREI CODRESCU

Au Bout du Temps

So late in the 20th Century
             So late in the 20th Century
        At the end almost of the 20th Century
  I sit in my home
           In my modest and meaningless home
           And worry about my penis
        ABOUT MY PENIS FOR CHRISSAKES!

In praise of biology
    In praise of visions . . .
Only a few years ago it did not seem
        so late in the 20th Century
           it did not seem very late
             in the 20th Century
        this saddest of centuries
maybe the 14th was a very sad century
        fin de siecle
           mal de siecle

mal de fin
        so late in the night
           so late in the century
             in the 20th Century

*

A Petite Histoire of Red Fascism

(for M. Brownstein)

All connections
are made by energy.
The inert masses
know nobody & not
themselves. Nobody &
Not Self are well worth
knowing but connecting
them takes energy
so they are known
only by their masks
of inert proletarian
matter—Bolshevik
statues. The people
with the most energy
employ themselves to
know the statues. The
statues are well-known
by the inert masses.
The people with just
a little less energy
are then employed
to interrogate the inert
proletariat. One energy
grade below, the police &
mental-health apparatus
employ themselves to
energize the inert mass
which is now for the
first time broken up
into individuals.
Breaking it up releases

energy—enough energy
to respond to questioning.
The police level then ex-
tracts a primitive narra-
tive from the recently
inert & this narrative
generates enough energy
& excitement to produce
a two-level discourse which
makes sense to the upper
energy level. New
energy is created & soon
the top echelons are
introduced to the dis-
courses of Nobody &
Not Self. Together,
the brass & the mass
envision the statues:
the energy of the mass
will henceforth be em-
ployed to make statues
of the brass.

✻

De Rerum Natura

I sell myths not poems. With each poem goes a little myth. This myth is not in the poem. It's in my mind. And when the editors of magazines ask me for poems I make them pay for my work by passing along these little myths which I make up. These myths appear at the end of the magazine under the heading ABOUT CONTRIBUTORS or above my poems in italics. Very soon there are as many myths as there are poems and ultimately this is good

because each poem does, this way, bring another poet into the
world. With this secret method of defying birth controls I popu-
late the world with poets.

✻

Against Meaning

Everything I do is against meaning.
This is partly deliberate, mostly spontaneous.
Wherever I am I think I'm somewhere else.
This is partly to confuse the police, mostly to
avoid myself es-
pecially when I have to confirm
the obvious which always
sits on a little table and draws a lot
of attention to itself.
So much so that no one sees the chairs
and the girl sitting on one of them.
With the obvious one is always at the movies.
The other obvious which the loud obvious
conceals
is not obvious enough to merit a
surrender of the will.
But through a little hole in the boring report
God watches us faking it.

✻

The Threat

I am not looking for your jugular.
Only for your eyes.

This isn't exactly accurate.
I want both.   And if you ask, as you should

if you like yourself, why do I go for such
ferocious treats, I must
admit

that there is something unexploded in my gut.

And it wants you because there is
an unexploded something in yours too.

A music box we swallowed when we were children?
The growing up? Which is
learning to handle terror?
Was there something in the food or is
the government responsible for it?

It's nothing I can stick my knife into and say:
"For sure it's this!"

And yet I want it out more than I want these words

*

En Passant

Having avantbiographed the world
To make another come right out of it
I have certain scribbler's rights
On the next one—endlessly impregnate
The self about to be designed.

I praise the lava holes

whence issued my first passport.

*

The Inner Source

All good things
       eggs & hashish
come from Molotov's eye
       & return to Stalin's.
What I'd like to see
                    he said
is a poem without Stalin.
       Me too.
There are certain kinds of typewriters
made for Ted Berrigan staccato poems—
       especially elucidating the question
of audience as singular.
                    The same machine
addressing itself abstractly to a theme
       or a plural audience (also theme)
                    would be more of a machine,
i.e., would be more aesthetic.
       Addressed
                    to you
                    it wobbles
betwixt the listening to itself & the void.
Likewise the telephone, said F. O'H., and true.
One gets his effects, said Lenin,
       from speaking to all as if all were one,
              thereby birthing the Hell's Angels.
But Stalin said
       entering the poem through the back
              that one must speak to No One
                    as if all were included.
It never occurred to Homer to include No One
       though he invoked his guises.
And F. O'H. took to eliminating No One from the address
       by putting a name in the blank,
              an intelligent listening.

A great deal of whistling wind between a civilized
address in a city with streets
& a steppe with horsemen picking teeth with lances.
Conquests instead of dentists
oneness instead of arthritis.
Detritus humanists stash egg in the aortas.
A word sucked from the air and lightning
spewed smoking out into the mouths
of a million baby birds
versus
the word ESPRESSO in neon and the rain
beckoning anonymously warm in Paris, France.
The verbiage of frozen butts upon the saddle of loud death
sugar crystallized above the hush
of cottony May evening *sur le coin*
de table.
History of what rounds (how many)
and what babble
before specific address
and hey, hey, that was me talking
to you walking
away.
Go on
while you still can
before they notice.
It is in this way
that the listener departed
a long time ago
from an address in the city
changing his number leaving no telltale traces
or tales.
The one Mongolian who tried was turned
into thin slices and worn under the saddle
till pastramied.
The N.Y. Deli on Second proudly serves him now on rye.
Consequently only good Mongolians tell long tales.

The epic-homosexual tradition
survives intact
in the unaddressed
without address
but tightly
packed.
The anonymous alienated prosaic use the full-page bourgeois
indigested aspirined and hebdo dramadaire Cointreau's sex
sated deconstructed (self) lophe
tell toted (melted)
on the spot
where addressed
where the telephone
was.
Imagine Stalin phoning up his troops one by one.
Imagine Mayakovski phoning up his fans one by one.
Imagine Dylan Thomas remembering each girl he fucked.
Imagine Whitman remembering each blade of grass.
Imagine Stalin phoning Mayakovski.
Imagine Stalin phoning Frank.
You can't imagine that?
Frank phoning Stalin?
Of course.
Let's talk mustache.
Let's hash the hush.

*

CLARK COOLIDGE

Risen Matters

And I should go and I should do and
    what should I go and do? and whether
Rods that attach to the wheat and are the wheat of sight
I have launched a new boat in the spirit of abacus
A level divide never to be gotten reading
The new old book on scenery
I live in the object between the pages subject to that
    and lift up my cap and hum and part

I have no cap and my thrust is to the thread side
    and all is divisions in the hope, the edgy desire
    to be done with singles
I live on the Mount of No Cape and thrill my sound
    through restless   not yet heartless
Here are no adamant ones enough to freeze the opal

Time's sides gone
Going a matter of done
Should is the what of strewn occasion
And and is the rod without
Which no field

*

Disturbing
the Sallies Forth

What has been brought to a finish
I do not want to see, face.
Watch the earth as a heavening ball
wound in hand to press the land,
be stumped! The works are alive.
And say, Drop your plans in waves of
thought wider than rift at the edge
of widening pact. Haul on reason
and snap. When did the change turn up
that makers found their materials
twins to matters? When did
we enter? Caught now awake
simultaneous inside and out there, nevermore
the need for such a travel, poised at the point
of a work in light lines of blood.
World, worlds, the shout vision of just another
ball wavers in the void of edged weights.
Nights the battery juice peers over the coiled prow.
I have an answer collection, patent leaning.
I lean a ledge on which apples are painted.
I jingle all histories in my anchor pocket
and stand by a window of birds erased by trees.
Happiness calls from cold mines beneath my sanity.
And wonder is a twine of wands lodged
to spine of nothing I know at least to hold.

*

Of the Confident Stranger

What can a man do that
will not be overdone by others?
(the thoughts gone into
the words and out again)
There is a picture of a pork pie
left on some plumbing, a profile with pipe
shadowed on a tent wall by
light of the desert zero

Incidents in c-sharp
minor as a virgin scatter
and the poets will write

❊

To Mind

for Ron

It's pleasant to remember that the world doesn't
know anything. We do.

Comes into my mind
with from time
to time a buzz.

Novel as a dime, a disc
inscribed with a "rear".

You wouldn't know anything
if you didn't say anything.
Me, I'm not telling what I do.

A cloud.
And pen, and no ink for that
matter but a snooze. Later
we'll enumerate everything
forgetting our language, too lazy for lessons
as if radar were likely or handy
as bedside

                as cough drops or slang.

*

Remove the Predicate

What if they knew nothing, or what they did
know held nothing for us? All the vaunted
spears of time dope, buried in a fault heap
under the cats' mistakes, nothing but hoops of tell
close enough to fear weed to keep matchless for us

I look under things here in a Rome all built
of under, no top to any of this but a quick
mistaken sky, full of even my god a blimp
or on a bright day the pure echoes of all you'd think
you've seen, I lie down beneath it and cash

Hand me the documents, no, those cut and parcelled
out of well water, that one pure spring interrupted
the Mythraic vaults, where they ate it is said to
increase power's pressure, as I walk past my
millionth trattoria, humming up coffee ultimacies
and the words to spell my name

None to walk farther than city, in this city
if it is?, it's close enough celled to be a town

when the sundown seethes into the ground and each
morning you forget, as if the bells couldn't say
which side brazen side of the same palmed one
the known is old and we are new

*

Rome Once Alone

Stealing along in this eyelighter city
the trials are hidden, far behind the near wall
the views constructed full hewn and tap block
high away as shoe is settled the squares fill to static
the square where the magic hood is bronzed

The horned toad in a box is not brought here
its blood was hired here, mined from perimeter
vines reached to glass and lamp concocted violet
the sow caught in the stone a part of the ambling language
and the Popeye held at the wire a high melancholic

Humour a rubber let loose in this backcourt reaction
times have so colored the river nothing greys
the center of all this marble a ruby prism
ashes tend by night a tongue by day
and the last time I pass will be by flashlight
and the last thing I rob will be a gong

*

Back Aways

A Twist of Childhood—

In wizened old terminal birth
I hold up a spalding lemon
is a pearl, is a whizzing point of land's end
laughing at me, and whirling me up
   a lap of the goodness

This the beginning of the toil term
the load of ingot and bland
the silly heave on the tip of turn it to true
whatever the collecting of lighthouses be saved as
the saintliness meditating on sand spits
the youth ope of eye on a bitter pear
oval of room on rectangular you

I stared at pencil edges, knowing them not
to be a parcel of see-you in doorspace
and who's edging there, the two
that misted you into frontal lobotomy, cheering
for free linger tootness blossoms
apparent to the bottom of the dare the glade
all in hoot buckets pointed
the sea, that amuses and frosts
the brink of allotment, one toy

Eyes that silent the bright band stripers
a later knowledge of snaky pens and men
standing bag-baggage back in shadow storm
rotters and kelpish standages near basement
   clot and ravage
but I didn't know
nor note to fend

The passing out of all clean care
the blond muscles in the cave
of name dare and rave
coddling under a stare, a gravid
pottled grounding of chondrules
sited before your muzzled beak
   lip light and hair
you wake to the finding of stains

And what did I see all plaining in my hand
   but the finer geckos
the ones with plans, and sheltered avenue gainfulness
   hovered about the spite long nose
longer than the spoon around the bottle in space
my siftiness of premeditative prolonged intent
when mystery is a whisper in the candy heart
nobody knows but nobody me

The glass nobody
the me without handles
the back-of-the-door infusion of placky particles
   borrowed from neighbors of the weighty adult
sun on and waiting for nothing
seeing the blend in motes of serious
   and universal smear of no-intent
   pocketless and on the smile
   the empty blast of regal fear
I lost my spoon
but pestiness lasted

Did I know heart when I wiggled in trees?
What did I tent within windows' glasses?
Weighted Monster of the Wiggle During
I saved a cap for my mate and tipped it never
hurled holes in the ground to sever
and berries of no-choice in the loam deck chested

I made them war for my manned tomorrows
   which never were plurals
merely white glance in tendon gloom glade
under hausers of parental distemper
notched a common in my beckons
powdered all stare

Mere underwear
I make the sign of the sun peck
and remark alert at its hybrid
no central palm in the mind
so sorry wider
the lengthen, clothesbody
you got to reach
by screen means to apple sturdy
no matter the hook bulb
   and closet study

The it bib
in avanti letter
capsulates the puke mule
his roentgen itch and fodder buried
alp to the hilt
and in flinch
a whole palm of parent
   in dauby door
in rate of cloud, clown sediment
and a corpuscle muscle
clads you in delve
   age stem
you rise, but you don't
lacking swerve
and a litter daze bulb clot eventuation lesson

And make it be your name, make that pumpkin disturb
he's lying on candy, says the satisfied doorway

oof of clad and rumple to the itch
baffled at tune glands and the grapple
seems as if it's trade hoot clear to the door
miles trumpet from the grassine lane
name was hoot bucket and traipsed on in
pajama clout out of minerals frangible
nape of Bucky Bug, it's possible

In the doorways there are nothing

Sad saw of afternoon in the edge lace of cryable ledge
under awnings of tree pots and crystal case
where ice is housed for your lemon leg
and care'll go over your day like a wheeled derrick
denying mystico printings of pad whelks and the tin on the
    door
of Grandness Little, the portico of these pictures

Adds up the icemen loafing
and leans from dormers the stories of them
as if you couldn't have tea
    with your head in a drizzle
cone pad of cough ladings
accoutrement to the phone
no illness head has ever so violet varied
and carps all violent in a copsey stir cap
the cartoons of Mister Pond, the shave

And coffee rose morn over all city breathe
was incinerator actual
as I giggled into my brain to feel who
was I to dare there, ectoplasmic in my walk
to loaf school and hair up to my witness lessons

Chuckle wise of those I knew there
sharp feeted by wall and wire and cokey delvings

housings gigantic of volumes, romantic of sheaf
festering through boilers of raretism day
level hope on the scald, and the run time of pirates
experiating at the love of fence broughten trees
and girls in parks, girls of the alum car

You see what I do, everytime I miss you
whole cold parting gyzm polluting roentgens
would stop by where my father parked
   and level his fold head
   and mystery up my dead

                                     bowed deed

Shambling off ramps, with half a cone to my fasten
the rooves of those blinds were flatten

                                     but I lasted

                  pottery blue boots
                  in the chisel dawn

And youth hone hours, tonguing tips the tooth
but rain off barn end I am loath
back to

                  the snakes the walls to my chisel dare
                  and apey stave

This is all a fizzing but has lasted
has made me full dare again the indigenous sud
New England of apple of harm and raid weathers

Putting the pages together in the hairy wetness
of stove bolts in rumple fights
you know, but I don't
being young
ink applied
spending the day in

bending try
        to remember
the hoses made my horses
my rug oval of train chug minute

But you'll all go off in a candle
and never fasten me again
and I'll sight stars never set
and remember gates shutless but on the lock
and trend myself back to barry baiters
and relegate my sadness to a yurl
and lemon the shadows
and kiss the migrant bat
and wait tight wait
for waters to witness my losted
                        (told fist)
    (adults are all relegators)

No knowledge!
all blows off in blues of furls
of slow dates so fast they smart
and cool banyan angles of the heart
my age
and another stage
all others
penitent partners
of the snake
whose sign is wall blank

Pushed grain past frond
    and knew it
    more than wait
assemblies of the slipping guard
remiss in its berry pebble clashness
things must shine themselves separate
from mass, from buttled arbiters
honings of the glove

and wait water white
blessing the nod and the dim open
to coin myself back to initial tip
and load loss with fume
meditant hung stepping
drapings the world let down

Displays
a grab at from my carey cage
all carried down like a case of my witness lessons

You'll be afraid of your own self I will
and tremble in destined plick of ghost coat avenue
recalling the nothing from the nothing gate

*

ANNE WALDMAN

After Li Ch'ing-chao

drinking strong *genmai* tea
a purple hairpin slips to the floor

bend downstairs in slithery robe
to telephone beloved far off

meditators sleep under new moon
snow coats lake & mountains

trapped at Seminary 2 more months
face ages around eyelids

slap on creams, paint cheeks
don lacquered comb with painted feather

discipline is rigorous
to bring the mind back

scent of incense & gong
inspire further practice

"I don't exist" "All is impermanence"
this haunts me

but I long to clutch my lover's body
& he sink into me

*

On Walt Whitman's Birthday

O strategic map of disasters, hungry America
O target for the song, the jouncing poem,
the protest
A long imperfect history shadows you
Let all suffering, toil, sex &
sublime distractions go unrecorded
Let the world continue to breathe

It's simple: a woman gets up & stretches
The world is her mirror & portal too

(Whitmanic morning task: waking the country to itself)

✳

July 4th

Wood green. Grandfather built it.
But Grandfather is dead. He puts
down the glassblower's tube to die
a Lutheran. He starts the black
Ford sedan one last time. He wears
working glass spectacles on his
pale face.

Metal holders are spread like
fans on the front of the house
supporting American flags small enough
a child can wave as the boats go by.

✳

Berthe Morisot

Toward the end of her life she said that the
wish for fame after death seemed to her an
inordinate ambition. "Mine," she added,
"is limited to the desire to set down
something as it passes, oh, something, the
least of things!"

A critic had written of the show at the
Salon des Impressionnistes singling out
Morisot: "There are five or six lunatics,
one of them a woman."

✳

Song: Time Drawes Neere

Time drawes neere
    love adornes you
        pours down autumn sunne

Babye I follow you
    sweete offspringe of
        nighte & sleepe

Pangs of the babye
    tossed in a bellie:
        birdies & woodlands cheer!

Eies gaze with delighte
    I hope I fear I laugh
        call you "rolling mountain"

Your roote is deepe, be you englishe
   rosie fayre or german darkly
      call you boy or girl?

I must have pillowes & musicke
   I must have raspberry leaf tea
      I needs must groan Ah me!

Ah thee! a secret growing
   I go no more a-maying
      I settle into my tent shift

Bursting at seams
   big tub, water barrel
      tossed as boat or cloud, gravid

Powre to claime my hart in
   bodye roome, powre to keepe
      me waking all nighte a-peeing

I ride you unscene wave
   wee rise together
      under daddye's roof & hand.

*

Number Song

I've multiplied, I'm 2.
He was part of me,
he came out of me,
he took a part of me.
He took me apart.
I'm 2, he's my art,
no, he's separate.

He art one. I'm not
done & I'm still one.
I sing of my son. I've
multiplied, My heart's
in 2, half to him &
half to you,
who are also a part
of him, & you & he
& I make trio of
kind congruity.

*

Complaynt

after Emily Dickinson

I'm wanton—no I've stopped that.
That old place
I've changed, I'm Mother
It's more mysterious.
How odd the past looks
When I reread old notebooks,
See their faces fade
I feel it everywhere
& ordinary too
Am I safer now?
Was other way gayer?
I'm Mother now, O help &
Continue!

*

Goddess of Wisdom
Whose Substance Is Desire

for Joanne Kyger

You want distraction's collar & necktie
She is something embracing a human document
but I fear you'll never twice spy land
modulating boredom & fatigue
with fashionable closet people
whose spasms of prudent laughter
are acute in your wake—No!
Won't do for you.

But she: gracious pleats, fits,
who owns all graces, slips, who is
no matinee twit, is a beam, who won't fall,
a supple frank movement, is a gracile planet
to know, circled by fixed heat,
benign of big eyes, obscure of sternness,
bears no ill labels, a pinafore hopping
on a leg, is mature of reason, who has a
sound reason, is a veritable pouch
of information, a saint

Also a bunch of winter traces,
glistening clips, is a clipper,
a bold one, a maiden to film
to smile to clasp to form your thoughts,
loath to make a plea of axis of world
shifting, mind's discreet parody of self,
slave to livingroom harmony, mine gates
are reluctant attitudes compared to hers,
profiles in wood to make a pleasure

quarter hum in pleasure garter to make
pleasure rather a saint too, she's got
a strange cook's manner for handling limbs

When women make concessions
who dares not dumbly bend
who dares not humble bread
or stumble up a cliff for it
to fondle her head . . .

Renunciation is sweet to her
checking out packages with a shiny face,
journeying without escort, without
a married name, wearing the cut cloth
of nourishment, traveling incognito's
seamy route of transport, dispel hot
tantrum, gum braids, triumphant
over gleaming mail, not in sense of manly
but mail of metal made
& substance of desire made woman

She feeds on rapscallion envy of this age
merriment & poverty smiling there
corpses, vultures, idiot grinning there,
impatience too, & ghosts smiling there
& lesser hells of deceit of many moons
& many mistakes there
& there—a tiredness, there—a charm
to fuck against bleakness, there—
accomplished treachery
there's no wink, gone slack
dizzy or stupid or vexed

No paths apart to cloak a fiction
to make an evil faction of this dire want
or wrath falling or plowing proudly
decked out like a male bird of the species

wolf music: come here tonight
arguments: go to the podium
owl song: friend indeed
mermaid: smooth a lash

Or lash against her pagan power
she whose substance, whose wisdom is desire
whose slaughter echoes laughter and earbone hisses
she who appointed herself to your distraction
she whose wish is in the light

A modest stipend, she is no mother diminishing,
her dreams are ornaments of sleep.
She's a sharp retina of perception
when you stray, when you are too peppery,
when you are not your blunt self
when you are a foil, a bitch
shrinking up like this itinerary's list
to arrive musically at rest
not a stag, not a suitor in jealous weeds
but optimistic & boosting speech.

*

Canzone

for Ted Berrigan, 1934–1983

I crisscross my feelings with a view
of street, people walking, some crazy looking, from a window
Some could be anyone, me, you, Ted, with your own "view"
Could anyone else share? Tinted clouds today. His view
which some thought extreme, distorted, stubborn,
making friends into Myth where they became viewed

with excessive scrutiny & magnified into situations in
    which only the Heavens dare intervene
He said, Propitiate the gods! They love to intervene
as you walk, sleep, talk, make love, drink soda in plain view
of them. I'll put in a good word, you show-offs! I have long talks
with them at night about you, no evasions when the muses
talk
This was the energy Ted sought by talk

As if there was no other way close enough to get a multiple
    view
of self, and tell some history through layers of talk
He would tell his heart to talk
& it did & enlarged the domains of art, his mind was behind a
    window
out of which he could throw propriety, then remake language,
    steal it from books, from fast elegant talk
to discover the power that lives in printed words & talk
is captive, you can re-invent the world, it's not so stubborn
but tongue-tied, shy, a young girl, gorgeous, funny, also
    stubborn
about bringing poems into focus. Huddle, team, to talk
Ted lying before his audience in bed, a practiced man, his
    memory then intervene
fundamental to the thing seen, the thing thought, then Death
    could intervene

Pugnacious, subversive, president of the adventure, Death
    intervened
to taste & magnify the ingredients, but also end talk
although I hear it still go on. Mysterious noises intervene
to shake the poet out of her sleep to recognize his cargo, & to
    intervene
of behalf of Ted who won't ever formulate a neat view
Here is a non-utilitarian cigarette, but it can't intervene
between us anymore, it won't intervene

as you once flicked ash on my lap (I was indignant), then out
    the window
Or you once beheld all of Boston from my airplane window
Did you ever belong to me? Could I never intervene
to make you healthier, less quivering with stubborn
love or pride? I loved you of course for being stubborn.

You were inhabiting the same stubborn
poems as I was. I can't look out the window
without missing you without being angry at you, stubborn
in a kind of grief that won't let me write now, head stubborn
& the typewriter waiting for a new oracle who will talk
vast magical ruminations spelled out from the moment, sing of
    a stubborn
time insistent upon war for chatter for stubborn stammerings
to make life more exalted, a point of view
which uses dreams because they are my imagination my view
now of you as a full citizen of this country no matter how
    stubborn
I breathe in the colors from the window
I stand in the early morning light of the window

Are you drawn back to look in my window?
If so, I'll be capacious, I want to ask you something stubborn
"I am a bountiful cotton crop" you wrote on your last postcard
    window
like a cartoon. Then my name and address: "Mt. Olympus,
    Near Bo-Tree, Manhattan." You draw an octagon window
Your handwriting makes me laugh, it would always intervene
optimistically. Did you mean to keep me in the picture? The
    window
is shut, I went away, a stranger moved into the apartment,
    no need to shout up at the window

I miss your comparisons, prodigious talk
We are as unlike as people can be in our talk

It is 1967. You call up at the window
with your rotund ambition, a cosmopolitan view
Let's get high, let's fall in love, let's ride uptown & see
    what the painters are doing with a view

Is it nothing more than strange antics, a view
I'll never own, nor you, nor greater intensity than talk
will ever do, when grief does spill over & intervene to the
    present?
My equilibrium is swaying as the 20th century stubbornly
    shuts down
I was there & I was there by the window onto you.

*

LESLIE SCALAPINO

That They Were at the Beach

A Sequence

She heard the sounds of a couple having intercourse and then
getting up they went into the shower so that she caught a sight
of them naked before hearing the water running. The parts of
their bodies which had been covered by clothes were those of
leopards. During puberty her own organs and skin were not like
this though when she first had intercourse with a man he
removed his clothes and his organ and flesh were also a
leopard's. She already felt pleasure in sexual activity and her
body not resembling these adults made her come easily which
also occurred when she had intercourse with another man a
few months later.

———————

When sexual unions occurred between a brother and sister they
weren't savages or primitive. She had that feeling about having
intercourse with men whose organs were those of leopards and
hers were not. Walking somewhere after one of these episodes
she was excited by it though she might not have made this
comparison if she'd actually had a brother. At least the woman
she had seen in the shower had a leopard's parts. In these
episodes when she'd had intercourse with a man he didn't
remark about her not being like that. And if women had these
characteristics which she didn't it made her come more easily
with him.

———————

She overheard another couple together and happened to see them as she had the couple in the shower. The nude part of the woman was like herself and the man had the leopard's parts so that she had the same reaction and came easily with someone, as she had with a sense of other women having a leopard's traits and herself isolated. The man with whom she had intercourse did not say anything that showed he had seen a difference in her and that made her react physically. Yet other women seemed to have a leopard's characteristics except for this one she'd seen.

Again it seemed that a man with whom she had intercourse was her brother and was ardent with her—but this would not have occurred to her had she really had a brother. Yet her feeling about him was also related to her seeing a woman who was pregnant and was the only one to be so. The woman not receiving attention or remarks on the pregnancy excited her; and went together with her sense of herself coming easily and yet not being pregnant until quite awhile after this time.

She also felt that she came easily feeling herself isolated when she was pregnant since she had the sense of other women having leopards' organs. They had previously had children. She was the only one who was pregnant and again she saw a couple together, the man with leopard's parts and the woman not having these characteristics.

Again she could come since her body was different from the adult who had some parts that were leopards', and having the sense of the women having had children earlier than her and their not having younger children now.

Her liking the other women to have had children when she was pregnant had to do with having them there and herself isolated—and yet people not saying much about or responding to the pregnancy. She thought of the man coming as when she caught a sight of the couple together—being able to come with someone a different time because she had a sense of a woman she'd seen having had her children earlier. There being a difference of age, even ten years, between a child she'd have and those the other women had had.

She happened to see some men who were undressed, as if they were boys—one of them had the features and organ of a leopard and the others did not. The difference in this case gave her the sense of them being boys, all of them rather than those who didn't have leopards' characteristics and this made her come easily with someone.

It was not a feeling of their being a younger age, since the men were her own age, and she found the men who lacked the leopard features to be as attractive as the one who had those features. She had the feeling of them as adults and her the same age as them, yet had the other feeling as well in order for her to come then.

She saw a couple who were entwined together and her feeling about them came from the earlier episode of seeing the men who were nude and having the sense of them being adolescent boys. Really she'd had the sense of the men she'd seen as being adults and herself the same age as them. The couple she watched were also around the same age as herself—the man being aware of someone else's presence after a time and coming. The woman pleased then though she had not come.

She had intercourse with the man who had the features and organs of a leopard and whom she had first seen with the group of men who lacked these characteristics. The other men were attractive as he was. Yet having the sense of the difference between him and the others, she found it pleasant for him to come and for her not to come that time. The same thing occurred on another occasion with him.

She compared the man to plants, to the plants having a nervous aspect and being motionless. The man coming when he had the sense of being delayed in leaving—as if being slowed down had made him come and was exciting, and it was during the afternoon with people walking around. He was late and had to go somewhere, and came, with a feeling of delay and retarding—rather than out of nervousness.

✻

RON PADGETT

Voice

I have always laughed
when someone spoke of a young writer
"finding his voice." I took it
literally: had he lost his voice?
Had he thrown it and had it
not returned? Or perhaps they
were referring to his newspaper
The Village Voice? He's trying
to find his *Voice*.
              What isn't
funny is that so many young writers
seem to have found this notion
credible: they set off in search
of their voice, as if it were
a single thing, a treasure
difficult to find but worth
the effort. I never thought
such a thing existed. Until
recently. Now I know it does.
I hope I never find mine. I
wish to remain a phony the rest of my life.

*

Louisiana Perch

Certain words disappear from a language:
their meanings become attenuated
grow antique, insanely remote or small,
vanish.
      Or become something else:
transport. Mac
the truck driver falls for a waitress
    where the water flows. The

great words are those without meaning:
   from   a   their   or
   Or   the   for   a   the
   The   those

The rest are fragile, transitory
   like the waitress, a

beautiful slender young girl!
I love her! Want to
marry her! Have hamburgers!
Have hamburgers! Have hamburgers!

*

High Heels

I have a vision
in my head of Cubism
and Constructivism
in all their artistic purity
joined with a decorative attractiveness
that exceeds deliciousness,
even more to be desired

than becoming a milkman
in a white suit and hat
delivering milk to the back door
of a white frame house
on a street lined with elms
and being invited inside
by the curvaceous, translucent lady
of the house, not once
but many times, too many times,
perhaps, for later her husband
will be coming home
with a sledgehammer in his hand,
the pink hand with light blue fingernails, oh
you have colored the wrong picture!
You were to put the pink and blue
on the beachball on the next page.

*

Ode to Bohemians

1.

The stars at night
Are big and bright
The moon above
A pale blue dove

The trees bent out
By windy shout
Of West Wind god
And the soldiers bolted from their ranks

—Did they o did they?—

And spilled across the countryside,
ants escaping some ant doom,
the final trumpet from the god of ant death. . .

while their wives were waiting in the kitchen doorway
in red aprons and yellow bandanas, really beautiful black
    ants. . .

2.

Two eyes bulging out with red lines
and rolling upon the ground. . .
all the better to see you with, microscopic weakling!
You rush below the microscopes of government,
the government of Russia, the government of the U.S.A.,
the horrible governments of Argentina and Brazil, the
           suspicious
governments of Greece, Venezuela and Turkey,
the governments strong and weak, a few weird bigshots
making you eat dirt and like it, buddy.
For me, I say "Fuck it."

I have a glass of red wine
and a beret upon my head,
I am tipsy in Montmartre,
my smock smeared with paint
and the lipstick of script girls,
and I salute zees life I lead,
O happy vagabond! O stalwart bohemian,
defying the ordinary rules of society
to express your inner self,
to tell those callous motherfuckers
what it's like, to achieve
the highest glory of man
and then sink back in its clouds

never to be seen again, like strange celebrities
whose caricatures grow dim and fade
from the pages of memory. Thank you, anyway,
colorful individuals.

*

Love Poem

We have plenty of matches in our house.
We keep them on hand always.
Currently our favorite brand is Ohio Blue Tip,
though we used to prefer Diamond brand.
That was before we discovered Ohio Blue Tip matches.
They are excellently packaged, sturdy
little boxes with dark and light blue and white labels
with words lettered in the shape of a megaphone,
as if to say even louder to the world,
"Here is the most beautiful match in the world,
by its one and a half inch soft pine stem capped
by a grainy dark purple head, so sober and furious
and stubbornly ready to burst into flame,
lighting, perhaps, the cigarette of the woman you love,
for the first time, and it was never really the same
after that. All this will we give you."
That is what you gave me, I
become the cigarette and you the match, or I
the match and you the cigarette, blazing
with kisses that smoulder toward heaven.

*

BILL KUSHNER

My Sisters

So what's love? I'd watch my 2 older sisters
Spend hours in front of mirrors, doing things
With their lips, incredible! they'd make
Their faces look down this way, up that way
& why? I'd hear them giggle crazily together
About this or that guy, then they'd dance
Together, hours & hours of going around & going
Around, then looking dreamy-eyed to a song
& then back to their mirrors & whispers & shadows
& moving their lips to uttering names, men's
Names: oh James, ohh Jimmy, no-o Johnny
& they'd sit for hours & write their names
then we'd dance, they'd make me lead them
Around & around some imaginary dancefloor & I'd
Look up into their eyes, their eyes so far away

*

Up

This? it's my Lounge Lizard look, very
popular in the 20's when I was but a thought
whether Flying Down to Rio or crossing Mulberry
I am I suppose what I was always meant to be
a slight eccentric with a bit of a tic
a sort of a gay Mary Poppins so thank you dear
America you've got taste you've got style

& you know a good drag queen when you see one
she sure can talk & she thanks everybody & I'm
so happy that 2000 years ago sweet Jesus died
for me, including my girlfriend Judy up there
in Canada & like to thank my mother & my father
for putting up with my noise all these many years I
love & thank you all for the best performance by a male

*

I Am

(can everyone hear?) a rum & coke girl myself
somewhere between dream night & afternoon
delight. Standing or walking stiff in New York
in the Biz called Show where life intrudes upon the poem
Steve Carey says in Calif "You only need a whistle"
all this Welsh spit, why I relish in it
big eyes of lives who've glowed & dim like feet
well, what sweet sweepy things going past me
hard in slow motion, intent on base relief
on my way from the general to the mess
Are my one line poems like one night stands
are people, yeah, one of my former great fears
this heartfelt sonnet stone drunk in the busy street
I feel pretty good, purty good, purr purr
aah Spring rub it in, here's a flower not in bloom
here in the glorious East where I rent a small room

*

SANDIE CASTLE

Mother's Day

Mother's Day Special
What's that mean?
Mother on a blue plate
Mother may I?
No you may not
Mother me smother me
Let's smother those mothers
Mother's milk
Mother's skirts
Mothers sulking
Mothers stalking men again
Mother's apron strings
Old Mother Hubbard
Mother's breast presented upon request
Mothers confess to anything
Guilty mothers
Quilting mothers
Organic mothers
nursing till their little nipples fall off
scoffing at bottle-fed babies
Well guess what *mommy*?
If yer little kiddie grows up to be a mass murderer
it's still yer fault organically grown or not
How's yer mother-in-law?
Don't ask me please
Oh fuck it man
Put me in the cupboard on Mother's Day
Give me a bone to play with
Where's mother's little helper?

She ran away that's what
Oh mother PLEASE
I'd rather do it myself
Mother's Day at Harborplace
Battered women carrying umbrellas for shelter
WHAT KINDA MOTHER ARE YOU ANYWAY?
Did you hear her son is gay?
Oh Mother of Christ!
What does she have to say for herself?
Do you know what lesbian mothers do?
Oh my God they don't!
Ohhh yes they do
I heard a Jewish mother saved her son's life
with a bowl of chicken soup
Italian mother caught with lover
gets shot to death while praying
Dope fiend mother nods out with cigarette
burns her little baby to death
WHAT ARE MOTHERS COMING TO THESE DAYS???
Oh mother really
Holy Mary Mother of God
where did you go after yer son's finale?
Well what's a mother to do?
Mother's always right
Mother's intuition
Oh no! Mother's an exhibitionist
Mother stayed out all night
We have to put mother away
Why why? She's changing life that's why
Ooooh oooh! Let's put flowers on mother's grave
Awww yer mother's dead I'm really sorry to hear that
Imaginary news flash . . .
Fifteen hundred naked pregnant women
CRASH Mother's Day Parade
with baseball bats
What happened to the girl
that married dear old dad?

Once you become a mother dear
you'll change yer attitude
Single mothers playing doubles
Unwed mothers are girls in trouble
What would Mother Seton say?
She'd roll over in her grave that's what
Nun's baby found dead in trash can
Headline reads . . . Bride of Christ Commits Adultery
Oh Motherland
Oh a mother's devotion
Oh mother really
do you have to be sooo emotional?
Did you say something mother?
Oh isn't that sweet dear?
Mother wants to make a motion
She's raising her little hand
Mother must be off her rocker
Motion denied mother-fucker!

*

The Blake Mistake

Oh *God* I really went and did it this time. Went and picked up a goddam English teacher. Shit I musta been crazy or somthin can't say a fuckin thing thout bein obscene. Might as well kick a dead horse as to try and figure this one out. Christ at least with the musician we both liked music. This guy starts talkin some shit bout some guy named Blake and I make the mistake of sayin I know him. Blake *shit* I know him. Robert Blake I watchim all the time. The English teacher he starts lookin real funny. So I sez you okay? Cuz he looked a little sick ta me all a sudden. So he sez *he sez* he's jus fine but he has serious doubts about whether I am. So I sez I don't know what the hell that's spoze ta mean. And he sez I didn't mean Robert Blake I meant *William*. Well I sez PARDON

ME I don't know no William Blake so I don't know how good he is but I do watch Baretta and he's terrific. That man knows everything goes down in the streets. Does William? Now I know somthin's wrong withim cuz he looked real sick like he's gonna throw right up on my rug or somthin.

Yeh I really picked me a winner this time. On top of all that he tells me he ain't even got no TV. Can you imagine? Now that shoulda told me all I needed ta know bout this guy. But I figure what the hell he's here now right? So I figure everybody eats right? We'll talk bout food. Seemed harmless enuf. I'm always hungry anyway. So I start talkin bout steak. I like ta think bout steak specially when I got baloney. So he sez. Get this boy I'll tell ya. He sez jus like it ain't no big deal at all. I don't eat meat. Can ya believe it? I don't eat meat. Now don't get me wrong I ain't had things easy but when you bring home a vegetarian you know you ain't gonna have no good time. I coulda died when he said it. I don't eat meat. Shit. So I start smokin my last cigarette in the pack and the only thing I'm glad bout so far's he don't smoke. Least I don't have to share it withim. So I sez. Jus ta make conversation ya unnerstan. I sez shit it ain't nothin worse than runnin outta booze after two in the mornin. Ya know what I mean? And I shoulda known better. Anyway he sez. Jus like it ain't no big deal at all. NO I wouldn't know. No I wouldn't know. SONOFABITCH. So I sez. I was pretty pissed off by then. I sez well you should know cuz it feels like pure hell and I least expected ya ta know how ta suffer some. Shit I sez and every time I say it he looks like somebody hitim with somthin. Fuck I sez jus for spite. How you ever gonna know anything worth a damn if you ain't suffered none? But cha see I'm changin my mind as I'm sayin it. Cuz he looked like he's sufferin *pretty good* by then. As a matter of fact I wouldn't be a bit surprised if he didn't learn somthin that night. I know I did. The next time I go lookin for some uh *company* I'mma bring home a plumber or somthin.

*

Hand-Jive

When sleeping alone
almost immediately following masturbation
I assume the fetal position
pull the covers over my head
and mother myself to sleep.

When sleeping with them
you know . . . men
almost immediately following masturbation
I lay in a prone position
throw the covers off the bed
and spend the night mothering them instead.

*

LEWIS WARSH

March Wind

The material of our lives increases, and
what others think of me
and what I do, approaching
you from the past with all my attitudes,
complexions and fears, making patterns
like rings of feeling around the sun, ring
true, like Saturn, or the moon
in the late afternoon. What
can I do to feel no caution, but
embrace each part of you, neither reject
nor deny, but step normally into my own shoes
not shoes two sizes smaller, while
the demons sit close by admiring
the sunlight as it dries
up the buildings, and the people lower
the blinds and themselves to sleep,
people with attitudes and plans and
designs, powerless people, power-
ful Redwoods and trees we look to embrace,
as I come to you out of a strange forest
as I approach you, shyly, at first
and you admonish me for mumbling,
as I hug you, or stare at your face in the mirror
hold you against me so we can see ourselves
in the future, like a sign in a dream
"do not awaken," written in haste.

*

Precious Mettle

One ends in ignominy because one begins mistakenly
virtue is angelic & vice makes us meek
we haven't drawn the lines around our hearts so clearly
it's impossible to tell where one begins & one ends
& it's hard to say "no" to love, or anything,
easy to imitate nature but what part of nature should
    we choose
the face of the passing stranger who runs her fingers
    along your sleeve
I think I'd like a drink but I don't have any money
the perversity of a tree whose leaves forgot to bloom
should we imitate the sky or go to our room
where the stars painted on the ceiling revolve in time to
    the music
which imitates our fears of feeling too much without
    knowing
if it's love of ourselves which makes us feel weak,
a person fainting at dawn on the street,
the scars of the person beside you in bed,
I trace your face with my fingers & you awaken
to the touch, pornographically speaking I love you less
or too much, deformed by wickedness like all of life
if one can define wickedness as the way other people
    think
& who can remember the night in December
we walked hand in hand through the empty street
struck dumb by the snow as it fell on our faces
this wasn't hell, but the outer traces
you paid your tab at the grocery on 6th
I bought a pack of smokes for the journey

*

Love's Will

I thought a life of solitude was in the cards,
solitude, & the levelling of emotional intensity,
& that I'd join the scholarly bards who fled
the ambivalence of love's propensity
to make the mind a distracted toy.
To think on things would give me joy
the blood would circulate in my head
the permutations of anything anyone said
seemed worthy of my time & energy. But
who am I to regret the promise
of feelings that belie another's destiny
& change a pattern that has no essence
like pyramids rising against the sky.
The brush of your sleeve is a source of happiness:
I crave the moments that pass me by.

*

4/13/79

Use words to describe feelings?
I wouldn't if I were you.
Tracing back the history
of a symptom to its source, the
world of memory beckons and
we turn to it feeling
rude as the heart quickens
for fear some stranger
might intrude, some presence
like a court filled with jesters
and fools performing a masque
Ben Jonson might have written.

A point of light cuts an edge
in two. Where once there
was solitude now there's
an Ecumenical procession,
heads of people carrying babies and food
from St. Ann's to Trinity to the Church
on the Hill. Some people
are classified "good"
by nature i.e. good people, while
others approach that state
after years of inner strife.
Think of buds struggling to burst
forth from the tips of branches,
or branches in which the buds
are imprisoned, encased in ice.
The cathartic method engages
our sense while resistance
fumes, head whittled
by an idiot out of a knot
of wood, the happiness that's
most apparent when it's
misunderstood, the surveyor's measurement
filed away for consistency under a full moon.
The comedy of thought animates the convictions
I know you knew, studying the classics
in a kind of take home test in self-
improvement, the amazing revelation
of a God you can see and who chooses you
to stand around and look observant, invisible
among those who know you and those who know
only the outline beneath the drapery like a
figure in a Renaissance painting, guarding the truth
or truth's symbol in the form of a chalice
or vase, this is what we do.
Odd that the air should feel odd
on Good Friday, exhaust
from too many cars surrounds

the steeple like a pod causing
static between bodies proportional
to the square of their roots, or
commodities becoming virtues which
exist to test our resistance
to speed or the whiskey
that made me clairvoyant
not virulent or virile
in the sense of having more
babies, let's get on
with our lives. As Milton
described "the parsimonious
emmet—in small room
large heart enclosed," so
the world consumes itself as
it multiplies, building walls
moats and turrets around
feeling mechanisms that were
inferior models to begin with.
Too comatose to know the difference
between what's secret
and what's real, I wake from a bad dream
and fire off a leaf to the master
whose name is plastered to the window
like an astringent. Lights
in the houses along Cliffwood
go out for the night, the
people we know by sight
turning over beneath the blinds.
The immediacy of the message
is lost in the history of a daily
life, kindled in privacy
and sparked by a belief
in what lies beyond: the
UPS man who arrived
at the wrong door and became
a fixture. A pipe on the grass,

different makes and models and brand
names attributed to gods and goddesses,
the anecdote splashing around in a pool
of associations back to who knows when,
following the thread beneath the door.
Who would take innocence to be more
than a reflection, an attitude towards night
as lightning approaches on waves of sound but
misses the point where even thought
could do no damage,
rummaging about like a pen
poised mid-air above a pad.
Body, restless as a flag, condition
some normal beauty to define
these eyes so hollow and sad,
linger longer than the weird
taste, or testament, of the past
which recreates itself as a series
of integers in the shape of dowagers
walking through a town square with
buckets of water balanced on their
heads: it's laundry day, the
shabby housecoats blowing across
cobblestones, impermanent
beauty raised to the highest
power, at peace again.

*

ROSEMARIE WALDROP

The Ambition of Ghosts

for Dorle Englehardt

Remembering Into Sleep

I. Separation Precedes Meeting

The cat so close
to the fire
I smell scorched
breath. Parents,
silent, behind me,
a feeling of
trees that might fall.
Or dogs.
       A poem,
like trying
to remember, is a movement
of the whole body.
You follow the
fog
into more fog.
Maybe the door ahead
divides
the facts
from natural affection. How
can I know, I meet
too many
in every mirror.

2.

When I was little,
was I I?
My sister? A wolf
chained,
smothered in green virtues?
                          Slower
time
of memory. Once
I've got something
I lie
down on it
with my whole body.
Goethe quotations, warm
sand, a smell of hay,
long afternoons.
                          But it
would take a road
would turn, with space,
in on itself,
would turn
occasion into offer.

3.

For days I hold
a tiny landscape between
thumb
and index:
sand,
heather,
shimmer of the blue between pines.
No smell: matchbook.
Sand as schematic as

Falling

into memory,
down,
with my blood,
to the accretions
in the arteries,
to be read with the whole
body, in the chambers
of the heart.
The light: of the match,
struck,
at last.

4.

Concentration: a frown
of the whole body. I can't
remember. Too many
pasts
recede
in all directions.
Slow movement into
                Distant boots.
Black beetles at night. A smell
of sweat.
        The restaurant,
yes. You've no idea
how much my father used to eat.
Place thick with smoke.
Cards. Beer foaming over
on the table.
        And always
some guy said I ought
to get married,

put a pillow behind my eyes
and, with a knowing
sigh, spat
in my lap.

5.

The present.
As difficult as
the past, once a place
curves into
      Hips swinging elsewhere.
Castles in sand.
Or Spain. Space
of another language.
                Sleep
is a body of water.
You follow your lips
into its softness. Far down
the head finds its level.

6. *Tropisms*

Inward, always. Night
curls the clover leaf
around its sleep.
Tightly.
The bodies of the just
roll,
all night,
through subterranean caves
which turn
in on themselves.
                Long
tunnel
of forgetting. Need
of blur. The air,

large, curves
its whole body.
Big hammering waves
flatten my
muscles.
Inward, the distances: male
and female fields,
rigorously equal.

7.

The drunk fell toward me
in the street. I hope
he wasn't
disappointed. Skinned
his sleep.
　　　　　November.
And a smell of snow. Quite normal,
says the landlord, the master
of rubbish, smaller
and smaller in my
curved mirror.
　　　　　I have un-
controllable
good luck: my sleep
always turns dense
and visible. There
are many witches
in Germany. Their songs
descend in steady half-tones
through you.

8.

You'll die, Novalis says, you'll die
following endless rows
of sheep into your
even breath.

Precarious,
like Mozart, a living
kind of air,
keeps the dream
spinning
around itself, its
missing core.
Image
after image of pleasure
of the whole body
deepens
my sleep:

fins.

9. Introducing Decimals

A dream, like trying
to remember, breaks open words
for other,
hidden meanings. The grass
pales by degrees, twigs
quaver glassily,
ice
flowers the window.
Intimate equations more complicated
than the coordinates of past
and Germany. The cat
can't lift its paw,
its leg longer and longer
with effort.
A crying fit
is cancelled. An area jelled
in the larynx.
Nothing moves in the cotton
coma: only Descartes
pinches himself
and every fraction
must be solved.

*

MARJORIE WELISH

The Servant in Literature

I could always rely on the continuity
of her being there, as continuous as the sand beach.
It often happens that crowds leave,
removing their hampers, small groups
unevenly going away, some sand deducted.
More plain and more pleasant from above,
the beach has a basic gradualness
and utility like a counter,
the "soft life" seeming to lie on top.
Footprints, an unmade bed, a talent
for biography lie in abeyance;
they should be saved.
It often happens that when crowds leave
the heroine moves across space
as a sign she is separating herself
into two bowls. Her robe and she are towed
across the interval that the form demands
to a chair. She will speak
to her maid as if to herself.
As a type, the attendant is lenient
and softens any failing, a civilian
usually of the same sex as the main character
whose action, "in conformity to the situation,"
gives way only superficially.
Once when I was fourteen and not very reliable
my mother offered to write down

whatever I said. Saying she would listen
struck me as her willingness to step aside
and give the chair to me
and my unspoken perturbations, even these.

*

Picture Collection

IMMIGRATION, WOMEN IN INDUSTRY, AGED,
COSTUME—1870s—AMERICAN,
MUSIC, TITLE PAGES—MUSIC,
UNEMPLOYMENT, CROWDS, SPECTATORS,
NEBRASKA—1899 AND EARLIER,
NEBRASKA—INDUSTRIES, IRON AND STEEL INDUSTRY,
COLLEGIATE LIFE—1970s.

The troop trains. It could be the jitterbug the way the soldier
hoists the girl to his window to kiss her, two guys
doing the boosting. But in most photos
the man and the woman are in a smash up,
and on the platform, out of their territory, a buddy
stands inside his duffel body.

Each folder is like the miscellany on your desk,
disrespectful when you search
for some one thing. Here is an engraving,
titled, *Entrée du Duc d'Alençon*, 1582.
But you are not looking for this.

ARRIVALS AND DEPARTURES—some categories
hurt more than others,

the truly painful not being
the SUICIDE, but the folder when she comes back,
all of them sitting around the table
telling her how to behave.

Here is an engraving
titled, *Entrée du Duc d'Alençon*, 1582,
but you do not have the strength,
for this nor for
the envelope of the man at the desk,
intercepted by other business,
never quite absorbed in you.

Even so you notice everything.
As if it were spring the duke is received
by budding cannon. All along the wall
deciduous clouds,
and today, for him, the heavy municipal buckle is open.
Sheaves of spectators are watching the long suit
on horse, and on foot, carrying lances,
carrying crossbows, seeing it lead
and finesse the climactic horse.

❖

Careers

How long we sit in front of them.
Compared with experience, this is gentle.
As if we are going on a long, persistent cruise
to be worn down.

My nephew thinks a fireman is a person
who starts fires. Wonderful.
Then a waterman is someone putting them out.
One composition goes like this:
"The fireman is someone who starts the barbeque.
Arriving with his lighter fluid
he is cheered by everyone, including mothers and fathers.
Then his face grows serious.
He goes over and ignites the grill."

The hardwood in the fireplace is insurmountable.
The first blaze of newspaper shrivels.
We begin again, using spurs and branches
to trap the fire, and then we try a jack
and a stirrup made from our hands,
filling a blue book with wild guesses.
Meanwhile someone comes forward to study the principle.

"It was not, of course, human."
The fireplace, like a "low, pinched braincase"
stared into the room, a container with no memory
of body heat and no feeling for it.
When building a house people embedded a skull in its center;
for centuries they warmed themselves by this contradiction.
With even points like a violin phrase repeated
and ignited over and over for a half hour
each attack vigilant—the combustion
is what makes the piece, while the most uneven theme
is our attention, which tends to back away,
succumbing to middle distance, asking what else there is,
yet returning. Looking into it, even looking for it.

Toying with pastimes, and in relation to them, our masterful
    size.
The adult games self-contained
in a plastic cube are attractive.
The wave, for instance, a section of which

in a case, tilts, the blue-tinted water
crashing one side, then leveling off
before piling and mechanically crashing the other.
The section of anything is interesting.
Another everyone has seen is the shallow oval of sand,
two different weights, two different colors.
The smokiest possible heap
does not deter gravity from sorting it all.
Tableaux from which we draw morals,
the diminution that transforms the ignored
natural occurrence into an object,
thereby a goal. The fire in the fireplace
and the others of the pantheon, the earthquake,
the tidal wave, should in turn while we sit around
play in a recessed place in the walls of our homes.

Sometimes during his youth or during the course of an evening
someone shows an aptitude for it and is allowed to preside,
and it becomes his phenomenon. He literally stirs the wind,
the warmed water swelling into a canopy of water,
sending uncatalogued feelings in advance. When a storm
        develops
on its own, he sits down. "The torrential rains begin."
Stones and rocks strategically gathered
into bulwarks withstand the slicing
rains for quite a while before giving up.
The point is to build something
not so that it lasts forever but that it dies
in the most developed way possible.
That is why he gets up and uses the bellows
to fuel the wind.

Beyond the smiling, seated man, in a sense within
the property left over from his L-shaped pose, there is a fire
"raging" throughout a house, and a company—No. 7—
pulling a hose towards it.

*

LORENZO THOMAS

Otis

Some women think
A man should hunt for them

Some women understand it

And some men think
Return a wondrous thing

She must be waiting

The dude goes out,
Is gone all night
She knits and yearns
Till gray dawnlight
Her girl friends say,
"That trifling
                blank
Ain't coming back"
And help undo her
                        work

That's the kind of cat,
You know,
"No man can take
My place"
Instantly trucks his shadow

Through the door
Catches a fit
That blinds him
Even further.

Folks like that
You hear about them
On the News.

Some women understand it.

Another dude,
you know,
Is gone for days.
But she sits, humming
At first a moan
She knits and polishes
And frets.
She frowns at friends
Then sings a gleeful song
As they fidget they
Whisper, "Girl,
Is you gone mad?"
So all of them chorusing
"That trifling
                blank
Um hmmm, I knows
                a man!"

Some women

Man, by the time
My man tipped in
She had damn near enough
Macrame string

To make a hammock
That sleep two
                on top
Three on the
                bottom

Some women
                think
And there is beauty
In the knit
                of thinking

Some dudes know
How to treat a woman
Right

Some don't

Some women understand it.

*

Shake Hands With Your Bets, Friend

Every bookie
On the phone to Vegas
Odd
But all the trunk lines
Are tied up,
Sorry. This trunk is not seaworthy, sir.
In all good faith, I cannot
And other blasts from the past
No sir no good no sir
Such accents no longer seem strange;
Simply, they take their places
Next to the treasured linen in the trunk

Clean linen was prized so.

And silk, symbolic. Heraldry
Amid the horseshit; oriental mystery
Shining out imperial futures
Come a cropper in the knots of the dragon
Appliquéd on the blouse
So carefully folded second down to the linen
And the silk tinted gold to go with the uniform serge
Of the master's desire for glory
Infecting all the crew with inertia
Obedience to the odds against survival
Cutting the Captain cutting
All of this loose, drifting free.

From the slaveship dock
Down dusty streets to auction block,
Awash in a chance for survival
No sir no good no sir
Until such accents no longer seem strange
He trudges

He drudges himself into choices before him
Using instincts and applied mathematical factors
The best advice is ask the winner
Bub, your guess as good as mine.

The choice is not acceptance nor adjustment
Nothing defiant definite at this time,
But give me a call in a day or two, he says;
From then on what? sack-cloth and cinders
Sandaled feet and a threatening sandwichman sign?

That's horseshit,
You either beat em or join em
Pays your money and takes your choice
Everyone's a winner

EVERYONE'S A WINNER!
And other stale blasts from the past
No sir no good no sir
You'll be out there all by your lonesome!

Silks and silver fittings,
Your lonesome!

Riding free
To the roses, arched into the lucky horseshoe
A horticulturist piece against natural resistance
Circular winnings of really knowing the odds
Not even enjoying *A Day at the Races*
As it appears on late night tv yet again
At least the umpteenth time, but a respite
Of inexorable glee and the usual horseshit

Resistance is natural, at first
Its lifeless monument
Suppression seems to rule
That's the usual horseshit

Show me a man

I sit here, for some reason, listing
Possibilities and ideas for packing a trunk
Or a kerchief
But leaving now is really going nowhere
New, not phrased or worried so bad
But confusing, that's what runs through
My mind concocting an elegant logic

Show me any slavery

A confusion of mail-order brides arrives
With careful trunks of hope and promises
Clutched in the letter packets in their hands

As dreams go sailing
Well damn how many *did* you send for sir
No sir no good no sir
You've got to choose

Off-track betting parlors are stormed!
Jostling
Throngs pushing and shoving
Thinking, soon he will choose.
Every bookie on
The phone to Vegas
People getting trampled down in the streets
In the mad rush to the window
As dated futures fling themselves
Into space from the top of office buildings
State capitols, from islands of pompous parkways
Skirting the miserable ghetto
They fling themselves on ignorant traffic
Short-tempered, sacrificial and vain
The drivers cuss the winged hopes on their heels,
Hoping to get home for supper
Before something else ruins their day
Knowing that when he chooses he will choose
As he has chosen
As they have themselves
Finally, to dare no more than one dares
To live so that one will not be forgotten
Buying that piece of immortal stroking
Piece by piece, by smile or favor
By appropriate chastisement or unnotice,
Not knowing though that though his choice is set,
This time when he places his bet
He's dealing with a new measure of chance,
But he doesn't know it may be the last time.

*

MMDCCXIII$^{1/2}$

The cruelty of ages past affects us now
Whoever it was who lived here lived a mean life
Each door has locks designed for keys unknown

Our living room was once somebody's home
Our bedroom, someone's only room
Our kitchen has a hasp upon its door.

Door to a kitchen?

And our lives are hasped and boundaried
Because of ancient locks and madnesses
Of slumlord greed and desperate privacies

Which one is madness? Depends on who you are.
We find we cannot stay, the both of us, in the same room
Dance, like electrons, out of each other's way.

The cruelties of ages past affect us now

*

Guilt

No longer the feather
She used
To be, her breath still sings

But her head on my pyjama sleeve
Is heavy with confused
Determination & vague hurt

My heart
A stone cast in a lake
Catching a sudden freeze
Prisoning the stone
    Half in half out

Rings
Of ice which won't melt

    The rarity of what we've felt
Seems done

In the morning's radiance
When we wake,
She's unsure of my silence
As she chats about the weather

But all I want to talk about
Would be unspeakable things

       *

Canzone

Strained daybreak breaks in past the blinds
You have your sexy moments with the sluts
And then the sensual response becomes a habit

Birds out of habit utter their sun spells.

Your habit strains
As her delusion finds
Your way to bland
Disgraceful petulances

Blocked. The tape feeds tacit
Arrogance to habit. Madnesses.
The radio announcer's pains
of authenticity. We understand.

She walks out with Janis Joplin's CHEAP THRILLS

As local "music of the Renaissance" abuts
Her vocal memories of the Shirelles.
O Lord, how vain we are! Ghost music fills

Our Sundays with whatever is at hand
and Idries Shah's THE WISDOM OF THE IDIOTS

*

The Leopard

The eyeballs on her behind are like fire
Leaping and annoying
The space they just passed
Just like fire would do

The ground have no mouth to complain
And the girl is not braver herself

She is beautiful in her spotted
Leopard ensemble. Heartless so

To keep her fashionable in New York
Leopards are dying

Crude comments flutter around her
She sure look good
She remembers nine banishing speeches

More powerful than this is the seam
Of the leotard under her clothing

Her tail in the leotard is never still
The seam!
She feels it too familiar on her leg
As some crumb says something suggestive

The leopard embracing around her
Is too chic to leap and strike

Her thoughts fall back to last semester's *karate*

Underneath, the leotard crouches up on her thigh
It is waiting for its terrible moment!

＊

Faith

She said she don't want no man
In her house. But
She ain't yet called
On God to notarize

Anything. And she smiled
So beautiful

She was 122 percent black
Except for calling on God

Someday it may happen you will lose
Something so precious
To you you will say Jesus

But you will not ask me to go

＊

Historiography

Bird is a god of good graciousness.—Ted Joans

1

The junkies loved Charles Parker and the sports
And the high living down looking ones
Those who loved music and terror and lames
Who in Bird's end would someday do better

As the Bird spiralled down in disaster
Before the TV set some would come to prefer
Out of the sadness of Mr. Parker's absence
Never again hearing the strings of Longines

Symphonette

Without hearing the keening cry of the Bird
Nailed to the wax they adored. In the memories
And warmth of their bodies where our Bird
Stays chilly and gone. Every cat caught with

A white girl wailed Bird Lives! And the dopies
Who loved Charles Parker made his memory live
Those who loved music made his memory live
And made the young ones never forget Bird

Was a junkie

2

We lost others to pain stardom and
Some starved at vicious banquets
Where they played until the victuals
Was gone. Pretty music. For all that

Pain. Who made the young ones remember the pain
And almost forget the dances? Who did that?
Steal the prints and the master and burn down
The hope of his rage when he raged? It was

Not only pain

There was beauty and longing. And Love run
Down like the cooling waters from heaven
And sweat off the shining black brow. Bird
Was thinking and singing. His only thought

Was a song. He saw the truth. And shout the Truth
Where Indiana was more than the dim streets of Gary
A hothouse of allegedly fruitful plain America
Some will never forgive the brother for that. Bird

Was a junkie

3

According to my records, there was something
More. There was space. Seeking. And mind
Bringing African control on the corny times
Of the tunes he would play. There was Space

And the Sun and the Stars he saw in his head
In the sky on the street and the ceilings
Of nightclubs and Lounges as we sought to
Actually lounge trapped in the dull asylum

Of our own enslavements. But Bird *was* a junkie!

Liner Notes to "Historiography"

*Because it is conceived as a tonal evocation of the spirit of Charles
Parker (1921–1955), "Historiography" is a poem designed for oral recita-*

tion. It is a solo constructed in the bop saxophone style. The poem was written to be performed with a jazz orchestra of 3–7 pieces, using traditional 1940s bebop instrumentation. In its own way, the poem is an investigation of the sonic developments pioneered by Parker and his associates.

"Historiography" has been performed in New York City sittin' in with the Wes Belcamp group at the Village Door (1972) and with the Ric Murray Trio in a poetry and jazz program entitled UNION at Sir James' Pub (April 18, 1974). The piece has also been performed with Lanny Steele and the Texas Southern University Jazz Ensemble at the Westheimer Art Fair in Houston, Texas (September 1974).

(L.T.)

*

Wonders

I know where I belong
But I been away so long.
Sometime I wonder.
Will I ever hear
Nostalgia In Times Square
Again, in some Avenue B
Break-in 1/2 bath flat
Will I ever sit
In the sun, high
On a Lenox terrace
And watch the Harlem River run
Away from the dope and the crime
To the gray East
Again? And me
With some Boone's Farm
Meaning no harm
On anybody
Sitting there digging
Eddie Palmieri's
Hip conversations
With Obatala.

Sometimes I wonder
About that.
Or to be freak again
Be in the Bronx
Stoned on the rocks
As Jr Walker strain
His voice and young girls'
Credulity. Again?
Oh girls I can hear
Your radios
Loud at midnight
In Harlem or Elmhurst
And the smog a gangster
To ask proud
Stars give it up.
Girls
Check it out
When you pout and talk bad
Think of me, exiled
Almost a year
From the life
Lord, and don't be so hard
Sometimes I be distracted
When I think how you style.
Hold it. I should like
The Browning of America!
I feel so simple to be thinking of Harlem
New York, the apple
Where we had our own Adam
And damn near all
The wonders of the world

Saigon, VNCH

✳

DICK GALLUP

40 Acres and A Mule

I can hear the wind whistling
    Between my ears
Among the shards of defunct civilizations
    In a museum

    In another civilization
The home of the Packard and the Straight-8
    I was a cowboy
And went from Fort to Fort
    Secure in Victory

Now like an Indian on the warpath
Long after the path has been paved
And turned over to nannies and their prams
I find myself out of my element

Strangely unconcerned
When all sides of the matter
Become equally bad
No matter what the subject

    And an inertia of defeat
    Whirs out from the center of things
Catching me up in its clutter of pointless motion

    Under fire and over water

Like a hopeless aborigine
Exploring the universe
Without a gun

And so I wake up one morning
To discover I'm morose
                              And uncommunicative
And heartless
                    And selfish
Cruel
        Critical
                    Hopeless
Helpless   Stupid and scared

As the night goes by like the last century in Germany
Only all at once
                              Compressed into the sound
    Of an ancient Volkswagen
Trying to park across the street
    For about 90 minutes

And about then I begin to realize
It's nearly as unpleasant outside my skin
As inside
              Where the tune is changing key
    Endlessly

Outside
                The bright days get recycled
                Like day-glo red swizzle sticks
                Into someone else's drink

While I just get older and a little more desperate
    To find something worth celebrating
        With a good cup of coffee

*

On the Meatwheel

At the edge of the forest
   She sings with her pale lips
While taps play
   In the country

   Full of mites
The lady sparkles
   Steps curl upward
   Away
In the faces of the men
   Her world turns with her

Birds in the trees whistle
   For ages past
The soldiers stand
   Hearts tattered, at ease

With ragged bitten nails
   They sag
At the edge of the world
   On white hollow wings

They live there in rags
   Their arms are broken
They see little
   Beyond what they do see,
They trust

   While the musicians
Stand the fire on end
   And sit down
   To a mean meal
Which flies through their bodies

You're a pip
They say
If you can breathe

*

Backing Into the Fan Mail
(Unreceived)

Such power there is in drawing breath
Knowing where this ends and that begins
The power of knowing how your body
Goes down into your boots
Pushing toward the edge of the buckled landscape

The frozen earth takes umbrage from the sky
In the bright thaw sodden and spongy
Last year's twigs clatter in the wind
Bless the man who invented windows
What pleasure there is in keeping the cold out

From the side of the house
Blinding white in the horizontal light
Icicles gleam
Sparkle in wonder of how they came to be so long
A dripping winter dagger in the side of early spring

But then I always did take everything to heart
The time I got an atom bomb in the mail
And when I took it down by the furnace
It didn't work though it was a lovely
Red and black bomb to look at

That was my first disappointment with the US Mails

*

Where I Hang My Hat

for Alex Katz

It's like in the art galleries

Where I can see the real thing

Occasionally

            a classless integrity

Of being

       Huh?

     At last the studio

Lots of toads

       a birthright

It is a good wrist

     Something to eat

      a people canvas

I mean paint

     Sunlight

a blowtorch

A pleasant and other reckoning with things

Second Avenue or any other

blueprint of the future

✣

Relaxation

So gay on your lovely head
The hat cradles the specialty
Of the house brand new
And hedged with the flowers
Of the past we have somehow
Got through. If night
Should fold in on us
Here in the day dripping
Down the fire escapes toward
The ground like poetry
In search of the common man
In all things, smoky and
Vapid insight coming near
To what I can't keep my eyes
Off, the fragile jaws
Of antique life, a fretful
Crowd of messages delivered
Long ago in the pouring rain

Then night would find us
As we are, bright lives
Dancing in the somber light
Of history, shiny pencils
At the edge of things.

*

PAUL VIOLI

Whalefeathers

for Buster Keaton

An octoroon eating a macaroon.
The waitress immense, her weight
compresses her voice:
"What'll it be?" she squeaks.
"BLT-rye-down with a swipe of mayo!"
And here's a girl nibbling a sandwich:
hunched over her plate,
not raising her head after each bite
but keeping her mouth close to the crust,
she cups it in her hands,
her fingertips right next
to the bitten edge, her teeth
just missing her nails.
Guy farther down mumbles to himself
while he eats: a gargantuan orangoutang,
he's reading the *Times*.
And there's the Generalissimo's picture
on the front page
. . . the deceased Generalissimo . . .
And it's not a bad picture (for the *Times*).
But that girl eating the sandwich,
she's holding it even tighter,
fingertips pressed into the bread,
(her pinky pink). It's not going
to fly away on you lady—

Good Christ, there it goes!
She just relaxed her grip a second
and it took off. Unbelievable.
I'd say it's a tuna-salad-Ampersand-bacon-on-white.
A few flip-flap circles over the counter,
it drops some mayo, slams into the window, squish,
slides down the glass
and flops dead hissing on the radiator.
She's crying. Everyone rushes over
to console her. Me too. I don't know
what to say. I say don't worry,
it's just one of those things;
chalk it up to experience;
they won't make you pay for it;
there's a lesson in this somewhere;
they'll make you another just like it;
live and learn; you'll
look back at all this someday and
. . . then I notice the Girl Scout emblem
tattooed on her arm,
figure she doesn't need any advice,
then backstep, fading into the crowd,
and head off to work.
But passing a news stand
I see the *Times* again,
think I'll buy a copy
or maybe one of these magazines
with pretty nudes on the covers.
I start flipping through them,
but the paper man tells me
no reading allowed and I tell him
I'm not reading aloud,
I'm not even moving my lips.

✳

Outside Baby Moon's

The Kelly Square Smoke Shop closes its doors,
a porter empties the ashtrays
in the lobby of the Gold Tooth Hotel, a grate is drawn
over the Wonderhorse Bar and Grill.
The last van has entered the garage
of the Reliable Music Factory,
the plug's been pulled on the jukebox at Baby Moon's.
Someone sweeps the aisles
of the Fluxus Total Impact and Window Cleaning
    Company,
the Rainbow Caste Systems and Storage Concern is dark,
members of the House of the Intimate Ultimate
have sung their last hymn.
The tower next to Sleazy Victor's
and the Cougar Belch Correspondent School
looms blacker than the night sky
and a neon fixture flickers in a showcase
at the Admirable Admiral Demolition Project.
Only the sign on the Soft Dart Prelude
remains lit, the Stardust Furniture Exchange
and the Frost Collision Works are deserted.
In just a few more hours, the first customers
of the day will enter the Kelly Square Smoke Shop,
shades will rise on the windows
in the Gold Tooth Hotel, a fleet of vans
will pull into the Reliable Music Factory.
Long fluorescent tubes in the Rainbow Caste Systems
and Storage Concern will soon be switched on
and secretaries will be madly typing away
under Sleazy Victor's vacant eyes.
Old men will unfold crisp newspapers
at the Frost Collision Works
and blue prints will be re-examined
at the Admirable Admiral Demolition Project.

Toes will be tapping at the Soft Dart Prelude,
wide-eyed, winsome girls will be dancing
on the roof of Baby Moon's, but you,
Faithless Reader, you'll still feel like a leaf
lost in a pile of gloves.

*

"At the Corner of Muck and Myer"

for Jim Shepperd

Green light—Go.
Red light—Stop.
Yellow light—Caution.
Blinking Red light—Strong suspicions.
Blinking Blue light—Apprehension.
Yellow light with bells—Mounting fears, accusations.
White light—Sweat, speechlessness, ranting isolation.
Steady Violet light—Sunlit fragrant rooms, visitors,
                              casual interrogations, short
                              walks with attendant. . .

*

GARY LENHART

The Old Girl

The first time I visited your parents' house
Your mother walked out of the bathroom
And before we were introduced announced,
"I've decided not to live any longer.
I've just drunk a bottle of iodine."
When she spoke I could see that her mouth
Was painted orange. Your brothers
Were playing checkers on the floor
And your father was washing dishes.
Nobody so much as glanced in her direction.
"What's wrong with this crew?
Somebody call an ambulance!" I screamed.
Your brother took me by the arm.
"Please don't be upset, Hilda.
She does this all the time."

My father used to take us to Plattsburgh
Saturday nights for ice cream cones.
We'd pile into the back of his pick-up truck.
My mother would sit beside him on the front seat.
One Saturday she was reading a pornographic novel
She'd brought home from work
And my father scolded her.
"You've got six children.
Why can't you wait until they're in bed
Before reading that garbage?
What kind of person gave that to you?"
As the truck slowed for a horseshoe curve

My mother flung the door open
And hurled herself from the cab.
My father slammed on the brakes
And ran to where she lay in a ditch.
He pleaded with her,
"Oh, sweetheart, please forgive me!"
The six of us were crying, "Mommy, please get up!"
It seemed forever before
Raising herself on one elbow, she declared,
"From now on, I read what I please!"

I remember when she was pregnant for Billy.
She was 26 and already had 8 kids.
She so wanted to miscarry
That several times a day
She would crawl downstairs on her belly.
When that didn't bring it off,
She stood on her head while Aunt Lily
Hung buckets full of water from her feet,
To no avail.

*

Satellites

The roof above JESUS LOVES YOU is loaded
With garbage chucked from the seventh floor

Rear window of the tenement next door
Often enough that, without being on the alert,

I've seen them several times. I rip
A piece of paper from the carriage,

Wad and bank shoot it off the fake fireplace
Into the wicker waste basket, reach left

For a blank sheet and in a corner of an eye
Catch them spilling a brown paper bag's

Innards, coolly pitching a beer can or empty
Orange Fanta into the Nevada-like dump.

Over the ledge they follow their breakfast
Leavings intently until plop, into a pile.

Wrappers sail aimlessly or with fluttering
Gumption descend to the street. Today,

Leaning out to inspect a recent menu, as
Pigeons poked among broken, mostly green, glass,

A Sugar Crisp box dropped past their heads
From a few stories up, riling them.

*

Around the World

It came from Pizzeria
Carrying one slice with pepperoni,
Onions, peppers, and anchovies,
Halted four flights
Above Vicanaida Jewelry,
Spun dizzyingly
About its axis
Like an acrobat
On a trapeze
Until it blurred
Into a volleyball hanging
Prior to a spike.
As suddenly as a balloon

Is blown to bits
By crowds of air,
It transformed back
Into a wobbling plate
Whipped presently to the street
By the bored with cardboard wind
Where it landed between
Two manholes and was pressed
Into pavement
By the Leo's Oriental
Fruits and Vegetables
White delivery van
Loaded with watermelons.

*

VICTOR HERNANDEZ CRUZ

Anonymous

And if I lived in those olden times
With a funny name like Choicer or
Henry Howard, Earl of Surrey, what chimes!
I would spend my time in search of rhymes
Make sure the measurement termination surprise
In the court of kings snapping till woo sunrise
Plus always be using the words *alas* and *hath*
And not even knowing that that was my path
Just think on the Lower East Side of Manhattan
It would have been like living in satin
Alas! The projects hath not covered the river
Thou see-est vision to make thee quiver
Hath I been delivered to that "wildernesse"
So past
I would have been the last one in the
Dance to go
Taking note the minuet so slow
All admire my taste
Within thou *mambo* of much more haste.

*

The Physics of Ochun

A group of professional
scientists
from Columbia University
heard that in an old
tenement apartment
occupied by a family

named González
a plaster-of-Paris
statue made in Rome
of Caridad del Cobre
started crying
The scientists
curious as they are
took a ride across
town to investigate
After stating their purpose
and their amazement
they were led to the
room where the statue was
Sure enough it was wet
under the eyes
Overnight, Señora González
told them, it had cried so
much that they were able
to collect a jar full of tears
The scientist almost knocked his
gold-rim glasses off his face
May we have this as a specimen
to study in our laboratory?
She agreed, and they took a taxi
with the jar to Columbia
They went directly to the lab
to put the tears through a
series of tests
They put a good amount of
the liquid under their
Strongest Microscope
Lo and behold!
What they saw made them loosen
their neckties
There inside the liquid
clearly made out through
the microscope was the

word: JEHOVAH
No matter how much they
moved the water they
kept getting the word
They sent for a bottle of
scotch
They served themselves in test tubes
They called the González family
to see if they could explain
all the González family knew
was that it was the tears
of Caridad del Cobre
They explained to Señora González
what was happening
She said that weirder than that
was the fact that her
window had grown a staircase
that went up beyond the clouds
She said she and her daughter
had gone up there to check it
out
because, she told them, a
long white rope had come out
of their belly buttons and some-
thing was pulling them up
What happened? the enthusiastic
scientists from Columbia University
wanted to know
We went up there and were
massaged by the wind
We got hair permanents
and our nails manicured
looking a purple red
My daughter says she saw
a woodpecker designing the
air
The scientists put the phone down

and their eyes orbited the room
We have to get out there
Incredible things are happening
They rushed back out
and into the González residency
They entered
It's in the same
room with the statue
They rushed in and went to the
window
So amazed were they
they lost their speech
All their organs migrated an inch
Clearly in front of them
a 3-foot-wide marble stair
which went up into the sky
The scientists gathered themselves
to the point of verbalizing again
They each wanted to make sure
that the other was "cognizant"
of the *espectacolo*
Once they settled upon reality
they decided that the urge to
explore was stronger than their
fears
One decided to take a writing pad
to take notes
One decided to take a test tube
in case he ran into substances
One decided to take a thermometer
and an air bag to collect atmosphere
Señora González, would you please
come up with us?
They wanted to know if she would
lead them up
If you could see it you could touch
it, she told them

She went out first and they
followed
The marble steps were cold
They could have been teeth of
the moon
As they went up the breeze smiled
against their ears
The murmur of the streets dimmed
They were climbing and climbing
when they felt a whirlpool in
the air
For sure it was the hairdresser
Señora González sensed the odor of
many flowers in the breeze
The scientist with the test tube
saw it get full of a white liquid
The scientist with the air bag
felt it change into a chunk of metal
The scientist with the writing pad
saw a language appear on it backwards
printing faster than a computer
The paper got hot like a piece of
burning wood
and he dropped it down into the
buildings
It went through an open window
and fell into a pot of red beans
A woman by the name Concepción was
cooking
Frightened she took it to a doctor's
appointment she had the next day
She showed it to the physician
who examined it
He thought it was the imprint
of flower petals
so even and bold in lilac
ink

The dream Concepción had during
the night came back to her
I know what's going on, doctor
I'll see you in nine months
Walking she remembered forgetting
to put the *calabaza* into the beans
and rushed home sparkling in
her yellow dress

*

Listening to the Music of Arsenio Rodriguez Is Moving Closer to Knowledge

The researchers will come to
research the puddles of water
that we have turned into
all over your room

Doña Flores
who is next door
is not innocent
She too begins
to *liquidarse*

Warm water so good
Listen to the box
It is damaging
everybody

Opening like a curtain
the air in front of us
whistles

in the thousands of afternoons
that everybody is
nervously plucking
transformationally swimming
to where it is safe to dance
like flowers in the wind
who know no *bossordomos*

Inside your brains
each cell stands up
to *dance el son*
as the explorers come in
to research
yelling:
Where is everybody?
Are the windows opened?
Has it rained?

*

Confusion

A moth
landed on
his hand

He immediately
saw
that it had
4,269 specks
of dust on
its wings.

*

DAVID ANTIN

Radical Coherency

don wellman wrote asking me if i would write
something   do something for an issue of a magazine he
was putting out   something on or rather approaching
radical principles of coherency   and i wasnt really
sure what he meant and i suspected he wasnt either and
i liked that   so i thought i would certainly do it
because i wasnt sure of exactly what he had in mind
and he had said to me in the letter   why for
example did you stop working in the way that you did
in a book like *meditations* say and how did you get to the
talk poems youre doing now   and i hadnt thought about
this very much   or not recently   maybe never
and i liked thinking about it now   especially
in the light of the idea of radical principles of coherency
which i hadnt thought about much either   up to
now   because i had been working in what i felt was
a sensible way   taking pieces of language that had
been parts of continuous discourses and assembling them
putting them down next to each other   one after another
in accordance with what i would call collage
strategies   and don wanted to know why i had stopped
doing that and why i was doing talk pieces instead
and whether i ever did any of the other work anymore
and the answer to that couldnt have been terribly
simple   and i suppose he was aware of that
though its easy to give a simple answer to anything
but whether its an answer i believe is another
story   though the issue of my belief may be

extraneous   i give you an answer and then its your
     problem   you believe it or you dont believe it
          but i wanted to think   about this   not so
much about why i stopped doing one thing and then did
     another   but i wanted to think about what i was
doing and what i used to do in the light of the notion of
     coherency   which i specifically wanted to think
about   the idea of what we consider coherent   why
     we consider it coherent   and the different ways
     of thinking things are coherent that are based on
     different organizing principles   and it occurred
     to me that the way i had been working   the way a
lot of people still are working   taking pieces of
     things that were once parts of certain larger things
          usually continuous things you would consider
coherent   like discourses of some sort or another
          and i was taking pieces of language from these
     discourses   and putting them together   or next
to each other   in new ways i thought interesting
          and when i did this i kind of thought of myself
as a reader as much as a writer   that is i thought
of myself as taking this material and laying it down
          and enjoying what happened when i did it
          or not enjoying it so much as looking to see what
happened and then going on   now taking something
     from here now something from thcrc   sometimes
changing what i was taking either by taking or breaking
it loose   or in laying it down   or sometimes just
     changing it by handling   and i would read it
          each part or the sequences of parts and i would
     enjoy them   each part or the sequence of parts
          or maybe not   sometimes i would simply regard
     them with a kind of interest in the curious way they
came together   because this was new   they had
     never been together before   and i wasnt sure what
     made them go together now or while i was putting them
together or next to each other   except that they had

made a kind of quick sense while i was doing it   and
   now they had to be interpreted or read these things that
once were parts of different things and now were together
        and the problem of course or one problem was that if
   i took a piece of something from a manual on aeronautics
and something else from leonardos writings on water and
   something else from the jehova witness magazine
              i would   when i heard these fragments coming
              the jehova witness travel guide to paris
              leonardos reflections on the motions of water
              recognize the sources the continuous discourses
   from which they had come   and since this was of no
great interest to me i was not the best audience for my
   own work   and there is a certain way in which i found
this a little depressing   not being my own best audience
         i like being my own best audience   it is one
   of the greatest rewards of a poets work   the
possibility the likelihood or even the inevitability of
   being the best audience for his work   though some
      might consider this a disastrous condition and a
      dreadful reward for serious work   but i do not
         i like being the best audience for my own unalienated
   work   and in this case i was not   the audience
would surely not recognize all the sources   the
      original discourses   from which these pieces had
been drawn   though they might recognize some
         notebooks   leonardos notebooks are surely known to
   some subset of the people who read my poems   and they
      might recognize these fragments even if i mangled them
   a bit in handling   changed something here and there
when i felt like it   but the others wouldnt know
         and even fewer would have read the *watchtower* or
   awake   or if they had they would not necessarily
   have attributed this spiritual tourist guide to that
   source   and if they did it would be unlikely that any
   significant portion of my audience would have identified
      both the jehovas witness guidebook to paris and the

notebooks of leonardo   and somewhat more likely that
they would not have known either   but i would really
   not have been able to tell which of my readers knew
which portion if any of the sources of my pieces of
   discourse   and i could hardly tell what organizing
principles my readers would employ to make sense of the
   poems i wrote   and so there was a kind of free
relation between us   me and my readers   and i liked
that and took pleasure in it and thought it should be
   beneficial to us all   and i think that probably
many of the poets who are now called "language poets"
   have some of the same pleasures   of not knowing
what their audience makes of the constructions they put
   together   while they are aware of the sources from
   which theyve taken them and probably enjoy taking them
         and sometimes perhaps the poets are lucky enough to
forget where theyve taken them from   and then they
   enjoy their work even more   and it occurred to me
that this was something like a situation that i encountered
   the other day when i took my mother shopping   my
   mother is an elderly lady   about seventy-five or
-six   whose memory is becoming regularly worse
         and she called me desperately   that she needed
to go shopping   she had holes in her shoes she said
and needed shoes   now she was not short of money
      she could have gone to get shoes but shed become
bewildered as to where to go to get them   shes having
   this kind of trouble   so i said ok ill come and
   help you get shoes ill take you shopping   i said
there are other things you need too probably   she
says "yes i need underwear   and a blouse"   and i
   said ok and i figured id take her to a shopping center
      so i got into the car and went to where she was
   staying   a kind of hotel for elderly people
      and i got her into the car and she said
      "i really have to have shoes   you can see these
   are falling apart"   and they were falling apart

and i said "ok well get you shoes"   and i took
her to the sears store at university town center   and
      i parked the car in the parking lot   and first of
all this shopping center doesnt look like anything shes
      ever seen before   shes never seen one of these
places because shes from new york   where they dont
have california type shopping centers or they didnt in her
      experience   and shes suddenly arrived in what looks
      like an enormous drive-in movie parking lot   and
she may not have known what that was either but there
are all these cars   and we get out and there are cars
      coming from all sides   coming slowly but still
coming and she clings to my arm as we walk through the
      lot   and she says "is it that big building?"
      and it is not a tall building but a long and wide
building long enough and wide enough to house an
      armory   though it doesnt look like one   and i
say "yes its that big building"   and we walk in   and
i look at her as we are walking in   and were entering
between kitchens and workclothes   mens workclothes
      i see her looking at   a shower stall
      a spinning ventilator for a kitchen roof   one of
      those cylindrical shafts originating from the top of
the oven and projecting through the roof and surmounted by
      a little crown shaped fan that spins your waste gases
away   and this   surrounded by various sinks and
      marbleized counters in the section on our left   and
      on our right mens denim work clothes   and my mother
is holding my arm and walking by all this   looking
to find where shes going to get the things that she needs
      as we proceed straight toward a leather shop
      and i realized that i needed a band for my wrist
      watch   so on the way past i glanced toward the
leather counter and saw that they had big brimmed leather
      hats   and belts   and no saddles   but they
      didnt have any wrist watch bands i noticed as we went
by   and i led my mother toward an area filled with

shoes   and my mother looked at the counters and
cases and racks of shoes and she said "well im not sure
what kind of shoes i should get"   she said "maybe i
should get something comfortable like tennis shoes"
          and i said "well maybe so"   now there were two
parts to the section of shoes   there was one part
clustered around the central counter and cases where they
          sold shoes   and there was a second part where they
sold bargains in shoes   and every kind of shoe
was there   there were running shoes and shiny high
heeled shoes for dress wear and dull leather oxfords
for smart business wear and there were alligator leather
shoes and patent leather shoes and dull brown and clay
colored plastic shoes with squat heels for indiscriminate
wear   and there were oxfords   and sandals and
wedgies and slippers and sneakers and tatamis and thongs
          and they were arranged in display cases and on
sculpture bases and on counters and in the bargain
section lying tangled in piles on shelf after shelf
          and my mother stood there and looked   and she
couldnt see any shoes   so i said "maybe we should
get you some other things you need first   how about
underwear"   she said "i must have a brassiere"
          now im not a great authority on brassieres because
my wife hasnt been wearing brassieres very much since
the origin of the womens movement   and thats been a
long time   and nobody i know wears brassieres very
much except on special occasions   but my mother comes
from a time when women always wore brassieres   so i
said lets go find one   and we go looking for brassieres
          but she says "i dont want to spend a lot of money"
          and i dont really know what a lot of money is for a
brassiere   but i know better than to ask her because
she will tell me one or two dollars or some price that she
remembers from an earlier time when she went shopping for
brassieres   so we make our way to a section of the
store called the budget system   because it appears that

there is a section of this store or rather a subsection
   of the clothing section of this store that is the
budget system   here everything sold within the section
is summarized by selection of examples from each subsection
   only sold at a lower cost   in other words
      examples of all kinds of clothing are sold here
together but cheaper   and there is a kind of
   boundary   a boundary terrain that separates the
summarizing budget system from the ordinary subsections
of the clothing department   theres a boundary between
lounge wear say   lounge wear is where they sell
   kitchen robes and mumus and terry funwear and terry
   jumpers   and it doesnt look to me like the place
where they would have underwear anyway   but not far
   away   next to it   and not separated from it by
any boundary there seems to be a place where they sell
      what they call   intimate apparel   which gradually
eases into terry funwear mumus and kitchen robes
      and they have lounging robes and shorty pajamas and
   all sorts of sheer and diaphanous and maybe comfortable
clothing thats mixed up with other not so sheer but
      comfortable clothing like kitchen robes   which as
      i think of it ive never seen anybody wearing   but
across this boundary like a river of terrazzo flooring
      terry funwear seems to continue   on the other
side   though its within the domain of the budget
   system   and when you cross the river it gets
   cheap   or maybe it doesnt but is supposed to
      so we crossed the river and it didnt seem to get
   much cheaper   but it got complicated   because
terry funwear immediately disintegrated into levis
      mens shirts for women glamourous tie-around crepe
   blouses with puffed out sleeves   and i knew my
mother wouldnt like them   nurses uniforms
      the nurses uniforms approached another boundary
line at right angles to the one we had just crossed
      at the edge of that boundary line were greeting

cards   and on the other side i could see books
        but back across on the side of the terrazzo river
    that we had just crossed and around the turn of the wall
behind lounge wear   there were giant bottles of coca
    cola and a place where you could apply for credit
        and if you looked further   further over
        if you got desperate you could buy cheese   and
    i realized that was outside our domain   and it was
        beside that   on the other side of the river   so
    i figured lets leave that alone and get back over here
    near the nurses uniforms   because bounded by the
nurses uniforms and the cheaper version of the terry
funwear   somewhere toward the center of it   no
        it wasn't actually toward the center   because at
    the center were the glamourous crepe blouses   but
edging into the corner there was something white and sheer
    that looked like it might have been brassieres   so
i said to my mother "well lets go find you a brassiere
        what size are you"   she said "im a 36 b"
        so we went looking for a 36 b   and when we found
    it she said "i dont like that kind"   and it was to
my unpracticed eye a more or less ordinary white brassiere
    except that maybe its surface was decorated with a kind
    of lace "well" i said "what kind do you want
        dream fit?   cross banded?   contour cupped?"
        im reading off the signs and shes looking at the
    contour cups   the strapless   the wired brassieres
        the wireless   telegraphy bras   after all
they have "legtricity" stockings why not telegraphy bras
        but she says "no i just want a maidenform bra
        and i said "maidenform?"   and i seemed to
    remember that when i was a kid in new york there were
    lots of ads in the subways and on the buses in which you
would see a picture of some crowd scene like a prize fight
or a museum or zoo and all the people would be sitting
or standing around appropriately dressed and doing whatever
    they should be doing except for one beautiful girl

who would be doing whatever she should have been
doing but wearing only her snappy looking underwear
"i dreamt that i went to the ballpark in my
maidenform bra"   and i suppose my mother also
remembered those ads   "i dreamt that i went to the
zoo in my maidenform bra"   and also remembered a
snappy looking bra which maybe shed also once worn
but that was a long time ago in new york and we
were in california now   i said "mother i dont think
they have maidenform bras here   look theyve got
dreamfit   theyve got shadow patch"   she said
"i dont know"   i said "why dont you try one on
36 b its going to be 36 b"   and i pick one for
her   but she says "isnt there a saleslady here who
can help me out"   and there are no salesladies who
can help you out in this place or i cant see any
but edging off toward the fringe of the budget
terrain there is another terrain called the fashion
place   and over in the fashion place there is a
very slim glamourous young woman who looks as though
she might know about such things   and i figured there
was probably a fitting room around the corner over there
where my mother could try on her 36b and see whether shes
grown or shrunk or remembered correctly the size that
she used to be   so i gently steer her over toward
there while shes looking around at the clothes that we
are passing or for a lady to help her   and i point her
toward the glamourous young woman at the counter of
the somewhat more fashionable place   and suddenly my
mother is out of the area that was the budget place
she crosses the border which is not noticeable
its like going from la jolla to pacific beach
or rather like going from pacific beach to la jolla
two towns grown together distinguishable only by a
gradual upward shift in price   there is nothing to
cross but you cross it   at one point you were in
pacific beach and now youre in la jolla and everything

costs more and looks costlier   the fashion place
was suddenly overwhelming and my mother was overawed by
these vaguely fashionable clothes that suggest subtly
the 1930s   as in other more fashionable stores
similar subsections would suggest this more emphatically
and we enter and i say to my mother "i think they have
a fitting room in there where you can try it on"
and my mother looks doubtful so i ask the lovely
young woman and she smiles reassuringly at my mother a
very lovely smile and assures her that the fitting rooms
are right around the corner   and my mother is even
more overawed by the slender loveliness and fashionability
of the girl and her smile   and she looks at me
uncertainly as the girl takes her arm and gently shoves
her toward the fitting rooms   which my mother moves
toward obediently but tentatively   looking back plaintively
all the way   and as i see her disappearing into the
curtained doorway she looks very sad   a little
white haired lady with an orange hat   wandering
around the corner tentatively attempting to try on the
bra that shes holding while still walking around the
corner with her clothes still on   and i keep thinking
shes going to figure this out   shell finally get
into one of those little rooms and try it on and well
find out whether or not it fits   and i wait an
awfully long time   and the girl is smiling at me
itll be all right   your mother will eventually
get the bra   everybody buys bras and tries them on
and they eventually find one that will fit   but my
mother finally comes out and she says "i dont really
think this brassiere will do"   she says "you know im
not very big   maybe i can sew it to make it fit"
and the girl says "but they have many more bras in
all sizes over behind loungewear   they have a bigger
selection there than in the budget place"   my mother
looks doubtful   "i really could take it in by
sewing it here"   she says "im very small"

and the girl says "so am i but there are sizes for
everybody"   and while were having this conversation
im thinking   i figure that maybe i should take her
    through to intimate apparel over behind loungewear
        but my mother hates the idea of crossing that river
of terrazzo flooring once again   passing through
terry jumpers and through junior coordinates and the
    perfumes   the perfumes colognes and toilet waters
on the left as you sail up the river to the left of
loungewear and pass perfumes and toiletries   the
    exercycles the electric shavers and face brushes and wind
up near luggage once again across from bargain shoes
        and i see shes afraid of that voyage   and its
    a tough voyage   so i say "mother the selection is
better over there because they have more expensive ones
        and more of them   its really ok we can afford it
        the money is not a problem"   she says "i dont
    know if i really want to"   but i take her arm and
insist that its all right   well go over there and well
    find one and it will fit perfectly   and then i start
        looking all over again for her size and we find it
        but she doesnt like this one because its cut too
    low and that because its too sheer and shes a little
        depressed by the luxuriantly flamboyant bikini styles
crowding her on all sides   which dont look appropriate
for her station in life at seventy-six   and shes
feeling depressed by all this and she says   "cant we
    just go home?"   and i say "but mother you came here
        because you needed to buy things   at least lets
    get you shoes"   so i steer her away from the depressing
lingerie and we travel over to the shoes   and she
comes slowly along with me and she stops here and there to
        look helplessly about while i keep trying to get her
    to the center of the shoe world   and finally i
leave her for a moment to finger through the stuffed
    shelves while i scout on ahead to see if i can find
        something more or less plausible to show her

and when i return to where i left her shes standing
there looking quite cheerfully at a pair of blue sneakers
with a picture of snoopy embossed on them   and in round
bright letters the word   "boss"   "these look
wonderful" she says "i think id like a pair of these"
          and i say "what size are you?"   she says seven
and a half   and i go scrambling through the pile
of sneakers to find a seven and a half   and i cant find
one   but i take heart that shes been wrong before and
i find her a six and a half   finally it turns out
shes a six   which we eventually find   and i say
to her "are you sure this is what you really want mother
          i thought you wanted shoes"   she said "these
fit wonderfully   i like these"   so shes got a
pair of blue sneakers with two little snoopys and the
word "boss" printed on them   and i said "dont you
need socks"   she said "yes i do   what i do is
cut down regular stockings and make socks out of them
ankle high"   i said "we could start by getting
you anklets and it would save you the trouble"
          she said "oh do they have those?"   i said "yeah
lets go through the hosiery section"   and we
look through the legtricity and sheer and dark panty
hose and we can find knee length stockings and thigh
length stockings and panty hose or socks for athletes or
children but no anklet stockings   i ask somebody
else   i manage to find another handsome young woman
walking among the shelves and i ask her do you have any
ankle length stockings and she says   "we do but were
out of them but we have calf height and knee height"
          and now whats beginning to interest me is that once
there was a kind of coherency   a fully articulated
system of hosiery that included waist height stockings
          panty hose   and obviously thigh height stockings
          and knee stockings and calf stockings and ankle
stockings   and maybe also toe stockings
          but whatever the system contained   at this

particular moment   all that is left of the system
is whats left on the shelves   and such logical
  structure as we can infer from whats left   and whats
   left turns out to be calf height   and my mother is
  once again getting depressed   so i grab three pairs
  of calf height stockings and assure her that she can
cut them down to anklets when she gets them home
     but she thinks theyre a little too light   too
sheer   "well" i say "theres the smoky type"   and
i grab some of the smoky style and i give them to her
     shes got three of them now   and she says thats
  too much money   i said "mother take it   lets get
out of here and get the rest of the things you need
  how about a blouse?"   and i start grabbing blouses
  from the other side of the river again   "this is a
nice looking blouse" i say "why dont you take it
    how about something glamourous looking   mother
wouldnt you like one of these to stand in on the terrace
  of your house overlooking the ocean while youre having
  cocktails with your friend the real-estate broker and
  his friend the lawyer and the neurologist   and youre
all looking at the sunset"   and i take one of the
  tie arounds and give it to my mother   "youll look
  great in it im sure"   she says "i dont want one of
  those i couldnt wear it   i have nothing to wear it
to"   i said "what if i take you out to dinner in a
fashionable la jolla restaurant   youll look glamourous
  there holding a margarita in your hand smoking a
cigarette in a holder   it will be wonderful"
    "no" she says "i cant really   its too expensive"
    "no" i said "its cheap   theyre selling it at
fifty percent off   it says so on the label"
    she says "what was it originally"   "fifteen
dollars"   "thats too expensive   thats seven and
a half dollars thats terrible i dont buy blouses for that"
    "well" i said "what about shoes   now youve got
sneakers you still need shoes"   she says "i want to

go home"   now thats one of the reasons why i abandoned
    collage   which is organized around something like sears
        by and large   and while it is sometimes entertaining
or illuminating to consider this kind of organization
        to inspect the parts from which it has been assembled
and speculate upon the discourses from which they might
have been taken   to restore the missing parts or
    merely take pleasure in the juxtaposition and collision
of these fragments of otherwise unrelated or arbitrarily
    related things   that are now parts of some new
and totally unfamiliar yet partially familiar thing
        and this can be something of a pleasure and even
    dazzling   this simultaneously incoherent coherency
this sense that you are considering some precarious
unfamiliar thing that is always about to dissociate
    itself into bright shards and doesnt   or a dazzling
    jumble of shards that keeps threatening to assemble
itself into a fairly dull familiar thing   which you
    hope it doesnt   and i understand this pleasure in
    regarding sears as a work that was done for you
        yet there are other kinds of organization   that
i find   interesting   banal coherencies for example
    that can become somehow suddenly interesting   there
        was a professor when i was in college   a professor
of french literature   a balding little man in an
ordinary dark tweed jacket and gray pants and cordovan
    shoes   who one day appeared wearing a gray chamois
    glove with a pearl button   now there he was in his
    professional tweed jacket and his ordinary striped
    shirt and tie with a stickpin   but wearing a
single gray chamois glove with a pearl button   and it
    was not especially noticeable except that he didn't take
the glove off in classes or at coffee with guest lecturers
or in conferences in his office with students   and
    while no one made very much of it no one could figure
out when they thought of it why this dumpy little french
professor with the watery blue eyes and slightly

bulbous red nose was wearing one gray chamois glove
     but soon things became slightly more coherent
     he started appearing with two gray chamois gloves
     and some time later   apparently having found
his way to a thrift shop he had bought himself
     perhaps for seventy five cents or a dollar   an
old alpaca morning coat in splendid condition   but he
still looked funny wearing his blue or pink striped
     shirts and the thin dark tie with his morning coat and
chamois gloves and the cordovan shoes that professors used
     to affect in those days   but before long he was
wearing black pumps striped trousers stiff white dress
     shirts with a softly knotted flowing tie   then he
     acquired a walking stick and disappeared   which is
     to say that he had acquired a banal coherency that was
not so banal at new yorks city college in 1953   and he
     had acquired it progressively   growing more and more
coherent each week   and more banal   till the final
     moment   at which point he disappeared   and thats
     also a form of coherency i have found interesting
     or rather a movement from and toward coherency
ive found interesting   at one time there was at
city college a conventional coherency of which this man
     was a part   at some point he began to become less
     coherent   for a time he became a form of
incoherency   that gradually evolved toward an absolute
     if discordant banality and at that moment disappeared
     and this movement i have also found interesting
     but not so much nowadays   now i am more
interested in the kinds of coherency that develop
     sometimes rather startlingly   out of the way
the human mind works as it faces the exigencies of everyday
     life   that is im interested in the way the mind
     works   because i dont know how the mind works
     in this area i am very ignorant   but
     fortunately   as i find   fortunately or
unfortunately   so is everybody else   specialists

in the working of the human mind dont know very much
about it   which surprises you   or rather it
surprises me   it may not surprise you   it
surprises me because things happen with the human mind
that are very peculiar and startling and reveal
unlikely situations that require nearly no cultivating
only to be attended to   and sometimes you cant
help attending to them   my little boy   hes no longer
a very little boy   blaise   hes thirteen years old
he was going to sleep and feeling sentimental
he was sleepy and couldnt sleep   and in spite
of being thirteen he was being   sentimental
usually hes a cheerful noisy kid who sounds a lot
like the poet hes named after   blaise cendrars
thats his name and its turned out to be the right
name for him   but today he was being young and
sentimental   and he said "you know daddy   why
dont you put on the sleepy music   you know the
sleepy music you always put on   that record by fields"
"fields" i said "fields?"   "you know" he said
"WC"   and sure enough it was the flute viola and
harp sonata that we always used to play for him since he
was three   by debussy   so it occurs to me that
there are ways that the mind organizes things that are
rather startling   that are more surprising than what
you can do mechanically   that are more surprising
than what i can do by planning to sit down and cut the
pieces up   or surprise myself by shaking them in a
hat or getting a machine to shake them in its hat for
me   and i like shaking things in a hat no matter
whose hat   but you dont normally come up with
things that are quite so surprising when you do that
or at least i havent for a long time   by shaking
things in hats   and i think   sometimes
even trying to formulate   merely to formulate a
kind of sense   out of someones most conventional
narrative   just to try to make sense of it

appears to produce a radical coherency that i had
never anticipated   for example when my grandmother
was dying   and i had never fully understood this
my grandmother was a very very elegant lady
a sort of high class european style lady
from a kind of european but jewish background
and she was dying   and when she was dying she
was dying for awhile   she was weakening   her
faculties were weakening   and she had taken to
bed   now she was a very lively lady so she was not
someone who liked being in bed   and at one point while
there   and i came in   she was protesting
and at the time i thought that she was protesting
being in bed   and it would have been very much like
her   to say to hell with this thing and try to get
up and do something   but she was protesting obscurely
she kept saying over and over again   "theres not
enough room   not enough room"   and i kept trying
to listen because she had become very weak and was
speaking vehemently but very low   "go away theres not
enough room"   and i couldnt tell whether she was
chasing away the people who kept coming into the room
her daughters who were coming and going and trying to
help her   or me   and they kept asking her
"mother whats the matter mama   whats the matter"
and she says "not enough room"   she says "give
him some money"   and they said   "what?
what do you mean money?"   she said "put it
in the can"   she said "theres not enough room
go away"   and they werent sure whether she was
yelling at them   or driving something out of the
bed   she said "give him the money and let him go
away"   she said "take it away   at least take off
his hat"   and they kept staring around   whose
hat?   what hat?   she says "its terrible"
she says "that black beard"   black beard?
she said "please give him the money   every year

i give them money"   every year she gives them money?
who?   and i never heard any more of this story
she died   and recently   recently thinking
of this scene   thinking of this rambling set of
words   it occurred to me that i could imagine a
coherency   i mean i have no conviction about what
she was really talking about   yet   i knew that every
year   every year   she used to give money
to an orthodox jewish organization   for which
she had no particular affection and no special interest
in   and they used to come around   always
one guy in a long overcoat   with a big hat
ear locks   and a black beard   used to come
with a tin can   and people used to put money
in it and give him a glass of tea   and my grandmother
always gave him money and a glass of tea   and i
suspect that probably   if she had given him money
she might have survived and he would have gotten out
of her bed

*

JESSICA HAGEDORN

Motown/Smokey Robinson

hey girl, how long you been here?
did you come with yr daddy in 1959 on a second-class boat
cryin' all the while cuz you didn't want to leave the barrio
the girls back there who wore their hair loose
lotsa orange lipstick and movies on sundays
quiapo market in the morning, yr grandma chewin' red tobacco
roast pig? . . . yeah, and it tasted good . . .
hey girl, did you haveta live in stockton with yr daddy
and talk to old farmers who immigrated in 1941?
did yr daddy promise you to a fifty-eight-year-old bachelor
who stank of cigars . . . and did you
run away to san francisco / go to poly high / rat your hair /
hang around woolworth's / chinatown at three in the morning
go to the cow palace and catch SMOKEY ROBINSON
cry and scream at his gold jacket
Dance every friday night in the mission / go steady with ruben?
(yr daddy can't stand it cuz he's a spik.)
and the sailors you dreamed of in manila with yellow hair
did they take you to the beach to ride the ferris wheel?
Life's never been so fine!
you and carmen harmonize "be my baby" by the ronettes
and 1965 you get laid at a party / carmen's house
and you get pregnant and ruben marries you
and you give up harmonizing . . .
hey girl, you sleep without dreams
and remember the barrios and how it's all the same:
manila / the mission / chinatown / east l.a. / harlem / fillmore
     st.
and you're gettin' kinda fat and smokey robinson's gettin' old

so take a good look at my face / you see my smile
looks outta place / if you look closer / it's easy to trace /
the tracks of my tears . . .

but he still looks good!!!

i dont' want to / but i need you / seems like i'm always /
thinkin' of you / though you do me wrong now / my love is
strong now / you really gotta hold on me . . .

*

Chiqui and Terra Nova

such a strange girl / chiquita / hangin' out with the likes of
terra nova / a man / woman / what polite people refer to as
transvestite / terra nova / bundled up in technicolor crocheted
doily shirts / outdated sixties' bellbottoms / dressed in the
outdated chic / of rock stars' old ladies / like chiquita
remembered seein' / in the backstages of fillmore east and
fillmore west / when jimi hendrix was still alive / some shy
young man with blown-out hair everyone ignored / in those
days
      but jimi was dead / and terra nova reigned / in the streets of
new york city / carrying her bundle of technicolor clothes and
opalescent jewelry / new york city / the only city that
mattered / in terra nova's serene opinion
in terra nova's serene opinion
      "it's not as if i haven't travelled" / she would say / "it's not
as if i haven't been to kansas-st. louis missouri-grand rapids
michigan-new jersey-or cicero illinois . . . i've even given
california a whirl . . . some old man took me to paris for a
one-night stand near the folies bergere! but i couldn't stay . . .
everything was too historical and they kept egypt locked up in
some museum basement . . . san francisco's too slow for me . . .

oakland too much to handle . . . los angeles far too spatial! i
like to walk at night . . . but l.a. cops are trigger-happy in the
wrong way. . ."

and terra nova would flash her famous smile / at chiquita /
who she now accepted as a friend / after all / it was chiqui who
named this spirit / new earth / a found poem / in rags / they
haunted streets / together / sometimes peering into cars /
parked along the river / in the late night / watching men / jack
off men / languidly / nervously / or desperately

but **jimi was dead** and what about transsexuals? chiqui
often asked her friend / terra nova was proud of the fact that
she was not one / or the other

"i hesitate to speak on the subject" / terra nova replied /
"only because one never knows, one never knows . . ." like the
weather / one of terra nova's favorite subjects

chiqui and terra nova would lean against a car / parked on
christopher street in the early morning / and discuss last night's
t.v. news / terra nova had a crush on ed bradley / and was a fan
of CBS / "he seems so kind and unapproachable / **a real man**" /
she would sigh / but it was the weather report that infuriated
her / snide and smug weathermen and women who predicted
sunshine / five days in advance

"how could they know?" / terra nova cried / "**how could
they know!** and how dare they disturb my atmosphere with
BAD NEWS" / BAD NEWS / terra nova had no room for that /
in her life

and whenever chiqui asked about transsexuals / which she
often did / bein' a young and fascinated woman / curious about
silicone breasts / artificial vaginas / and stitched-on penises /
terra nova would refer to one of her cherished movies /
"frankenstein" / any version would do

"now / you think about that / GIRL / you
think about that" / was all terra nova murmured
closing large almond-shaped eyes and nodding her head slowly /
her dishevelled mass of curls / shaking this way / and that /

how melancholy overcame her as she marvelled at the world
and **jimi hendrix dead** so many years

once / when chiqui had some money / she bought terra
nova a new wig / a royal peacock blue wig / and terra nova
threw back her head and laughed and laughed and embraced
the smiling chiquita / "my chiquita banana" / terra nova
crooned

terra nova wore her new electric blue wig to washington
square park and danced for a giggling crowd / sang stevie
wonder songs out-of-tune / but didn't care / was joyful even
when the rain came down and the crowd dispersed

chiqui and terra nova collected more quarters and dimes
than any hustler in the park that afternoon / strolling down the
streets arm-in-arm / like tropical apparitions / only visible to a
few

*

BILL BERKSON

Ode

1

Midnight moonlight mobbed Dante's bridge
Nights you are arduous
to ward off cheap distress
anxiety earned like yesterday's pay
Correction can't dramatize itself
probably shouldn't
January passing maples in a car
provisionally bright alive
and at the controls
wrong, no worries, except
motion prevaricates
there isn't much of it
in the right places
a little of who you are
suspected to involve
If I could I would do so out of excess
not necessarily a bad thing
cue me and I'm on
clue me in and I'm yours
now I'm going to name that tune
suggest a title, indicate
strongest love-and-hate scenario
first sign of spring
first serious encounter
by chance with the rich and strange
Whoever scribbled white markings

on the floor at our feet
was shameless and
lacked character
I'm just peeing in the wind
meaning resilient, dizzy and frayed
rain hammers pearls
on the skylights
in a pair of red rainboots
decalcomania
under ordinarily visible
penises and breasts
One house actually had a barometer
although it never did any work
neither rising nor falling
the steady-as-she-goes
on the surface of the wall in the grand
living room behind the sofa
in a well-polished mahogany frame
Easy does or easy doesn't
Inspirited takes care of fathoms dense
with passing hims and hers
amassed around the alcove
"Watch the hook. Beware the hook."
Hemming a summit
pulsing white tusk, sky's maritime dray
"Bub!" my father's voice, wristbone shivers
dreamed I hopped off a big white truck
Queens Boulevard and lost my gear

2

sunlight fractures the plexiglas
fanning around sturdy trunks and boughs
sly shadows of bush in the yard high noon
cow trails wild thought has mapped
rain sorrow brainsweat and fatigue
eagerness of insane

whomsoever eyes take in and fix
requiring required
coordinated gales of laughter light and love
on the way home from the sleepyheaded
    doctor's office
a fish that eats
birds that freak in unison
bugs at their labors
do the dirty work
a rapid boil
politesse du coeur
politeness of or from the heart
in the assembled body
assuming the bodily appearance
of a body or two
the small boy rolls some marbles around
on the floor of the house
one gets lost
a pointless story
but suffused
with recognizable colors
that travel far
time is important
making as it does
elbow-room for happenings of note
to occupy quasi-permanent niches
in estimable space
probably you knew all this
because something tells us
as is its wont
and the occasional savage trance-like state
of people in the process of singing
being heard

*

A Fixture

Not ever knowing what she does in the shower,
a frictional sorrow like bedding in dark
feeling brows flex over wireless concerns,
not hers.
A stone in the river you can't move moves you.
And the postholes wobble. Glaze is permanent.

In her partition is the stairway of unhunched love,
a muscular mouth.

*

Bubbles

I was a bathing beauty in THE AMERICAN VENUS.
My dream of becoming a great dancer: How sweet he was then,
a brilliant, laughing young man of the world, his heart
so tender: "Get married!" I cried, bursting into fresh black
tears: Glittering white sequins: I put no value on my beauty.
Somedays I thought I would run away from Hollywood forever—
to Miami to Havana to Palm Beach to Washington D.C. no less!
Now we are in the air, warriors of the sky, burning the beans
and WANTED FOR MURDER: No rehearsal, no retakes:
His actors cry real tears: He wanted Dick to cry too and
Dick was not a spontaneous weeper: Breaking out of his grasp,
I grabbed a shotgun and killed him with dramatic swiftness.
That developed his character: Stars shimmering by beasts
in the black sky: His jaw muscles hunched closer to deliver
his monolog: "You're a lousy actress and your eyes are
too close together." I shoved him away, saying "Are you
trying to make love to me?" "Why not?" he said furiously,
jumping up and backing away to the door to make his exit.
"You go to bed with everyone else—why not me?"

*

Dream With Fred Astaire

I'm in a large movie theater. I go to the john.
Standing at one of the urinals next to me is Fred Astaire.
He zips up his pants and says "I'm a loser!" I look deep
into his sunglasses, their mirrored lenses, and I say
"Oh you're doing alright!" he is visibly moved by the
open-hearted and believable way I say this.

*

Star Motel

Inside I could hear
a party of people
the aimless cars
and in the middle distance
inexorable murmurs
of the ice machines.

*

Familiar Music

A pair of dark blue panties
among hairbrushes.

*

Baby's Awake Now

And now there is the lively sound
Of a panel truck heading due southwest
Along Elm Road, edge of dusk—
The densest light to see to drive by.

The underbrush has brown fringe
And small silent birds.

I saw the rainbow fire.
I saw the need to talk.
I saw a unicorn and a red pony.
And I didn't want any deviled eggs.
I drove home with my collar up.

We're alive. You do alarm me to the fact.
The light is on the window in the air,
And breath comes faster than the hounds
To sanction what remembered, what stuck.

*

Fourth Street, San Rafael

There was an old man at the bank today
Standing beside the paying/receiving window while his wife
Cashed a check or made a deposit she wore a light
Blue dress black shoes black hair
Not a sign of white or grey in it
But from the curve her shoulders made a weight sunk
Down to her ankles she was probably of a certain age
Though a few years younger than her husband
Whose ripened aging was no way disguised

A stiff olive drab fishing cap visor above his long bony face
And around his neck he had on one of those thong ties old
    gents wear
With a metal clasp at the collar and blunt tips at the ends
Loose hung sports jacket and baggy no-color slacks with a belt
He stood talking seriously to her about their money matters
And whenever he wanted to make some special point
He would place his hand firmly on her back and pat or caress it
With such decorum he would be her constant lover any time
Healthy wealthy and wise, and so it seemed
Stepping up to the adjoining window next in line

*

TOM CLARK

Dispersion and Convergence

Like musical instruments
Abandoned in a field
The parts of your feelings

Are starting to know a quiet
The pure conversion of your
Life into art seems destined

Never to occur
You don't mind
You feel spiritual and alert

As the air must feel
Turning into sky aloft and blue
You feel like

You'll never feel like touching anything or anyone
Again
And then you do

*

Rec Room in Paradise

Those men whom the gods wish
to destroy, they first make
mad, and then, when the first white flecks
of foam speckle the men's lips—the spit
of bewilderment, of overpowering visions—the gods
throw their heads back and they
laugh and laugh, they laugh and they
laugh, until they are rolling on the floor
of the heavenly TV lounge

*

Alpha November Golf Sierra Tango

From coast to coast
Voices of flight control
Are getting anxious

What is wrong suddenly
Is that I swallow a cold
Blast of air, I mean fright

Spill coffee on my book
And hear the kinks
In the great universe

The warp in the coffin
Phantom men fly out of
Anywhere in this world

Come in, come in, they call

*

Climbing

My heart in pieces like the bits
Of traffic lost in the blue
Rain confused I roar off into
To learn how to build a ladder
With air in my lungs again
To be with you in that region
Of speed and altitude where our bodies
Sail off to be kissed and changed
By light that behaves like a hand
Picking us up in one state and putting
Us down in a different one every time

❊

The Process

Two crows sew themselves onto the lace flag
Of that flying cloud, whose cosmetic grace
Adorning the Plain Jane face of the day
Pins them in an unlikely halo of pale light
After one blast of which they dance away,
Croaking shrilly as abandoned divas
Whose black scarves flap in the breeze
Over every home and panorama, dark precise
Signs washed up on the air to be noticed
Out of a continuous process of succession

❊

Final Farewell

Great moment in *Blade Runner* where Roy
Batty is expiring, and talks about how everything
he's seen will die with him—
ships on fire off the shoulder of Orion
sea-beams glittering before the Tannhauser gates.

Memory is like molten gold
    burning its way through the skin
It stops there.
        There is no transfer
Nothing I have seen
will be remembered
beyond me
That merciful cleaning
of the windows of creation
will be an excellent thing
my interests notwithstanding.

But then again I've never been
    near Orion, or the Tannhauser
gates,

I've only been here.

*

Arc

It turns the corner
like a smoky plume
and runs out
to loop around
the dead moons of Jupiter

This street is named
the New Angel
after the one who
cut it through me

The angel who preferred to free men
by taking from them
rather than making them happy
by giving to them

*

ISHMAEL REED

Sky Diving

"It's a good way to live and
A good way to die"
From a Frankenheimer video about
Sky diving
The hero telling why he liked to

      The following noon he leaped
      But his parachute wasn't with him
      He spread out on the field like
      Scrambled eggs

Life is not always
Hi-lifing inside
Archibald Motley's
"Chicken Shack"
You in your derby
Your honey in her beret
Styling before a small vintage
Car

Like too many of us
I am a man who never had much
Use for a real father
And so when I'm heading
For a crash
No one will catch me but
Me

The year is only five days old
Already a comet has glittered out
Its glow sandbagged by
The jealous sun

    Happens to the best of us
    Our brilliance falling off
    Like hair from Berkeley's roving
    Dogs

Even on Rose Bowl day
An otherwise joyous occasion
A float veered into the crowd
Somebody got bruised over the incident
Like a love affair on second ave.

It's a good lesson to us all
In these downhill days of a
Hard-hearted decade
Jetting through the world
Our tails on fire

    You can't always count
    On things opening up for you
    Know when to let go
    Learn how to fall

         *

The Katskills Kiss Romance Goodbye

    1
After twenty years of nods
He enters the new regime
The machine guns have been

Removed from the block
The women don't wear anything
You can see everything

2

Hendrick Hudson's Tavern
Has slipped beneath the
Freeway where holiday drivers
Rush as if they've seen the
Hessian Trooper seeking his
Head

3

They get their goosebumps at
The drive-in nowadays, where
The Lady in White at Raven
Rock is Bette Davis and
Burton apes Major André
Hanging before the Haunted
Bridge

4

A New England historian has
Proof that King George wasn't
So bad.
Gave in to every demand
Donated tea to the American needy
Yankees are just naturally jumpy

5

Where once stood madmen
Buttonholing you
Gentlemen think of Martinis
On the train to Mount Vernon

6

R.I.P. old Rip
Cuddle up in your Romance
Your dog Wolf is dead
Your crazy galigaskins out
Of style
Your cabbages have been canned
Your firelock isn't registered
Your nagging wife became a
Scientist, you were keeping
Her down

7

Go back to the Boarded Up
Alley and catch some more winks
Dreaming is still on the house

＊

Skirt Dance

i am to my honey what marijuana is
to tiajuana . the acapulco gold of her
secret harvest . up her lush coasts i
glide at midnite bringing a full boat .
(that's all the spanish i know.)

＊

Dialog Outside the Lakeside Grocery

The grocery had provided him with
boxes of rotten lettuce
He was loading them onto a
yellow pick-up truck
He was frail white man and
wore a plaid woolen shirt and
frayed dungarees
I was sitting in a gray chevrolet
rent-a-dent
"I have eight adult geese and
twenty-six ducks," he said
and i said
"I'll bet you have a big management
problem," and he said
"They're no trouble at all. My
wife raised two of them in the house.
When she goes near their pen
the geese waddle towards her
and nibble the lettuce out of her
hand"
"I'd never think of killing them"
he said
"They keep me out of the bars"

＊

GLORIA FRYM

Training for the Apocalypse

for J

Consider the will to love
as the decision to survive.
That's how the agents of Eros operate.
They sneak into your dreams
just before the world ends.

✻

Season Ticket

In the circle of your intentions certain spars
Remain that perpetuate the enchantment of self with self
John Ashbery

The experience that eludes you intrigues you more
than the one you're currently having. It's just
over your shoulder. Pain is the least interesting
part. They deaden the vein and draw the blood.
Pints quarts gallons graham crackers and then a
glass of Tang. They replace all of it,
for a while you are out of circulation.
Now you are strong enough to pinch hit for yourself.

For this you held yourself in.
For this you have lowered the bucket
into the well and drawn the luckiest penny.
Your pens are also full of ink.
Your sink full of dishes. The chopsticks on the table.
And the dinner bell rings.

Never mind the sacrifice of lilacs in California.
For two minutes in late summer
before your skin turns the velvety petals brown
you may bobby pin a gardenia
behind your left ear and everyone
will ask you to cater their lawn parties
and evening barbecues with avatars
of your presence.

At times the big world seems to narrow
into the little self then explodes
and the shrapnel hits your best friends
who only want to hold your hand along the way.
Did you want to stay a professional child indefinitely?
Intention hails the uncommitted virtuoso, you do
know what you want, don't you? And if you don't
you'd better have the final say silk-screened onto
your gold lamé tee shirt.

What triggers declivity is so confounding
you can only proceed to eat asparagus
and pee out the impurities of bad weather
inside your spring cranium. New day
and isn't it blue-green? Is there no place
safe from the self, one narcissist asks another,
yes, the self as it indefatigably keeps company
with its own low life, bopping from
one sleazy foreign hotel to the next,
with no time to learn the future
of its own currency.

Be grateful that your friends are so interesting
that exotic mushrooms grow in the back seats
of their leaky convertibles.

You can write anywhere
and you will always say what you must say since
your name is the same, isn't it?
Have you done anything separating the him from the her?
A new hybrid of tangerines
is not still called mandarin oranges.

Forget that love lies in botanical ruin.
A life could change in a day
if the couriers bring new information and day two
could find you in Paris dangling your toes on the Seine
instead of chaining your pinkies to a typewriter in Dubuque
hacking out that cash crop. Oh just
a little truck garden please, and don't forget to plant
the heavenly blue morning glories reaching toward
a vacant but highly perfumed heaven. Hope springs
because the genes contain all possible geysers
and it is up to you to crack the safe
at 3 A.M. and conduct the dawn from
your highly promising podium in
the most dangerous orchestra pit. The pianos are breathing
heavily, Nijinsky awaits the tap of your baton.
Anna Pavlova rises like a phoenix
instead of a swan especially in your honor
tonight.

*

JANINE POMMY-VEGA

Rites of the Eastern Star

Ladies reading
from little books
What are they saying?

We sit
in the first row holding hands
The family of this man
in the coffin
The privileged watchers
in velvet chairs, the scrutinized,
the bored and visiting royalty.

I warn you we must have
passion! Open the floodgates!
The merciless seas!

The rigid semi-circle
of women in white uniforms
fans out in front of the coffin
Clutching flowers, dogmatic verse
they give us a tepid theater piece
vague sermons hang in the seams
of their garments. Give us
violent theater I tell you!
Draw back the curtains!
Release the hounds!

The great tragedians
knew how to wring the necks of swans.
You could hear the cracking of bones
from the seventh row

*

The Voices

Something under the bones is calling
dragging me down to the root of myself
I stop on street corners
taking telephone numbers from men
who could be lovers, it does not change
I seek out every face I've ever loved
as carrion, food for the bones
It only widens the crease to a
scar on the waters.
If bones were soft, it would be
in the bones. This is under that,
like a sea on a flooded meadow.

I have grown lean and bend with the wind
like a green stem whose flower is
plucked waves in the grasses
I look covertly for promises from total
strangers in the street, the soft place
under the bones dark and rippling.
Murmuring sounds like the lowing
of cattle far off over the hills
move through my footsteps
As though I could equate the bricks on both
sides of an alley with the sliding through,
and still not reach the yard.

The body gravitates toward darkened corners,
foxholes where the wounds are licked
and licked again
The worker wanders from his tools and is found
sitting in a chair with limp hands
watching the rain slide down a window
A valley of quiet graves in the moist ground
murmurs under root and footstep
Hovering over the sound is a mother buried
inside me, her bare arms cover the sea.

*

JACK MARSHALL

Glimmers

of Leeuwenhoek's
drop

of water,
my first

lens,
tense, trans-

parent globe, condensed
sky

to see
through, continuable

point, free-
flowing window

you could draw
from the kitchen tap, through

an eye-
drop's worth, close-up, see

smooth white folded
nap, linen tablecloth's

woven waves, knotted
wood smoke, the moon

itself, pale window or marble
well, another

matter. And what
worlds more

wondrous with each downward drop-
let blooming

a knot
open in the grain

of vision! And from that wood
a leaf's threaded net-

work of lacy veins
retracing those in the hand

holding it, and the eye
stunned wide

at twelve seeing
Tchelitchew's celestial tree,

drawing radiant embryo
boys out of fiery air, take

root, live melting or molding luminous
foliage, their nerve-waving faces'

peeled eyeballs a shimmer
of molten ganglia, soaked bloody

space aglow, the inner
core heat consuming stars. . .

What were they beginnings of
but faces of dread

and desire still
to come—summer's ice-

blossom cornea, crystallized,
staring

within
the webbed wood's center

at her whose reach they elude
yet are drawn to, surround,

silently mouthing,
warning, wooing, as if

calling for help,
and plunging

were about to be-
come soaring,

and midway is
tangled branches, brain, stem.

How brightly
expectant

they hover! as if in a gathering

sense that being seen
by such unblinking

eyes of air and water
is to shine, be given

power. And he
who in that light

sees you—see now
through his eyes

the many-eyed sun-
flower

head of a fly
through a microscope,

its flickering
green-gold

iridescent wing
cells like tiny

conical bricks
in a wall that flew! Imagine—

protein-bonded vapor
spun

over eons
into tissue

withstanding
swipes of wind, hand, spun

out of microbes like those
thriving

in a waterdrop—live
hair, hook-tailed, locked looping

as curved sweeping scimitars of
Arabic calligraphy

your father wrote out for you
one day in rapid flowing

script. Where they, too,
linked or fleeting

strands of barely familiar
code all the more

dream-like for being
so close at hand? Might those

lenses once have been
steadily concentrated on

by the hand and consciousness
of free-thinking, stubborn,

damned Spinoza
dividing infinity

into axioms
and rays

of rational harmony? Divinity
embodied in a mathematics

deemed heretical, but,
to a boy, so chaste, incorporeal,

I couldn't begin to understand,
nor why heresy? Only that

this gentle excommunicant
and terror of Talmudic rabbis

I studied under
and hid

my reading from,
called by his fellow townsfolk

when not trying to lynch him,
"This Jew,

the only man among us
who talks like Christ,"

too solitary and shy
for a hero,

this feverish, tubercular
silkworm in his cocoon,

could for hours be totally
absorbed watching spiders

battle in corners of his attic room
in Amsterdam. Eternity looked on

that world, too,
abandoned by the sun

from where Vermeer's poured milky
glistening

pearl-
drop earrings

an eye
still

shining through
sand and pigment, beckoning

testament to the untouchable
blue

veil,
light and air. Blessed

Baruch, in the rays
of that illumination permitting

what is forbidden, did he
grind for twenty years, for failing

Dutch patrons' eyes, lenses to find
dust before breathing himself

an early grave
on February 25, 1677, anniversary,

two hundred seventy years later, of my birth.
Axiom: in the beginning

Elohim
created by contracting

Light Without End
to nothing—*tzimtzum*—but a dimensionless

dot, the heavens and earth,
in a mastery so absolute as to be

invisible. Proof: visible and
invisible, the hazardous dread-

fulness of reaching twelve convincing me
I'd reach no more

than twenty-five, and am already dogging
twice that, dogged by

a weight as of a sea
that brought us

here, tide pushed on by
tides behind, pulled

forth by tides forward . . . ocean
given different names

on the different shores
it washes, serving

the pin-
hole

hollow pupil
of the chambered nautilus

as eyeball. There, down under
then, regain

our sight? and, between
dropping

or diving, as we choose,
go

into better
armed than empty-

handed? So the body, fed
on illness—if the inner disturbance is

great enough—creates
its health, increasingly

fragile, increasingly
complex, a higher order. Imagine—

two particles, one in contact,
separated even to the ends of

the universe, change
instantaneously when

a change in one of them
occurs. So,

heart in mouth, feel
the speeding music's

measure slow, if not for which,
how would you know the lovely

touch of time's caressing,
shapely, shiftless

body? How
slipped

through your fingers it may
be placed in your hands again . . .

"Water," said David at six,
"burns fire." With that. Now

between dimming and flaring
glimmers backing up, see

the cardboard-stiff black cat
found at curbside

you buried deep at night
in the raving widow's grape arbor—

our fort and arsenal
against the huge

blunt cars, like waves of
invaders in those World War II years—

their Atlas-
bearing hoods aimed speedily

down streets so wide,
what hordes did they imagine,

on what air-
swollen wheels, would have the right of way?—

breaking up our games: the wild
delirious animal

elasticity running
a batted ball

down barely
within reach. Not till

now seeing those hidden
dangers: late

one summer afternoon
in those days that seemed to stay

aloft forever, beneath
the lightning-

winged Mobil Pegasus
hoof-raised

three floors up, outside
our bedroom window,

its silver-blue fluorescent
tubes not yet lit

for neon night-
flight, high

on running bases, Joey, showing off, holds
the oily orange gasoline pump's

hose close
up for a look, spills

a drop, screams,
clutching the runny

sunset flame in his eye, jumping
to put it out.

Or those chimes
of the eagerly awaited

immaculate Good Humor
truck, fragrant of vanilla,

on that, or another, sunny day,
which struck

Eddie's lovely blond five-year-old sister
down, hers the only eyes

closed, head hard-wrenched
far away in the light of the sun clean-

clawing the carnivorous street.
Weeks later, dug up

the cat, saw the frightful
white worms wriggling

inside the shape that had been, gut-
emptying gleams

dimly even now
lighting that darkness continuously

tunneling from birth. And I remember,
I remember as if having to go under

for air, not the wind waking
for the low roar

of years—night, solitude
no blindfold

but an eye conscious
of being an eye,

inheriting the past
of your nights and the awful

mounting dread at the courage needed
to be born.

Through an opening
bloody or bright,

you enter yourself
as you enter the night: birth

either to choose or wither
on the vine. . .

Years later, feel the eerie
undersea tug again,

reading in Ferenczi's *Thalassa*,
when the primal oceans receded, drying,

and our gill-breathing ancestors evolved
organs for breathing

air and protecting the embryo—
the danger not of drowning

but desiccation—
and with seeking the aquatic

existence of which they had
been deprived, came the impulse

for the first time
to penetrate

into the body
of another. Sexual

combat began as a struggle
for moisture? Fucking

to be intra-
uterine again? for the parasite's

fear of birth and the pleasure,
finally, of surmounting that danger?

If, in the child, sucking, touching,
being touched, looking, being looked at, provide

complete satisfaction, in the adult
looking, kissing, sucking serve

genital eruption.
Unless the pulse of

gladness gather, quicken
periodically to be

released in rhythmic rapture,
the eye would be absorbed

in endless looking, the mouth in sucking,
the hand in touching, leaving the body

open
to attack.

Does limiting intensest pleasure
to a single organ increase

efficiency and make adapting to threat—
to catastrophe even—possible?

Might there be, then, no part of the body
not represented in the genital,

when in the moment of libido
back-flow occurs that ineffable

feeling, "oceanic bliss," bringing
solace to the struggle,

giving strength and inducement to
further toil? . . . meaning, for instance,

now. For in't this
the future you dreamed of all

the time?—small, frail
vessel now

thrown
together at sea even as the journey—

and not over
gentle

blue water always nor through
long lingering low—

lidded looks
beckoning just a little

ahead of your reach—even as the journey
proceeds, eye meat

eating the meat of vision, demi-
paradise but for our blindness,

not its absence, turned back
each moment into history bringing us

shakily from
sleep and roughly to

our feet before sending us
flying—the eye not

quick, not
physical enough to see

no break in the dream
dreamed by a single being wherein

all the dream creatures also dream
of no longer dreaming

but of living *in* the dream.
In the heaven of Indra

is a network of pearls
so arranged, if one is looked at,

all the others are seen
reflected in it, each

made of all the others,
each link's

pull on the whole
moiling

seafloor-yoked
ensemble any midnight could steal

the heart out of
any or all

our hands held together, desiring
what never was, anxious

for what is no longer . . .
Between stars and salt of the deep

dispersed body whose
skin we are—

though the way repeatedly
forgotten and heart's blood hinting

home, sung to
in crooned or stuttered

music that never had reason
to begin

any more
than to end—all

oceans to it are
one

drop.
To trace beyond

would be trying to tell
the story of the sea, dark

blue depths, darker within and farther in,
nothing.

I don't want to hear any more
about eternity . . .

This moment
is not enough?—then

eternity won't be either.

*

SUSAN HOWE

from Speeches at the Barriers

1.

Say that a ballad
wrapped in a ballad

a play of force and play

of forces
falling out sentences

(hollow where I can shelter)
falling out over

and gone
Dark ballad and dark crossing

old woman prowling
Genial telling her story

ideal city of immaculate beauty
invincible children

threshing felicity
For we are language   Lost

in language
Wild sweeps over the wheat

mist-mask on woods
belling hounds drowse

Iseult of Ireland
Iseult of the snow-white hand

Iseult seawards gazing
(pale secret fair)

allegorical Tristram
his knights are at war

Sleet whips the page

flying leaves and fugitive

Earth of ancient ballad
earth as thought of the sea

water's edge to say goodbye

2.

Right or ruth
rent

to the winds shall be thrown

words being wind or web

What (pine-cone wheat-ear
sea-shell) what

volume of secrets to teach
Socrates

Banks of wild bees in story
sing in no wood so on

cornstalk and cornsheaf

prodigal benevolence
wealth washed up by the sea

What I find
signal seen by my eye

This winter falls froward
forever

sound and suggestion speared
open

Free will in blind duel

sees in secret houses in sand

each day's last purpose
each day's firm progress

schoolgirls sleeping
schoolboys sleeping and stemmed

I will dream you
Draw you

dawn and horses of the sun
dawn galloped in greek before flame

fugitive dialogue of masterwork

3.

sabbath and sweet spices
seaward so far and far

The woods seem to thicken

Merry men in Arden
(foresters feared foresters)

forage cold earth bescratcht

noise and noise pursuing power

Temper and Order
The leashed stars kindle thin

perpendicular
Clear space of blackness

between us
(grey leaves grey gusts)

Dust people hover
Iceberg setting of universal

impending
(The enemy is always riding by)

figural shadowing of invisible

Wassail
tatterdemalion revel

houses containing vision
houses of recognition

trim father nodding to trim mother

remembered name in Quiet
remembered precepts

4.

Twenty lines of

boughs bend into hindering
Boreas

the thin thaw wanders off

Presence
October drawing to its long

late edge
Understanding of time endlessly

sliding
(trees hung with false dreams)

endlessly running on

Distant forget
Tiny words of substance cross

the darkness

Who are they
(others between the trees)

falling into lines of human

habitation
Tread softly my misgiving heart

To chart all

Versimilitude
Throw my body at the mark

Parents among savages
Their house was garlanded with dead

theologies
(fierceness of the young)

Then to move forward into unknown

Crumbling compulsion of syllables

Glass face
caressing the athwart night

5.

Torn away from number weight

and measure
Ten adventures here forgotten

never touching

To go forward downward
Search for the dead

Benevolent woods and glades
hamadryads

plots and old-plays

A fictive realm
Words and meaning meet in

feigning

without a text and running from
true-seeming

Florimell flees away into the forest

Hide her there
an illusion (fiction)

Beauty of the world
becoming part of the forest

and the reeds
(thousands of years)   Night

monadical and anti-intellectual

no clock running
no clock in the forest

evanishing of the actors into

one another
Am in a simple allegory

Reaching out alone in words oh

peerless poesy

*

STEVE LEVINE

A Gothic Gesture

for Paul Violi

Is this the movie in which James Mason
Slams his cane down on Ann Todd's fingers?

Because she is playing piano? Yes, it was
A gothic gesture and made Mason a matinee idol

Overnight. One night, nights
Passed, we see him first

Meditating on a record by the Troggs, then groggy
Putting his fist through the ballroom window

In a sudden frog-like fit of Angst, his features
A concentrated form of melancholy, green. . .

Green and lumpy landscaping, brooding
Piano, parodistic weltschmerz.

*

Tiny Catullus

By myself I walk today
Maybe to stop and joke

To mingle gaggling gee-whizzery
With babble, or just plain talk.

Then suddenly you fly into view
Stop and quiet I
Cop a glimpse
Of our planet's random grace

And guess that you're a dancer—
Legs slimly styled, not mildly
Blessed, but muscular as I imagined
Are the best! And you, yourself

Are genius too—for flying
So fully into view
So singularly among
the thundering numbers.

*

Pure Notations

Above, on the wall, sexy frescoes are her intentions

Clearly exact, where she'd couch and cup my balls back.

*

Or awake, articulate, late tonight, she'll write

Something like life's pure notations, being taken.

*

JOHN YAU

The Kiss

Was it a "please urge" or "a police purge" or some combination of both? She was too busy seeing everything in the mirror but herself. In the upper left hand corner a man's voice combs the few clouds that visit this part of the state. Along the highway are towns whose inhabitants have forgotten why a river separates them from their neighbors. In order to solve their dilemma they had to agree where one ended and the other began. The rest of the fragments were delivered by the new mailman. One resembled the park, while another resembled the mayor's garage. He wondered if it still contained the magazine with a picture of a woman about to undress. He sat where there was supposed to be a sofa and turned the pages, until they began turning themselves, faster and faster, as if a destination would arrive.

*

Instant Coffee

In the woods behind the city they saw a parachute snagged high up in the branches of a Douglas Fir. The crate (with the word ABSOLUTELY stencilled in fading red letters on all sides) dangling from its leather harness was too high for either of them. They stepped back for a moment and were as casual as beer cans.

They did not hear the usual noises falling from the branches; birds dismembering their diagonal anthems, sun articulating hallways of leaves.

Chris thought this box meant that hope was still a possible solution, a place marked off where anyone could go and be alone. Jan, however, figured this was a clue to a puzzle that had not been constructed yet.

They had started out that morning by looking for the story that most resembled their own, or was it really the other way around? Neither of them could remember. After many attempts, they left behind their notes, partially erased, like snow around a plane crash.

*

Shimmering Pediment

An overloaded circuit—lightning
Jammed the horizon, and for days
The echoes remained in my eyes.
But the brightest star is to begin
Anywhere. "Among the peonies,"
As an ancient Chinese poet wrote . . .

Near where the river pirouettes
Past the airplane graveyard
I wandered in as a child;
A fenced-in field; the broken
Fuselages and crumpled wings
Reclining, like sunbathers, in
Haphazard rows of damaged magnificence.

Actually, I never played on this knoll,
Though I think somehow I must have.

For around supper I felt compelled
To return to that silent and empty
Amphitheater, my plane spiraling
In a diminishing circle, as I flew
Parallel to where I am now standing.

*

January 18, 1979

So often artists have painted a woman
washing, or combing her hair.
And nearby is a mirror.
And there you were, crouched in the tub.
It was cold in the apartment.
It is always cold in winter.
But you were brushing out your hair
and singing to yourself.
And, for a moment, I think I saw
what those artists saw—
someone half in love with herself
and half in love with the world.

*

FANNY HOWE

The Nursery

The baby
        was made in a cell
in the silver & rose underworld.
Invisibly prisoned
             in vessels & cords, no gold
for a baby; instead
eyes, and a sudden soul, twelve weeks
old, which widened its will.

Tucked in the notch of my fossil: bones
      laddered a spine from a cave,
the knees & skull
were etched in this cell, no stone, no gold
where no sun brushed its air.

One in one, we slept together
    all sculpture
            of two figures welded.
But the infant's fingers
squeezed & kneaded
          me, as if to show
the Lord won't crush what moves
on its own . . . secretly.

On Robeson Street
        anonymous

was best, where babies
have small hearts
                    to learn
with;
        like intimate
thoughts on sea
water, they're limited.

Soldered to my self
    it might be a soldier or a thief
for all I know.
The line between revolution & crime
    is all in the mind
        where ideas of righteousness
and rights confuse.

I walked the nursery floor.
By four-eyed buttons & the curdle of a cradle's
paint: a trellis of old gold
    roses, lipped & caked
where feet will be kicking in wool.

        Then the running,
the race after,
cleaning the streets, up for a life.
His technicolor cord
hung from a gallery of bones,
    but breathing, *I'm finished.*
    Both of us.

And when the baby sighed,
through his circle of lips,
                        I kissed it,
    and so did he, my circle to his,
we kissed ourselves and each other,
        as if each cell was a Cupid,
        and we were born in it.

The cornerstone's dust
up-floating

by trucks & tanks.
White flowers spackle

the sky crossing the sea.
A plane above the patio

wakes the silence
and my infant who raises

his arms to see
what he's made of.

O animation! O liberty!

❧

JIM BRODEY

Little Light

for Eric Dolphy

*"He was like an angel
that came down to Earth
played his saxophone
incredibly, and passed
too quickly."
Clifford Jordon, 1966*

There's
A
Little
Light
Over
The
Con Ed
Tower, Eric, and it's you. Too bright
to be a star, total capacity
brightens a still-raining sky, & I'm
on stand-by, waiting for your horn
to come crashing down on Manhattan.
                              Tonight, in the bath tub,
Listening to your ancient sides, rolling over, scrubbing
my back with your delicate clarinet breeze, oh so blue,
the rain beating on my eyelids, big drowsy drops shaped
like coins, that lay their own tattoo on my palms as I,
too heavy to rise beyond as you do in your uniqueness
while the soot-tinted noise of too-full streets echoes
and I pick up the quietly diminishing soap & *do*
myself again.

And, right now, it's noon in the tropics, as
a great big hand fondles the cherubs that cruise this ashen
    light,
one big whooshing sigh knocks a fleshy heave towards what
    snow
glides in on a severed tongue still singing, so beautifully
deranged, and squeezing some more difficult light
to dry my glazed flesh with
                    some of your happy brilliance.

*

To Guillaume Apollinaire

Ah, Guillaume, my friend, and greatest of predecessors, if
    we'd have met, say, on Le Pont Mirabeau,
And had a sweet cup of emerald tea, laced with some not
    so-mild but truly agonizing potion, we'd
Have frolic'd together and sang of the days when men
    and poets brought the night to a standstill
Beckoning across this great abyss of years to Homer and
    Whitman, each a saint of viable lamentations.

Ah, to have walked in your shoes of such mirth and sorrow
    joking with the Mona Lisa under our coats,
Knowing the entire world suffers without love in a dark night
    in which our voices flutter and groan, then
You'd take me to meet Max Jacob, mad Jew of delight, who'd
    sing of the distinguished liaison between
Truth and writing, that only poets know and hunger for.

So, my angel of purity wails, searching for your light, in
    this night where Montmartre and the East
Village undergo similar changes to be the disappointed world
    become less dangerous to our souls, writing

Is the torch we each choose over any art, none so immediate
    and unimitatable as a bridge over 'troubled
Waters,' wherein our blackness shows through the dizzy muck
    this world heaps on we, her heroes.

It is an angel's face we preserve, in our papers, scratched
    by a quill of disinherited light, as
You knew by a magistrate's bitter, how many times you thought
    them to fuck off, pitying the average
Knowing the extremes our insight carries us to, great voice-eye
    crooning gypsy passion, in the names
Of robbery of the species, theft of the untouchable, murder
    of the weird and triumphant syllables we sing.

Ah, Guillaume, we know the omitted lightning sandwiches,
    that the little birds turn into verse, have
Indeed affixed their cries to our spiritual radiance, auras,
    pelican wings, coyote teeth, moronic scrawls
Leaping from the holy book we take our menus on, turning,
    turning in our mental property, to a foam
Bloodied, and saved through all eternity that verses we conjure
    as happiness erupts from every pore.

Let these hands embrace you as the brother I never had,
    the father I never knew, the mother
Lost to me through love's isolation, the sister I dream
    draining testimony from brutal trial,
As life is my witness, we could stand on that lonesome bridge
    and gaze through a future in which your writing
And mine, "Alcools," and "Panda Heart" sing together, and take
    train into this wilderness of prisons & anthology.

*

Noh Play

to Robert Creeley

No sense like the strong magnetic feel
    of self.
No new hair restoring miracle drug.
No books on any shelves.
No typing machine. No stereo.
No radio slicing this quiet
    with electronic death announcements,
    what skulls were raped at Kennedy
    Airport, another girl found in a
    New Jersey swamp.
No food in freezer, just big ice hunk.
No cat to creeow hungry tantrums.
No phone bill. No rent on geometric cell.
No ultimate plan. No ideas.

No restless hungry feelings.
No food. No necktie parties. No waterbed.
No girls banging on the front door
    cause they're locked out.
No appointments. No telephone withdrawal.
No cigarettes. No more ashes.
No music (except for the brain breeze).
No heartbeat. No halo. No shrimp.
No interviews with the already sleeping.
No indecision. No wine.
No missionary work amidst
    the uncivilized planets.
No breeze floating away all
    bitten up. No neon
    hauling ideas back
    from Kalifornia.

No grinning pressure cookers
   of absolute waste
   mowing down candidates
   for the funny farm, with
     an overweight
      uppercut.

No more night clouds. No more Junes.
No more endlessly wondrous headspin
   achieved by poems.
No H-bombs. No fantasy hells. No ice.
No rainbow flames smeared into sky.
No tilted gravy train of nuptial peace.
No invigorating twilight dance with the Mayas.
No audience with truth. No shadows.

No glistening monk on Union Square
   soundtruck intoning self-lib-
   eration OM vibe shout.
No Pope Panda. No Bruce Springsteen.
No unlit. No burnt. No boredom.
No mantra is silent after we stop
      singing.

No more saintly opus than tender
   intimate sexual barely-moving
   teeth touch trembling loin-tingle.
No winged monitors. No clitoral charades.
No underwater rodeos. No dry lake.
No cocaine. No nerves.
No goose step remedies. No toothache.
No more Heckle & Jeckle
   colossal animation
     fuckups.

No pitiable lower dark moods.
No Peter Townshend. No hamburgers.
No fog-colored Dover Beach or Agate Beach
    stapled to Bolinas shorecrest.
No more Kerouac, O'Hara, Duane Allman
    Lee Crabtree, or Buddy Holly.
No winter in California.
No use taking on so. No more. No more.
No more movies. No machines. No pulse.
No pain. No cold water. No pencils.
No armrest on this spinning eternity.
No pubic hair bouquets. No duets.
No pain. No known terror.
No nothing.

No gas chamber.

No geometric verse.
No electric waste.
No shampoo. No worthwhile
    hammock of dreams.

No photographs.
No sunlight.
No exterior boundaries.
No score in six innings.
No known gods.
No rhythm. No melody.

No words.

*

BOB HOLMAN

One Flight Up

Weapons alone
      go to war

Crazy people
      try to stop them

They are killed

             Eventually the weapons
             destroy themselves

A may playing chess
      falls off the roof
But luckily turns
      into a paper boat

Next we are upside down
      looking down
The wrong end of the rifle
      is into someone's eyes

             Everything
          is a
                target
The pigeon lands
      on your hat
             The hunter aims . . .
(We are the hunter, too)

As you fall
        you don't turn
                into a boat

A camel leads the coffin
        incredibly fast!
We all
        race madly
                after the coffin
                        This is all true
                        & happens very slowly

                Luckily we are at the movies
                Watching *Entr'acte* by René Clair

People everywhere,
                you too can race after the coffin!

        THIS IS NOT THE END

                *

CYN. ZARCO

What the Rooster Does Before Mounting

Gustavo said,
"Your poems are like samba,
some even tango on the page
as if part of some strange ritual—
what the rooster does before mounting."

Gustavo said,
"In Argentina, I was in love
with Che. Even my father,
the old prick, gave him money."

Then, said Gustavo,
"You did not choose me; I chose you,"
and made me sit down while he took over
my kitchen.

I say in a yellow chair
and watched him chop vegetables—

carrots   bell pepper   onions

✻

Flipochinos

when a brown person
gets together
with a yellow person
it is something like
the mating of a chico and a banana
the brown meat of the chico
plus the yellow skin of the banana
take the seed of the chico for eyes
peel the banana for sex appeal
lick the juice from your fingers
and watch your step

❉

Emergency Poem 1973

for Nicanor Parra

Today's American car
is like a woman who won't
start until she fastens
her seat belt.
She screams
when you leave the key
in the ignition
long after the ride
has ended.

❉

Poem in Nueva York

phantasmagorillaorgasmiasmacharismamama
diaphragmdiarrheacatarrhcatatoniccatastrophicmascara
maracascaracasbarakastrakatakas
attack us
attack us
attack us
atticalunatica
bakitkanapakaloka
guayabano y banana mo
mi alma y tu almo
en mi poema
sorpresa

*

Nights

When I'm without you
I sleep on the couch
or in my bed with books,
pen & paper.

I can't decide
which I love best—
you lying next to me
like an open book
or an open book
lying next to me.

*

Saxophonetyx

I've heard all about musicians
They take love, don't give love
'cause they're savin it for the music

Got to be so one night I was watching him
take a solo, and when he closed his eyes
everyone in the club closed their eyes
The first thing I saw was my shoes
float out of his horn
my favorite leopard-skin high-heel shoes
the left foot, then the right one
followed by my black silk stockings
with the seam down the back
my best hat and all that
were floating in the air like half notes
like they belonged to no one
least of all to me

I tried to close my eyes
but I couldn't
Out flew my blue silk scarf
my alarm clock
my alligator suitcase
even last month's phone bill

He kept on playing that horn
as if nothing even happened
and when I slowly closed my eyes
I saw his fingers wrap around my waist
my spine turn into saxophone keys
my mouth become his mouthpiece
and there was nothing left in the room
but mercy

*

FAYE KICKNOSWAY

Rapunzel

An old woman, her butt spread on the stoop,
Scratched her knees and Jesus Christ
The sidewalk:

"The gentamin usta tamper with me reg'lar,
The asssuckun bastards, reg'lar. Came struttun
Their spigots, riddy ta piss in my pipes
Like I wuza goddamned privy.

Get me bloat bellied 'n' forsake me till
I'd dropped their brats 'n' then they'd
Sashay back, the motherfriggers,
Wantun ta dung more seeds ta life.

They pinched my tits till lumps growed
'N' screwed scars deep inside me,
Then laid me in an O.R. room 'n' chopped
My sex ta slops.

My diddlun days 'r' done, but you,
You hoteyed babes, purrun bareassed
Where I usta lay, you'd do well ta cool.
Let 'm pocket-pool."

*

Old Man

My energy is going, been spent
in nickels on telephone calls out of here,
telephone calls from so long ago
it makes my head ache
to think of it.
Couldn't stand the corridor.
Couldn't stand the bed.
Kept feeding those nickels in.
Anyone's voice
that answered.
Said hello

until I ran out of nickels.
Sat on the stool in the booth,
fished my finger
in the hole.
No coins.
Did it
maybe five times
a day.

Don't want to say
any of this.
Don't mean nothing.
Never has.

*

cats is wheels, fur
wheels prayun the world away.   birds
n dogs n hogs n men dressed
like shotguns
get lost in their bodies.   cats

piss metal
when you push the valves
in their teeth.   airplanes n tanks n
submarines.

cats. cats. cats.
the door bushes out
like whiskers n the moon
looks in n its the bottom of a

cats paw
right near where
the cats claws
lie sleepun.

*

After Hilary, Age 5

1.
Fat men
eat horrible food
like toads & gravel
&
sit in the garage
like laundry
until your Aunt Doris
makes them leave.

2.
The woman who lives in Grandma's
china cabinet
eats large cats
and little children
between 1 and 4 p.m.
every Thursday.

Grandma lets her
because of the alligators
in the radiators
and the turtles
in her throat.

3.
If you spit at the Moon
it will lay eggs in your hair
and your mother will be gooseflesh
and your father will die

*

CLARENCE MAJOR

Inside Diameter

1

the position is so well-known
its variations do not count
unless you split hairs: people
become delirious in its grip:
gladiators lose their thrust,
battles are lost. People
praise the wrong works: those
early things, weeds or
whatever, inspired dullness,
somebody else's action.
Putting it in a silkscreen
doesn't make it either,
putting it under acetate
overlay doesn't reduce
the penetration.

2

Jokes about Noah's Art—
pardon me: Ark: proliferate
as the position continues to be
struck and turned. Watch
a horse's eye flutter
just above the buckle
on the strap: it is
an attempt to resolve conflict:

the outcome is the same.
Machinery rusts by contact
with warm flowing liquids:
now where do these fluids flow
from? across the room they look
exactly futuristic, held down
by a printer's correction color
with is applied, stroked on
with an instrument resembling a penis.
You can stick a well-known face
in the battle, place a sword
in her hand, let her gallop
forward toward the surface
with as much vigor as heat
rising from an opening
long identified with war.

3

The original position is known.
It's difficult to make it glow.
In holy wars the position
is rarely forgotten in favor
of other positions. In nightclubs
where women in black stockings
shake themselves at warriors
with hatchets in their belts,
the position is sometimes hard
to locate in the cathedral
of the imagination—which, itself,
is a cracked surface shaped
like Barcelona when it is not
immeasurable. You can see variations
on the position mashed and broken
in the desert (alongside fishscales
and Mediterranean masqueraders

from Algiers down on their luck)
under wriggling skies
still stinking of flesh plowed
with broken mirrors
in inexhaustible anger.

4

Battles are won and lost
in this position: crutches
are occasionally propped under
the performers after war
to keep them from falling out
of their own bodies. When
it happens prophets have their day.
The position cannot be faked:
a nun jumping rope in a room
with three inches of water
or one in the prayer position,
is not pretending *the* position.

5

The position is common.
Here, where they speak a language
I cannot speak well, the position
is spontaneous in gallic delirium.
People do not work at it here:
mates dislike such lack of trust.
Watch the horses' eye again:
everything the position means
is there fluttering anonymously
as if it were the act itself:
two tumid surfaces etching
their own postures in space
as they lose themselves.

✽

Dressed to Kill

They do move with grace:
with great sturdiness, these ladies
in hats, with uneven eyes, thin lips.

They move without moving.

Have you noticed their eyes:
their eyes move, too: tiny eyes
planted deep in the bone
of the skull.

Necks as long as a horse penis.
They turn slowly
especially in public
when one must be polite.

*

MICHAEL STEPHENS

The Good Ship

Susan is eating a mandarin orange Eiffel Tower that Jane and Walter brought back from their trip to Paris. The other day Susan was eating a cassis Eiffel Tower that Jane and Walter brought back from their trip to France. I want to assure her that the price of a lollipop is worth the price of our culture, but I don't want to seem cynical. Instead I tell her that she looks like Sophia Loren before her jewels were stolen. She is dark, fine boned, quiet, sexy. Her eyes are green and grey; her mouth is moist. Slowly her orange Eiffel Tower disappears. The peak melts in her mouth, the girders next, she's about a story up when I look at her again; soon all France will fall from her licking. First the cafes fold in an orange and saliva swirl, then the hotels, restaurants, taxis, salons, pissoirs, kiosks, and alleys. Next the provinces. Rivers vanish, hotel rooms filled with Algerian prostitutes wash away with a lick, an aging novelist with another. It drove me from her house to look in the candy stores of my city for an Empire State Building, a lollipop made of Grand Central Station, Port Authority, any memory I have of these New York places evaporates with her sweet tongue.

*

Mom's Homecooked Trees

Imagination as Nihilo frothed like salt foam, like waves breaking, rolling; like fucking, her thoughts were of such fine intimacy with her person, forever in motion throughout the afternoon, like beach grass, bending, blowing, an infinite interplay of changes and things in Nihilo and in wind—watching the moon pronounce itself like a sea of vowels above the ocean. "I will be as fancy as Flash Gordon," Colonel Duke commented as he slipped on the big white gloves of his space suit. Choose that which may not have changed your life, the wild beach rose said upon its knoll along the beach, but used properly changes the artist's vision of what his or her life was, lived according to the book of notions in a dream that starting at the coast, went warmly like an undersea current to the eels in the sea. Then this is what the scrub oak told Nihilo: the major work is selection; knowing what to discard (her heroes were Heraclitus and Descartes) in experience, and relegate your energy toward the actual instead of the temporal notion of what is real. Hoy, hoy, hoy, the sea birds called! It is also good to know that the seascape has an intelligence the immaculata Nihilo can understand too, that besides being a good movie, this planet is ovoid not round, and that it wasn't just good acting and directing but that birds, plants, wildflowers had a decent maritime script to work with. That the invention of neon does not concern Nihilo here, dreaming sensuously upon the moon and its Astronauts, the death of deeds as well as actions. She remembers the Astronaut John W. Young as he stepped from the Landing Craft onto the Moon: "There you are, mysterious and unknown Descartes and Cayley Plains. Apollo 16 is going to change your image." And then she recalls her love for Heraclitus like an imprecation to nothing; she calls to the sea birds, and she knows they will answer: Hoy, hoy, hoy!

*

JUDY GRAHN

The Meanings in the Pattern

The interior of the Arizona Indian museum
is cool. A woman stands at the counter,
selling her family wares. "I am a Pima,"
she says. "We have always been here.
People say, where did the Anasazi go?
But we are right here, we never left.
We were farmers, always.
We were promised water for our gardens,
now they are taking it. My daughter
made the baskets; only girls are taught
to do it. My son made this pouch."
She pats the small soft leather purse,
thick with close beading, red and white,
yellow and blue. The design: clouds,
a bird, a man, the earth.
"This pictures tells a story," she says.
Her black eyes looking inward and outward.
"No one who buys this could ever understand—
the meanings in the pattern. What it is
really worth." Clouds. A
bird. A man. The earth. Her fingers
feel the beads. "There is a story here.
It takes three days and nights to tell it."

*

They Say She Is Veiled

They say she is veiled
and a mystery. That is
one way of looking.
Another
is that she is where
she always has been,
exactly in place,
and it is we,
we who are mystified,
we who are veiled
and without faces.

*

Frigga With Hela

Her fingers
within me
    a spindle
my feelings
    woolly
her dear hand
    axis
on which my internal world
    whirls.

"She is making me"
on the whorl of her love
turning me out and in
transforming patterns.

So I say of her,
"she is making me,"
and I mean she is
making me over,
again.

*

JANET HAMILL

Autumn Melancholy

Catherine de Montchensi was a young Occitanian wife in the age of *l'amour courtois* and the jeweled sunburst on the Virgin's breast. The age of hell's bedlam—*janua diaboli*—the earthly woman awakened to her nature. She had been betrothed in childhood to an older man—a marriage arranged by her father in the interests of land. And at the age of thirteen she left her home in Pau to enter her husband's castle in Toulouse. Animated by a high spirit, Catherine quickly mastered the courtly conventions: hawking, playing chess, learning letters, singing, and playing musical instruments. But in spite of these amusements, her time passed melancholically. For although her husband provided her with every luxury, she resented her conjugal subjection, and longed for a love that was freely sought and freely given.

One day as she was training her goshawk by the river Catherine encountered Arnaut Vidal, engaged in the composition of a chanson. So strong was her attraction for the troubadour, that she released her hawk, letting it fly from her wrist. And the jongleur, feeling the same magnetic pull, dropped his rebec in mid-song. That afternoon they began an idyll, fearlessly following their heart's urges, making love in a grotto beyond the castle's walls. Three months of clandestine meetings elapsed before the romance was interrupted by Catherine's husband, who, having grown suspicious of his young wife, followed her into the fields. Enraged by his cuckolding, he reacted violently. Catherine was brought back to the castle, where an iron girdle of chastity was fitted to her pelvic basin. And the lord's hired men chased Arnaut to the edge of the fiefdom, where he was brutally castrated. The tragedy led Catherine to take up a veil of sorrow in a convent; and Arnaut found a refuge in monasticism.

Five hundred years after the forceful separation the remains of Catherine de Montchensi were discovered beneath the abbey in St. Guillem-Le Déserte, along with a box containing chansons by Arnaut Vidal. The exquisite lyrics praised the young wife for her beauty and refinement. They spoke of the ennobling quality of love, and described woman as the ladder on which to climb to heaven. As soon as the bones were found they were brought to the square in Pau, where a monument, which still stands today as white as a Pyrenean snowdrift, was erected—a beautiful female figure enveloped in loose drapery, reclining on a sarcophagus, with a face wearing a melancholic expression, and the body's posture suggesting a convalescent, eternally recovering from a sickness of the heart. Throughout the centuries the statue was perceived by its beholders as a saint of love. People brought flowers and placed them at its base, where they knelt and prayed for an intercession in their love lives.

Two hundred years after Catherine de Montchensi's remains were discovered the bones of Arnaut Vidal were unearthed beneath the monastery in Limoges, along with a box containing letters from Catherine. The letters reminded the troubadour of how much like an altar was the bed of consummation with his lady, and they compared the nourishment received from the spiritual fire of erotic love to that the lover of God received from the bread and wine of the eucharist. As soon as Arnaut's remains were found they were brought to Pau and laid beside Catherine in a marble sarcophagus, beneath the effigy of a magnificent reclining naked youth, with a face that wore an archaic smile. On the day of its unveiling a great ceremony was held in the square. Dignitaries attended from as far away as Paris. An orchestra played the overture to Wagner's *Tristan und Isolde*; and as the music reached its rapturous peak, the canvas cloth covering the statue was removed, revealing the lovers side by side, with the inscription *conjugium in aeternum* chiseled into the stone of their common plinth.

On the day following the ceremony the strange events began. The first thing noticed was the altered expression on Catherine's face. Gone was her melancholic look. It had been replaced with an archaic smile. And the folds of drapery covering her body had disappeared. Even more startling was the powerful pull one felt on approaching the statues. It was as though they were imbued with magnetism. Many were frightened by the changes. But many realized a miracle had occurred. And within days of the coming together in stone of the young wife and the troubadour a cult of love was initiated. People in love, and people seeking love, came to the square with flowers. They stood at the base of the monuments, where the aura was so intense one became endowed with the virtues of the lovers on the sarcophagi. Worshippers held candlelight vigils and slept at the feet of the statues, hoping that as they slept the spirits of Catherine and Arnaut would enter their bodies. Soon word of the miracles spread throughout the country. Visitors arrived by train from all over the continent. The existing hotels filled to capacity, and new ones were built to accommodate the continuous stream of pilgrims. Additional priests were needed in Pau to meet the demand for marriages, and the town swelled with intoxicated wedding guests reluctant to go home. Couples wishing to conceive a child started making love at night at the base of the statues. Then they were joined by couples wishing to insure their union. Strangers sought each other out during the day, waiting until nightfall to make love. But eventually the cultists grew too impatient to wait for nightfall. They started making love during the day. In broad daylight the square was strewn with naked bodies, orgies, and drunkenness. Until one day, at the height of the fever, someone castrated the statue of Arnaut Vidal. The same person broke open the sarcophagus, making away with the bones. The mutilation had an immediately sobering effect. The magnetic aura surrounding the statues ceased. The naked revelers filed out of the square. It was only after the pilgrims were gone and things were quiet that one noticed the statue of Catherine de Montchensi. Gone was her smile. It had been replaced with a melancholic gaze. And the posture of her body beneath the folds of drapery suggested the languor of a convalescent.

*

Carravagio

I'm in a small Mexican town outside
Oaxaca/the sun is crawling like an
orange serpent through the window
a white sail disappears over the jungle
I walk through the rooms in a green
satin slip/amulets on either shoulder
strap/bleeding hearts of Mary/Magdalene
laces in black are wrapped around my
ankles/Carravagio dreams in the bedroom
heat siesta/wandering the waterfronts
of all the ports in all the cities
of the world/his skin is flushed
with a mild fever/and blue gulf stream
fly-fish lie across his legs/the walls
perspire like the exhausted flesh of
a youthful Bacchus/damp indulgent
sheets/a parrot screams behind my back
the scarlet blood drops leave a trail
down my leg/the laces tighten
and I feel so sore inside
a raving barracuda/took a bit of something tender

*

SUMMER BRENNER

Natural Selection

First you feel along the bottom making sure it's not too soft. You find the center depression. It's the round entrance through the scaly folds. You press down on its softness. Not too juicy. Not too hard. You've found the one you want. You lop off its tree-top and begin to peel away the outside. The skin leaves brown knots in the flesh. The fruit tastes perfect to you. And it's so beautiful. You slice it into discs and sprinkle cayenne on it. The song of the sweet pineapple and the hot chile makes your mouth beat.

Laura says in Bali the women say not to eat pineapple. It makes the *bula* too juicy. Then men say there's no such thing as too juicy. Then magazines say it's something to worry about. Then Felix who is three says he wants to eat Thumbalina's *bula*.

I love to see women feeling up fruit in the market. Pinching. Poking. Rubbing. Smelling. Packaged produce is a great deprivation.

Choosing cheese is difficult. In France shoppers squeeze the cheese. My friend Jean-Marie told me if you're looking for the right Camembert, touch your eyelid. That's the way it should feel.

Once Laura and I were together at the Cheese Board. And they gave us a small sample of brie that smelled exactly like a man's come. We thought it was the most hilarious secret. And ran out giggling close as twelve year olds.

Plums are just about my favorite. In New Mexico one summer we lay out by the irrigation ditches. Everyday laying our bodies between the muddy bank and the muddy water. Our skin went from gold to brown to purple. Like burnished plums.

Years ago we used to walk home from the movies on Saturday afternoon. My cousin and I were in our early teens. One time a car rode by where we were walking. It was full of greasy men. One of them held a banana out of the window. I didn't know what it meant, but I knew it was awful and inviting.

Bananas. Cucumbers. Squash. The shapes of the things we love to eat. The things we love to feel. The dough rising. A smooth glass bottle. Jars of pickled peaches. Jams. Jellies. Preserves.

The variety of beans in Mexico is astonishing. And fruits too. Exotic ones. Rare ones that look like a monkey's bottom.

How many times has it been said that our country has lost the connection to what it eats, undergrown overdosed food. It's obvious people have had to give up caring about their lives, as they have given up caring about their food.

In Oaxaca I was loudly scolded for feeling pineapples too long.

*

Fata Morgana

The senses are much more fickle than the heart. It is their generosity that makes us twist and dive to get at it again.

Baby, you know what I like.

Every reality greeted with the divination of the senses. Smell the coffee. Smell the squealing tires. Smell the cloakroom. Where you fell on a pile of coats and came. Smell the tomato's leaf. Smell your smell before you get your monthly bleed. Smell sweat.

Now see. What do you see. The car tracking the edge of the highway around a concrete curve. The smile. At the gas station the way some of them smile. The stacked tiles. The pitched roofs. The window in the eave. The curtain in the window. The light in the curtain. And behind a thousand veils. Winesburg, Ohio. Gunga Din. The big Big Dipper. Dip dip dipping.

Sense is the stuff of our human being. Sensual. Risqué. Dirty. Sweet sensual love. Dirty slut. Loves her own smell too much.

It is that face. Those brows. That voice. Those hands. That back. Those thighs. That neck. Those breasts. That tongue. Those teeth. That chest. Those feet. That fur. Those paws. That tail. That beak.

Phantasmagoria. The body. Stand. Walk. Lay. Hunch. We touch. We don't stop.

In Paris on the Métro. Through the glass your eyes bolted mine. Drawn. Airtight. Shut out. Train east. Train west. My stop *Rue de Sèvres*. Yours the *Dixhuitième*. The single second of explosion from one lit orb, mine, to the other, yours. Love travels the speed of light. Train gone. No more. I almost jumped out to catch one back to find you. What did you look like. Heart of my hearts. Who took my face and ate it. Then threw it back through the subway window. A lesser reflection of myself without you, my double darkness.

The French inspire such things.

And us. All of us. Us the billions of Chinese. The Pygmies. The Kiwanis. We have our inspirations too. From the smell of old cheese. From the ocean. From cats in heat. From pigeons. From the stuff between the toes. From fresh-squeezed juice. From the choices. From taupe and midnight blue. Clean jade. Venetian red. Chinese silk.

Chemicals have done a lot to change our faces. Television is plastic surgery.

Get it. I can eat this rug. And you too. You're so sweet, I can eat you up.

Now come to your senses.

LO AND BEHOLD.

*

LAURA CHESTER

Correspondence

I want you to be reading this, as I make love to your cock. I want you to be standing there, reading this, looking down at the top of my head, engaged in the act of loving you, maybe looking up myself, to smile through half-closed eyes, only to sink again, into the pleasure of mouthing you, and I can feel you getting harder, wanting to push it in a little bit deeper, and I am getting myself aroused, reaching up to touch from your chest, expanded, down with curving nails, to where I can hold the stalk, and lick the tip and kiss your tightening balls. I want you to be engaged inside my orifice. I want you to feel me feel the meat of your buttocks, as you plunge, withdraw and plunge, as you collect my hair and groan—I want it to be so good you want to free yourself in my mouth. I want to you fold this poem, as if you can't stand to stand uncertain anymore, but have to let it go, allow—And let the paper fall, just as I make (imaginary) love to you—Real in the mail.

*

The Good Time Is Now

He reminds me that the good time is now, that we're together riding in the last light of day, and the air is filled with the exhale of flowers and the earth is green and moist. I feel such tenderness towards him, as he approaches his fiftieth birthday, protective of the child in him, the unborn thing, that comes to life within the kisses of my mouth, until he is a man and takes me, and dies the most familiar little death. I know now why this birthday hurts him, as if the years have not amounted to enough, though affirmation is his riding partner, and fifty is a kind of view. He remarks upon the soft olive green in the marsh field where the deer bound away like passing time, alert and afraid, with no intention of ever killing anything. He rides down the slope in his khaki shirt, the one I'm wearing right now, and I turn to look back up towards him—The softening sky is all a humid rose, and I think that he's the most handsome. He has learned that my love won't annihilate. Both of us, suddenly grateful, to see this awakening of earth life together, to witness the dogwood, alone, at the bottom of the path with its constellation of blooms. To me, he is just as wild and beautiful, as that tree floating solitary, still. A warbling fills the air, this time of night this time of year, and his birthday to me is a blessing. My man, with his shoulders shifting, as his horse descends. My man, with the thick, warm fingers, covered with dirt after planting. I wish he'd rub them all over me. Oh, to feel the drive of his passion, the power of his mouth, to make him feel as young as he actually is, not defeated, for this is a beginning place, and I'm dazzled with belief that the good time is now, and that it belongs to us both—Stunned, as the yellow of the mustard field, we galloped beside that evening.

*

Far Be It

Sometimes you have to pee *bad* at the beginning of a hayride, and sometimes you are giving a poetry reading and you hear someone laugh, and so you, the reader, chuckle also, thinking you are pretty funny, but the laughter referred to an incident in the hallway. Sometimes the most welcomed experience is when the dinner guest lies down on the sofa and falls asleep. Sometimes everyone else in the costume competition is awarded and you keep returning to the table of the judges, wondering when they'll notice little you. Sometimes you don't understand your own lack of patience regarding the small boy who is your son, and who is crying in his bed for no reason, until the next morning when he's obviously ill, when the log is found rotten white with fake weight, and the guts of the pumpkin's little snot that won't wash, and sometimes the radio blasts off at 4 a.m. announcing world disaster and then you dream someone guesses you are 65 when you are half that age, but don't look it, and sometimes you'd prefer to wake up without the aid of bouncing bodies, because sometimes the hole you dig isn't deep enough, and you figure that your life is just something you have to live with. Sometimes, when all the leaves fall, you can see that much further, but then you notice how far away you have moved.

✻

DAVID SHAPIRO

From Malay

Indelible lust (for you)
Two persons, two dim hints
Craving you monotonously
Oh gymnast sparrow

Two persons, two dim hints
Like sugar in a summer bicycle basket
Oh gymnast sparrow
Asleep on your twig

Like sugar in a summer bicycle basket
The newly dead are easy to find
Asleep on your twig
If only life and death were an eggshell like Princess Eggshell

The newly dead are easy to find
Craving you monotonously
If only life and death were an eggshell like Princess Eggshell
Indelible lust (for you)

*

Memory of the Present

Opening the knots of your braid,
I look upon a seething Atlantic
Behold, a luminous typewriter sails
into the air above the desk.

The desk likes to return to the thick forest
The autumn as a kind of reward.
Like whirling eraser fluid,
I have been blown far enough.
Here and there, Basic Spanish, Botany,
and a Panorama (Critical) of Proust.

It's hard to get desire on paper.
The earth pulls your body down.
It is time to fall. Galileo Galilei.
All of us have a special province;
all of us have the slight year;
all of us when properly excited
emit ceaseless atoms, housed
in a cabinet at night; most of us
have a body and with equal arms.
Stone fruit is fleshy fruit: cherries.

You must be as it were an evening star
As Sappho says in her *Ode to Hesperus*
through which variegated ivies were women,
flakes of likeness, lines of ice.
December follows November, as I follow
My soul is seeping through your braids like water
from the mirage of the November pool.
Hic et nunc
You have been before and remember it now
Sinking away with the same tone
You hate the flow, and yet it flows.

*

Sonnet

Ice over time

Loving your traces and loving to trace
teaching us tricks in the dusky light of your devices

On the margin of an indifference

Hippolytus Oenone travellers more or less
Absent of purpose on wings of chance
Neverness, sweetness, extraneous as the wind blows

The Alive with Pleasure sign has been torn down

replaced by Golden Lights in river haze
a mild Lucretian signboard

perfumes novelties displays
toying with you as you say Don't toy with me
my favorite mouth my favorite grey pen
I will pilot its razor point toward the page

¶

AMY GERSTLER

Direct Address

Malign my character, but do it under a willow,
with my ready-made mourner at attention, already bent at the
    waist.

Listen, peabrain, you have influence. Use it.
Do as I say. Start by kneeling. Tell him you're sorry
and you'll never do it again. Get him to spit out his gum and
    pay attention.
It's easy. Kiss him as if you're a little bit thirsty.

I was patiently waiting for you to explain these flowering
    phenomena.
Now I might as well be a prehistoric ear of corn, so ancient its
    kernels
are working loose like some old geezer's teeth.

Birds nest on the shores of a secluded lake.
Reptiles and waterfowl that populate the swamp watched
the skiff drift downriver, guided by the current.

The pastor receives letters from parishioners which pose
questions about heaven: 1. Will we be conscious
of the world's continuance? 2. Will we be cognizant
of those loved ones left behind?

"You go on ahead. I'll be out in a minute,"
she had said at the back door. She hated to think
they'd come all this way for nothing, so she went
upstairs, to have herself one last look.

❋

ELINOR NAUEN

Maine

I have to get in
a car right
this minute & drive
a thousand miles. With
no purpose but
to sing   the corn
sings. It could be
1976 when I
lived in town eating
cream cheese
listening to Bruce
Springsteen hiding
on back streets
wishing my lover would
call on me. The hot
air was yellow: I
owned a car, held
out, drove
to the shore for clams. We
served enchiladas & feuds.
I drove home
3 a.m. because
of the children, glistening

Quebec French 40s pop:
like songs
my mother
sang—happy
& betrayed.

*

The History of the Human Body
Winfield's Infield Hit
The Lassitude of the Infinite

Dear _____,
Hi, you can be in my new poem, if you're a Yankees fan.
Or, if you're a baseball fan (I just remembered
you're from the coast). Listen—as long as you're here
you might as well stay. It's just that I wanted
to write this poem about baseball
having 3 baseball titles & all
but one for you too, on the chance that that's
what it'll take for you to be in love with me.
I used to seduce this gay friend that way
a poem a day under his door—
the closest I got was the big IF:
if I ever, you'll be the one . . .

My stomach leaping like a trout
& all I know is your eyes & mechanic's forearms.
Yeah, but what about this goddamn famous oldtime
electricity: I haven't felt this way in years.
It's better than having a crush on
Lou Piniella & hooray
we're back to baseball.

José Cardenal once in winter ball
wouldn't play for 3 days cuz his uniform
wasn't tight enough
oh the sex object
Winfield flings the ball to the shortstop
who wings it on in to the catcher
swinging Rick Cerone. It's the springtime
of philogeny & my ontogeny
is throbbing in all its bristly prehistoric cells.
I'm either having a nervous breakdown
or falling in love.
Yeah, so my favorite number is 14:
Lou's Yankee number of course
& my Nicaraguan lover,
a power hitter who smashed a homer the night after
& tipped his cap to me coming into 3rd.
14—my skirts plaid & too long like my sentences
chalking Plato on the sidewalk, worrying,
without grace, this in between my baseball days.
At 10 I loved the Yankees cuz they won
at 25 loved them again
for what I can't do—no self-consciousness
of body or mind, like perfect
conversation late at night, seamlessly caught.
I need my time of grace
hunt the beauties who will love me
ceaselessly.

I'm a terrible comedian because I have no sense of   timing
I gotta always say everything I think of
Flaubert said he'd rather die like a dog
than hurry by a second a sentence not ripe.
I *like* those goddamn green bananas

❊

3 More Things

There is a tiny car on a tiny bureau by a tiny pink comb. The man with small ears kisses a tall woman with long brown hair. He smooths his right hand between her shoulder blades and on down to the little hollow above where her buttocks flare—the "small." With his left hand he folds her hair around her neck, then kisses her lips. Her hair is so long it wraps around her neck twice. He pulls hard, yanks till it completes a third revolution. Her pale peachy skin darkens into apricot. Her tongue flops out of her mouth & the kiss becomes limp on her part, ever more passionate on his. She flails her right hand toward the bureau, reaching for the rattail comb. She hopes to puncture his heart & thus be freed. Instead her hand lands on the tiny car. He gets in & hits the road.

*

If I Ever Grow Old:
Grim & Gleeful Resolutions

for Olga
after Swift

To be grumpy, grouchy, petulant, paranoid & mean: to hit out with
    my cane from my wheelchair at passersby

To clutch my chest, hold my breath, turn blue & be allowed
    everything

To insist upon senior citizen discount

To constantly remind the whippersnappers that if it was good
    enough
    in my day it's too good for them.

To remind the Young that I knew them when younger; to
    poopoo their feats

To make children kiss me on my scrofulous cheek & if it
      makes them cry
    because I smell funny, to slap them

To make them push me fast in my wheelchair but if they tip
      me they
    should've known better

To scare the wits out of the Young: It goes so fast, one day
      you're
    young, the next you're like me, old & feeble, how did I ever
    get to be so old, it'll happen to you. To never let them
    forget this

To give up shopping & dressing, as no one wants to fuck me so
      why
    bother

To help, with the accumulated wisdom & authority of my
      years,
    all those who suffer

To cut off mercilessly anyone who interrupts

To become extremely set in my ways, obsessive,
      hypochondriacal,
    opinionated, argumentative, obstinate & indomitable

To remind One & All of my various former loves &
      enumerate those
    once infatuated with me: nessun maggior dolore che
    ricordarsi
    del tempo felice nella miseria

*

LEWIS MAC ADAMS

Raw Honey

I.

Bumble Bees! Don't worry about the bumble bees,
they're not gonna sting the baby

& even if they do he's only gonna swell up briefly.

But Phoebe

says NO.

That beehive above the porch has got to go.

Well, fuck it.

I mean, if I could even rhumba with the bumble bees we'd be
the world's most famous:
We'd be Ecology;

And I can recall

Al Lurch of the World Environmental Systems
stepping through the door of the Bolinas Future Studies Center,
and recoiling
at the troupe of fruit flies
planeing through the dust motes
in the sun beams in the middle of the living room,
and saying

"Even in our experimental manure shed we have no flies. None!
            Because we have discovered a Cycle—
      eight different insects—
                  that when placed inside a supportive
environment;
                  i.e., a derailed boxcar.
                              reach a complete balance; i.e.,
                        No more fruit flies.

                        This way

                        WE have control."

                  2.

                              I guess I'm sloppy.

                  In fact, I know I'm sloppy.

But the two bees working deep in the dregs of
my coffee cup

            let me sing.

      Give me song to sing. Give me focus and legend.

and following their whirr outside I see unchallenged gold

in the waters of Bolinas Bay,

and the slight south wind surrounding

their departure brings me morning's second whiff of coffee

followed closely by your palm on my cheek and your voice

aching softly asks would I like a piece of fresh-baked bread and
  butter?

With a little honey?

*

Moguls and Monks

A dollar-green Cadillac limousine
pulls from the gate at Paramount
and turns down Melrose.
The mogul passenger leans his bald head
back on his head rest and smiles,
his face a mass of pure contentment

as two Buddhist monks bow by,
waiting at the corner for the light to change
so they can bow across Gower.
Though they don't
see each other, I am them both
as I turn up Highland, cruising
in the twelve spiritual
directions, with the
thirteen calls for cash.

But last night I met someone who was fine.

Fates, be kind.

*

JANINE CANAN

She Is Carefully Stepping Over the Important Communications

She is carefully stepping over the the important communications like cracks in the sidewalk. Even in the fluorescent lights she is inscrutable. She cultivates it: jaw down, mouth lifeless, melancholy cheekbones, eyes all depth. She wants the medal of honor. Nothing has shocked her. Nothing is more improbable than reality, she says. Fantasy can't hold a candle to it, that little dark room, crammed full with repetitions. She is prepared. She prays in case. Forgets all she can, keeping her eye firmly on the present. How poised, they say. How brave. She is a success at the piano recital. She gets straight A's—a few B's cautiously woven in to placate the authorities. She can be amusing at dinner, she can cook. A charming daughter. Earnest, determined. Someone who will do something with her life. Someone with a long list of demands on life. Who will demand more with every disappointment. Who on the last day would argue with God, we want something better. Someone who can't stop, can't stop wanting.

*

I Turned On the Hot Water

I turned on the hot water, filled the tub, poured in some bubbles, got your poems and just sank in, she said. As we nestled into our chairs in the dark and carpeted bar—Georgia in her little red and white polka dot dress, the piano playing Gershwin, the waitress serving champagne. I can imagine this book with a cover like a stuffed chair, a comforter you can open out in your lap, with colored block illustrations—this poem's satin, that one's woven orange. The important thing is to be able to organize your fantasy, she sighed voluptuously, voice trailing into the night.

*

Dear Body

Dear Body, gazing in the mirror it is you
that I behold with thankfulness.
You have been faithful these forty years.
With only a sore knee at puberty, some intestinal
rumblings before authority and teary outpourings
in the face of love, have you occasionally
asserted independence, disapproval, disregard of me.

Nor can I seriously object to the lines in your brow
that reveal where I have been thinking,
or to the downward curve of your mouth
that indicates grief I have carried since birth.
Your nose I thought too wide, has lengthened with time
that forces decision, and your white thighs
that frightened me, console me through darkening nights.

What good shoulders you have, I admit;
your soft breasts amaze me, and curving mortal hips.
When I see you naked so, still scarcely known,
I wonder, have I not served you well enough,
neglecting, depriving you of proper lovers—
surging, languorous caress of the bluegreen ocean,
the wild and powerfully exacting dance.

What a different story had I lived for you,
my devoted, solid, healthy Body,
with your hands of a potter or a surgeon,
strong enough to gather grain for a life of simple
satisfying eating. What patience you have shown
this lethargic, sedentary, moody being
who borrowed you, she claims, for higher reason.

Sitting waiting, while she thinks and dreams,
craving only quiet spaces, beauty in which
to lose herself on ever longer, more voluptuous
and deeper journeys, you must be a saint.
With your delicate, hyper-sensitive nerves—
painstakingly cultivated by erratic Mother Karma
who one moment forgets, the next grips violently,

so aware everything irritates or gives you
overwhelming pleasure, ecstatic wicked Body,
maniacally driven from one unreachable extreme
to another, isn't it obvious how, torn
between joy and terror, you became a poet,
passionately vibrating instrument, house
of the certain yet doubting, ever shifting eye.

Earthbody, brief spouse, what a strangely
inconvenient marriage. Yet you are my only
true support. And though you may never
fathom what I secretly am, may you—
who accepted the nature of existence itself—
stay with me, in your lovely halo of death,
till I depart, dearest Body, my slave, my queen.

✽

Diagnosis

Diagnosis: Emotional illness. Neurosis. Anxiety neurosis. Depression. Chronic depression. Depressive personality. Bad person, Hysterical features, obsessive features, schizoid features. Somatic complaints. Introverted personality. Borderline personality. Artistic personality. An intense need to create. A deep need to help others. Oral needs. Primitive dependency needs. Reaction formation. Counterphobia. Frieda Fromm Reichmann. She dreamed she was holding Frieda Fromm Reichmann's hand, walking through the hospital. She went to the library and checked out all of the psychiatric texts. She pushed the book-cart through the locked back wards. One of the senile white-haired ladies grabbed her hand, drooling, "You recognize me don't you, dearie?" The autistic woman opened and shut, opened and shut shut shut the sliding glass door. One of the students threw up at school, one slashed her wrist on the last day of class, one shot himself after the course was over. Three friends broke down in one year. Sister schizophrenic, catatonic on the bed, a knife in her hand wandering the streets. Fifty shock treatments. Mother a recluse. Father never came home from work. Starting medical school—she hated psychiatry, she loved it. The delightful old madwoman whose cat saw things. The whirling dervish in her office, hair cropped, cloak black, who brought sherry, irises and babyclothes, ranting exquisite chants. The aura that hung in her office at the end of the day. Viper that coiled in the corner. Vampires sucking in her drawers. Skeletons, she was getting thinner, or taller, one of the two. She opened all the drawers and doors and windows—and a cool bay breeze shot through.

*

SAM ABRAMS

The World Is With Me Just Enough

my seven year old friend
visited & tickled me
for an hour nearly

who needs the national
academy of arts & sciences

i'd rather be a pagan
tickled in a creed outworn

hurrah for alexa flaherty
mother of arts sciences magics
religions economies states
theories giggles

& of all these
the greatest is the last
by far

*

Cakewalkman

everybody   dancin
all the time as
     we have
     learned
          at
scott joplin
university

*

Not the Arms Race

i read in the new york times
in 1984
over 70 percent
of college educated married american women
between the ages of 24 & 31 say
they enjoy breast feeding
& performing oral sex

compared to only about 20 percent
in the sixties
for both giving suck
& sucking

finally
a clear sign

*

What the Sixties Were Really Like

we oughtta take somma these college perfessers
split open their head with an ax
& put some shit in so
they'll have something to think about

*

The United States of America We

have broken more treaties
than any other modern nation
civilian casualties were heavy this week
two generations since the first surrealists
walk a lobster on a leash
take drugs white men
are coming consciousness
& awareness are so different
you wouldn't believe

*

MIRA TERU KURKA

Crocodiles

Across the desk,
the insurance salesperson glowers
as I casually inquire about
taking out a small loan against
my paid-up policy:
"But ma'am, you must admit that $200
for an essential isn't much . . ."
I say, and smile beguilingly.
The salesperson glowers the more
she is filled with rage, inflating
like a Macy's Thanksgiving Day
Parade balloon and I think
I must be missing some point
or perhaps this is really my
mother I am asking money from, aha.
Before my amiable patter can continue
the insurance salesperson explodes,
accuses me of committing double indemnity
and in my disbelief and horror
I see that in her hands is a round
seed pod through which she has been
methodically tearing small holes
with her fingernails, sharp
as crocodile teeth.

*

Fruit and Government

The Pomegranate Surprise was a New Deal.
You peeled the leathery skin to find a
cabinet of rubies, or
so she told me when she got lost on
President Street. I had
instructed her to follow State,
parallel with Congress, until she
saw red on the corner of Washington
and Pineapple, but the bridge from the
abstract to the specific
was too much.

*

Under Which Heading Does All This Information Go?

under the bed
the smell of transmission
with ever-widening circles.

Mother, may I?
it's back to back
chain-linked,
rhinestones on the collar
with or without bells.

whiteout.
Talmudic chant, Chiang Kai-Shek,
mucho agua, watashi-wa,
watch the closing doors.

I'd like you to meet
my daughter, Nebraska.

*

JOHN GIORNO

I Resigned Myself to Being Here

Instructions for reading this poem:
each stanza should be read in one breath.

You're backed
up
in a dark
corner
and you don't
know
who's
hitting you
you're backed up in a dark corner
and you don't know who's hitting you,

and I'm sitting
all
by myself
inside
a taxi,
driving
down
Lexington
at 34th,
waiting
to get
downtown
waiting to get
downtown

waiting
to get downtown
waiting to get downtown,

you're heavy
and angry
and depressed
you're heavy and angry and depressed,

you've been
around
for a long
time
you've been around
for a long time
you've been around for a long time,

I always
live
with a woman,
I never
live
with a man,
and I make it
with men
and I make it with men
and I make it with men,
and knows
how to
love ya,
and I make
my women
go to work
and give me
money,
sorry,
I go

with a guy
only
one
time,

and you're making
drinks
for animals
and hungry
ghosts
and you're making drinks
for animals and hungry ghosts,

you're cooking
dinner
in a hell
world,
you're not
human
you're making
believe
you're human,
sitting
here
in this chair,

I'm walking
around
this party
with a drink
in my hand,
give me
just
a little
more
time
and our love

will surely
grow
give me just a little more time
and our love will surely grow,

beer
stink,
cigarette
smoke,
and music,
walking
to the bar
toilet,
you're the
only one
you're the only
one
you're the only one,
to take me
back
to where
we started
from,
so fill me
up
to the top,
don't you
stop
until I'm
overflowing,

and now
you're in
some American
re-incarnation,
and besides
not remembering

you're talking,
you're telling me
this story,
and not
only
can't I
concentrate
on your words
or understand
what you're
talking
about,
I can't
stand
the incessant
sound
of ignorance
in your voice,

and sleeping
next
to you
is like sleeping
next to
somebody
on the subway
and sleeping next to you
is like sleeping next to
somebody on the subway,
send her
back
home
to Brooklyn,
you gotta
get her
out of
the way,

and it's 5
in the morning,
you're stoned
and wired,
cruising
the sidewalk
cruising the sidewalk,
and I'm not
tired
yet
and I'm not
tired yet
and I'm not tired yet,
cocaine
and I'm alone,

and you're not
going
home
until you
do it
again
and you're not going home
until you do it again
and you're not going home until
you do it again,

uncertain,
and I'm sorry,
but I'm holding
on to
what
I want
I'm holding on to what I want
is right,
caught up
in wanting,

and letting it
go,

sugar,
alcohol,
meat,
heroin,
and cigarettes
sugar, alcohol, meat,
heroin, and cigarettes,
sugar, alcohol, meat, heroin and cigarettes,
I resigned
myself
to being
here,

your face
is puffed
and grey,
booze
and dope,
fat
and wrinkles,
and I'm
thinking
again
about
what
happened
today
and I'm thinking again
about what happened today,

when
you're with
alot
of people

you gotta
keep
talking
and when
you're by
yourself
you gotta
keep
moving
your hands,

you're in
some fake
category,
you created
for yourself,

so that's
what
happened
to the kid,
I just
want to
thank you
for a wonderful
time,

and you're not
gonna fall
down
cause you're
drunk
and you're not gonna fall down
cause you're drunk,
or nod
out
walking

cause
you're stoned,

and I made
one
big
mistake
tonight
and I made one
big mistake
tonight
and I made one big mistake tonight,

the bar
is closing
and there's
something
you dislike
about
everyone
in this room
and there's something you dislike
about everyone in this room,

but I'm
gonna
do it
one more
time,
too much
is not
enough,

you're my
toilet,
eat it
out,

I'm gonna
feed you
you're my toilet,
eat it out,
I'm gonna feed you,
you're my toilet, eat it out,
I'm gonna feed you,

and it's
the 1980s
and I can't
believe
I survived
the 1970s
as awful
as they were,
and if you're
gonna
judge me,
don't
judge me
lightly,

the politics
make it
completely
discouraging
the politics make it
completely discouraging,
and all
I want
now
is money
and all I want now
is money
and all I want now is money,

Buddha
Mind
what
happened,

and all
I got to
say is,
I'll see you
in another
life
I'll see you in another life,
doubtless
I will,
and I can
wait,

The Chicago
Conspiracy
and you were in
some filthy
jail
cause they
pulled
the wool
over your eyes
about some
dumb ass
anti-Vietnamese
War,

and in 1970,
I couldn't
believe
I survived
the 1960s,
and in 1970

I couldn't believe I survived the 1960s,
cause I
remember
jumping
off
the Empire
State
Building
with Lucy
in your eyes
like diamonds,
forever,
and you landed
on the concrete
sidewalk
on 34th Street
in an Andy Warhol
picture
in 1963,
now selling
for $80,000,

you were dead
in a hospital
bed,
and you get
up
and do it
again
and you get up
and do it again
and you get up and do it
again
and you get up and do it again,

I really
like being
with ya
I really like being with ya,
but I'm
only with you
for what
you can
do for me,
and never
forgetting it
is how
I endure you,
cause you
can't always
get what
you want
cause you can't always
get what you want,
but if you
try sometimes,
you always
get what
you need,

and I know
I'm living
with you
and you're rich
and famous
and I know I'm living with you
and you're rich and famous,
but I aint
here
for any
love affair
but I aint here

for any love affair
but I aint here for any love affair,

and as you know
I have a
batting
average,
you've had
the best,
and besides
their reputations
and media
visibility,
they weren't
altogether
that good,
just
like me,

and I pay
myself
the big
bills,
I own
this
place
I own
this place
I own this place,
but I'm
leaving
cause I
had enough
but I'm leaving cause
I've had enough

you're laying
in bed
playing
with your meat,
waiting
to go to
sleep
after somebody
you just
made it with
went home
you're laying in bed
playing with your meat,
waiting to go to sleep
after somebody you just
made it with went home,

good
morning
America,
how
are ya;
and my friend
got me
some good
clean
junk
and my friend got me
some good clean junk,
and he got it
from his friend
in Brooklyn
2 days
ago,
and that guy

gets it
for himself,
you weren't
a suicide
against
your best
wishes,
and you didn't
burn out,
or get
enlightened,

and I don't
feel like
standing
here
reading
a poem
to you
and I don't feel like standing here
reading a poem to you,
dragging
concrete,
it's like
having a lead
weight
in your heart,

and we've stayed
together
for 15
years
only
cause
we've never
stopped
fighting,
you've got

no other
place
to go,
and you know
what
it's like
waiting
for the bus,
I don't
know
why
I've faithfully
gone on
working
for you,
and I don't know why
I've gone on
servicing you,
cause
everyone
I know
who's done it
is a jerk,

you don't
even
pay
any money
you don't even
pay any money
you don't even pay any money,
and I'm tired
of your disapproval
and I'm tired of your disapproval,

making
love to you
is looking

in a bathroom
mirror,
and I keep
asking
for it
and I keep
asking for it
and I keep asking for it
and I keep asking for it,

and both
of us
standing
there
as empty
as each
other,

and I just
fell
asleep
for 2
hours
in the afternoon
and I just fell asleep
for 2 hours in the afternoon,
I was
eating
honey
and then I
licked it
off
my fingers,

you've been
in the front
line

for a long
time
you've been in the front line for a long time,
from the beginning,
not to
talk
about
the cross-fire,
you've been
hit
so many
times,
give me
a break,
and I like
my wounds
licked
and I like my wounds
licked,

you're the way
I like to
do it
you're the way
I like to do it,
whip
your ass
whip your ass,
and everytime
I slap
your face
you kiss me
and it sure
feels
good
holding
ya

and it sure feels good
holding ya,
you know
how
to love me
you know how
to love me
you know how to
love me
you know how to love me,

dreaming
I was
dreaming
dreaming I
was dreaming
dreaming I was dreaming,
like getting
to an itch
you've been trying
to get to
for weeks,
I said
I would
do it
I said I
would do it
I said I would do it,
I told you
I could
do it,

take me
home,
lots
of luck
and now
I'm going
to say
goodbye.

*

JEFFREY MILLER

The Day Glo Question of Identity

I summon something
                    when nothing works, except my heart
which always trudges on
                    like a paperboy
peddling wares through the snow and dogs
(The Detroit *News* won't even give you your birthday off!)
        I practice staredowns with myself and win!
I win!
        The real me jumps out of my face
                                    bounces back
and finally ends up sleeping in my lap
                    like the private eye who just stumped himself
                    with his own questions;
a master of the surreal chain-smoking.
                                    Whenever
I consider suicide I whistle, and I giggle
                    when horrified by the life I see spread out
on both sides of my eyes.
                    Thanks lucky stars
for these girls, these charmers
                    and the guy I call Jeffrey Miller.
        They keep me enthralled banging around in here.
A riot among friends.

*

Sexy Food Stamps

The country's depressed, I'm depressed.
Not that I give a rat's ass about farms in Kansas:
I'm out in my yard building a post office
merely to stimulate morning;
                                    tormented scrambled eggs
bounced by light and anticipated light
then wrapped in severely mangled love. Bonita
Linda, JoJo, you
and all the real names to boot, hello.
I'm not doing so good. It's bitter sweet,
this rainbow painted on the curve of my feelings.
It's candlelight caught in a pot of flesh.
Each wave with a counterfeit shimmer.

*

The Truth Made Breakfast

I could never dance until I met Rose at a party where
she and I fell in this drunk, funky
dance, right on time.
We did "The Dice" which is a new step where
you skid like 2 ice cubes across the place and melt
in a heap called "snake eyes." I stuck a rose
between my teeth and fandangoed
right out the goddamn window. When I got back
someone said "I didn't know you danced, do you waltz?"
"Me and Rose" I said
"we waltz, hully gully, anything." We then commenced
to display our talent,
off into the astonished wild blue yonder.

*

Jeremy

It must be hunky dory on Venus. The synapse,
an anticipated snap where your lover's tongue
goes bananas & clears out space like a broke
rubber band. No more headaches, click, click,
click, let's toast eternal imagination with
pink gin & stuff up the bod's homemade holes
with whatever's handy.
                    "Insects are evil thoughts" Lou Read
                    "The poetry of earth is never dead" Keats
& Jeremy, where are you
all these scams seem orphaned

                    *

Death

            here today
            gone tomorrow
            right around that corner
            o yikes
            o yikes

                    *

My fault's small, about the size of a pin prick
on a Trojan. Life (the unplugable)
is everywhere, at my door with a butcher's knife
always slashing at the cup of water near my bed
even when I sleep life pumps me for info
the moon concentrates on me particularly, bending
spoons against my sleep
and leaving proof that I was not really gone,
just acting stupidly; the water cup's empty

the toaster's ticking
the cat's been murdered.
I want to get out of life without any more violence.
It kills me to think beyond my death, how
will moss know the north side of trees,
what will my shoes do. I take no responsibility
for myself and I only defend myself
because it hurts so
being ripped apart by the force of this ragged universe
and in awe by the colossal beauty
of an empty room.

✻

Your friends come and go
but they don't talk about Michael
Angelo, they talk about baseball
and girls
and if you're hungry they give you money
and if you're broke they give you The World's Tiniest Hamburg

In this basically counterfeit world Alice
you're a real nickel.
Someday we should go down to The Pink for a drink.
(Someday when Whatchmacallit and Whathisface are "out of
    town.")

✻

Quite shy actually but obsessed
with not being one of those quiet jerks
who spend the whole night
thinking and scheming a perfectly obvious
point, these pretentions assholes
drive Volvos through the snow white
halls of Bennington, it's not so bad that
they will bore with their poetry, but

they want you to swallow their lives
to boot. Ick, I left that scene
long ago when I decided to assimilate my
delicate and scatter brained notions with anyone's
fancy. I don't believe in dichotomy.
I see hell as a collection of warm fires.

*

the night was clear and the moon was yellow
California was out of the window and inside
the old car too as you and I slurred down Hiway
One without a care, the radio reception was
great, Stevie Wonder was singing another great
tune, we both believe in God me and Steve
although he sees Him a little clearer than
me but no matter, I'm the Flint, Steve's from
Saginaw, we've both come a long way thank God
I'm not still back there like all those creeps
I went to Hi School with driving around in
Corvettes and having ugly kids. This car's from
Detroit, Michigan, no coast, no mountains,
just wall to wall snowmobiles and mom's 10
thousand worries. O and I guess I got about 10
thousand threats but you're not one of them. You're
fresh, like the first night we met, like California,
I picked you up hitchhiking, we smoked some
great dope, and you gave me a hand job as I
tooled on happily.

*

EILEEN MYLES

Dawn

I feel one tit
  well I feel two
erratic taps in my room radiator
    taps in my speakers
  so early and deep blue
I should have gotten out
  before I was in

    now I see trees going bare
against blue autumn sky
      I see me   I see me again.

    *

Medium Poem

I was the second of three children.
Born in middlesex county. Smack
in the middle of the twentieth century.
I have no womb memories
to the point of doubting my tenancy.
After-life seems a dubious conjecture.
I'll tell you when I get there. Paus-
ing in the middle of ladders

I smoke a cigarette for Wednesdays
when I am comfortable. And it is always
Wednesday. And I am never
sure. And I am always here.

*

Poetry Reading

I heard this "fucking beautiful"
reading last night. Bespoke
the flowers. I went to a bar
afterwards, drank white wine
beneath the sumach   it was
a pretty night out. I was
pretty happy to be with my
friends.

*

My Cheap Lifestyle

After a bourbon
I came in turned on the tube
Lit a joint and watched Monterey Pop
Nearly wept when Janis came on
Janis' legs kicking on stage is a memorable sight
Janis does her sweet little Texas girl smile as
Her act finishes. She kicks her heels
And Otis Redding is so sexy.
Millions of young americans experience religion for the first
    time
In their lives
Or so the cameras would inform us

I'm concerned about manipulation in this media
How one gains such wonderful power
But of course I'm too tired
Thrilled by the process of bringing down a familiar blanket
Upon my bed
Its nearly fall
Nearly winter
I expect the stars will be bright
The woods full of bears.

*

On the Death of Robert Lowell

O, I don't give a shit.
He was an old white haired man
Insensate beyond belief and
Filled with much anxiety about his imagined
Pain. Not that I'd know
I hate fucking wasps.
The guy was a loon.
Signed up for Spring Semester at MacLeans
A really lush retreat among pines and
Hippy attendants. Ray Charles also
Once rested there.
So did James Taylor . . .
The famous, as we know, are nuts.
Take Robert Lowell.
The old white haired coot.
Fucking dead.

*

Greedy Seasons

The whole idea of sanity is intriguing
to me. I should thank her for the
light. A man said he was in control
of his death and it was thrilling—
such a small death such a mighty
thing to feel. It was intriguing
to me. I felt the blood pound
in the veins surrounding my
heart and the autumn in New York
was bursting and I wanted to
darken too so much—there are
places I have not been, believe
me and I am so hungry. No meat
just hot gossip and soup. But
what soup. Just the soup
that I needed at this time.
The world is divided by back-
bone I learned. I liked
to lie down. From the top of the Empire
State building, an early high, changing
as the city got dark and flat-footed
I was jubilant, so were you, an old
friend from the other side of the street,
a great guy, but what you can see from
a tower, my eyes, my eyes. I blessed
myself for love and gratitude and nice
weather—even misty like this and the
spots of rain on my lenses made the
light funny—I could only take it
for a moment or two, I'm no kid.
When a woman moved into my body
I noticed it, dawn all around you,
your flesh. I couldn't share
my humiliation with you, who was more catholic,
standing next to you in line and I revealed

it was planned my favorite illustration
the brownies getting spanked. Look
at their asses, isn't it great.
He blushed and never spoke to
me again. The book was returned
to the library. I speak the truth,
it was great. Oh this morning
coming down the avenue in milky
blue light. My gratitude
began, was ushered in. Women with
wreathes of orange roses, violets
for me around my head. Secrecy
announcing corn splashing
into wine, fresh air, runes,
silliness and divine. Yeah,
the fantasy is wild, safe
in your arms, we're gathering
now in nothing flat the slow
incumbent steps ahead
to winter.

*

ELAINE EQUI

Condo Girl

The gold earrings,
the bronze pumps,
    the solitary female
    thin as an olive branch.
Cunning
    as the draft of cold air.
She moves like a she-tortoise
head tilted over
1983's Guide to Real Estate.

*

Girl Friday

I still get the urge
to wear uncomfortable clothes,
tall pointy hats . . . shoes
that pinch . . . cold water,

but after you've been burned once
at the stake
witchcraft is no big deal.
In those days I went anyplace

with shoulders round as a mousehole
I could unravel whatever I saw
be it pig or fence.
My talent was finding loose threads.

The old women called him "Boss"
but I can honestly say
I never saw the devil.
It was a dull life

except whenever we got dressed up
and occupied the forest
though inevitably we'd choose
neither evil nor good

like that moment after an orgy
of noticing the dirty windows,
summer is nearly over,
soon it will be time for another job.

*

For Hollis Sigler

I got this job
being a woman
but I could
just as easily
have been a hammock
practicing swaying and shade.
I could have been
coral or old wine.
Meanwhile in the city,
men are dancing with tape measures.
Building things,
without any flowers.
When they're done,
they'll want to hire some women.

*

Vampirella

At discos where I eavesdrop,
the conversation always turns to love
but please no talk of broken hearts
for certain I can say
that love does not reside there.
Centuries ago, my mother advised me,
even as a corpse a woman should be able to win
admiring glances from the mourners.
Full well did I heed her
when choosing my burial garb:
high-heeled boots, the shortest mini,
plenty of eyeliner,
and glad am I to have done so.
Because of such wisdom,
for the moment, I can breathe again.
It is not life exactly
but from time to time
I too make my excursions
into the land of the living
no different than anyone else.

*

Think Small

I wonder if all muses are assigned a poet to keep under their
coconut, like con-artist guardian angels. Then mine must be the
security guard in the department store where I shoplift. The mid-
dle aged, balding man that makes me remove my hat so he can run
his fingers through my hair. They have to check. They have to be
sure. Especially at this time of the year. There's probably a mil-
lion girls in the city running around with poems in their bras. But
I, obviously, know how to outsmart this private eye focused on

eternity. Blink, blink. He's so stupid, he really thinks I'm after immortal literature when I already own every poem in the world. All I want to get away with is the eggroll not the payroll. My biggest heist to date was only $18 which I still carry in my right hand as if I'd been born with it. I don't mind if my future is in petty theft. It doesn't mean I'm petty and it doesn't mean I want to get caught.

*

Hi-Fashion Girl

I'm swinging through a department store of the future because by then it will be possible to do that. I mean hear red. Dig the brass section of this cra-zy shirt.
Wait a minute. If this is the future, why am I talking like a ridiculous beatnick poet? The past must be following too close behind. Lodged by the cosmetics like a little Vietnamese girl with a grenade under her dress.
I'd offer chocolate but in the department store of the future all they sell is the potential for candy. The potential
                    to make Mom happy on her birthday
                    the potential to look terrific.
What is all this potential I keep seeing like landscape in a recurring weirdo dream? It must be the reason I ask you to style my hair, order my meals and supervise the movies I see.
    Yes,
so I'll be ready for the next big trend after death.
Glass elevators where you really do ascend into heaven but are kept around to serve champagne. Man, that is not modern. That was done in the Dark Ages.

*

PAT NOLAN

Doubt

I talk and no one listens

gee I dunno if I have the right to bitch
wander backyard garden and register growth
of peas cabbage broccoli corn tomato plop
ripe fresh strawberry into jaws with leisure
and majesty of royalty second cup of coffee
in hand I also check out the color composition
of this half lit early California morn and sigh

"Help me Rhonda (help help me Rhonda)!"

high noon

the bees around my self
a mammal of silence

flank of day bright blue
                against points of fir
and redwood

                        and oh!
                                the heat of it

                beercan hats

        sirens of summer
                calling down the highway
                        destination disaster

(the empty house's uneasy silence
of telephone rung unanswered)

but that's the way it is
you say what you don't mean
and mean what you don't say

"girl when you call my name
(I) salivate like a Pavlov dog"

(bass drum beat on first word)

hummingbirds at it again
little tiny winged sex fiends
doing what they do best

the refrigerator it takes a strong man to open
"nothing for sure but this brand new tattoo"
and why did I want to wait till later to write
 "the old folks around here like to circle
this twilit neighborhood their Cadillacs
on idle they slow boat around the block
their excuse for an evening stroll"

just lazy I suppose

like last night
                I should have written

                                                "doubt"

                when I had it

*

Exercise

Just as I stood up
I sat back down
again forgetting
what I stood for

*

Stone Age

I go to put a letter
in my mailbox
and pick up a rock
for the big dog
at the end of the drive

*

Exercise

get loaded
and climb
into the tub

*

Tea For Two

if I'm not too quiet
I'm just a bore

sickly sweet opium
vodka and a good woman

this stuff sweetens
the voices in my head

a body drenched with
concern for itself

pleasantly on edge
tea is a ritual

if I didn't hate gum
I wouldn't need valium

*

Home Life

You're paranoid she says
        and I might as well be
                I can't get any work done

I got myself
        into trouble
                playing the game of love

but that's another story
        I put the lid on it
                the problem is

I sit down to think
        and I've misplaced my smokes
                or the cup of tea

I was drinking
        when I was thinking earlier
                is empty or someone

comes to the door
          with a check they want cashed
                    do I look like a bank?

I'm not complaining
          I'm just saying
                    the baby cries and crawls

across the floor
          a wailing trail of tears
                    to the desk where I sit

with my thumb
          to my chin and pulls
                    herself up to my level

my thoughts are hollow
          in them echo
                    her wail and

through the wall
          the sound of the dishes
                    being done

*

Senryu

The bed creaks
as I make it

*

The Great Pretenderer

What I thought so unusual about today
I can't remember right now
but examining my pen I see where
the baby has left her teeth marks
maybe it was how sometimes firm
decisions are often overturned without
the slightest qualm or hesitation
or after a weekend of feeling like
the badly tuned image on a picture tube
(out of phase and shadowy)
all of a sudden I'm feeling great
and raring to go to town which I do
almost on the spur of the moment
and buy a notebook of the kind
I always thought too pretentious to own

       it took me years to figure out
what I was doing
           (smoke exiting slowly from
nostrils)
    form came later
           and I had to sit for hours
on end pen poised
with not a jot to my name
      if it hadn't been for the radio
          I woulda been long gone

    for instance

we were burying clothes. she thought
she should tell him. her legs showed
as she picked up the basket. I told
her I'd tell the kid. I got my guitar
out. it was going to be a long movie.

if it's not that it's cable TV
so I watch it every night and learn
the Chinese character for "trouble"
"two women under the same roof"
police as usual are looking for clues
hysterical madmen at the very top
National Guard called out

money messages go right over my head
"most of the world's phosphates. . . ."
an inkling of destiny as UFOs
in the East Bay glide into camera range
and to the left of the newscaster

> KING
> OLAF
> INSF

if I've learned
one thing
over the years
it's don't be such a fuckin' fanatic

"it's only money"
I keep telling myself
and "Let It Be Lowenbrau"

a heavy sweater and a wet blanket
describe me perfectly

in a newspaper I find an ad and
a clip-me coupon that reads "Mark
an X For Each Prayer Need You Have"
and lists
1.___Better Job
2.___More Finances
3.___Someone To Care For Me

4.___Happier Marriage
5.___I Need More Confidence
6.___People Talk About Me
7.___I Am Not Understood
8.___I Am Worried
9.___My Health Is Bad

after checking numbers 2, 5, 8, & 9
I decide what the hell
        and mark them all

"I've never seen anything like it"

a sunset the color
I wish they made pantyhose

       ✻

KEITH ABBOTT

Persephone, 5, Outside

She is using
language
so she does

not care
what it
means

so it means
the world
to her

if you
know what
I mean

*

Blue Mason Jars

Time gone
frayed things
that old

Fillmore flyer
from 1967
stuck in

the shabby copy
of Philip Whalen's
EVERYDAY

and the thought
of Richard's
apartment

"The Museum"
as Bruce Conner
calls it

canned pears
yellowing in their
blue Mason jars

patches from
the Hells Angels
a switchblade knife

blade carved in an
intricate design
and laid

in a velvet-lined glasses case
spattered
with red rose petals

*

French Desire

Read a little Apollinaire & love it
it's in French which
you can't read

worth a shit
how desire
attaches us to all

things
the sermon for today
& how much we

all love
to love
want to want

more and more and more
How I wanted to learn
French & how I

did
half-assly
and I thought

of it fondly
today thinking of
how much I love

to desire
to feel it in me
and feel it go

away
a finger, a tongue,
A DICK TRACY

Little Big Book
imago
mundi

muddy old boots
parked behind
the hallway door

you see
he sees
she sees

and it's love me
love me
love me

*

To an Old San Francisco Poet

How to remember you correctly when I'm not sure you're dead
Yet on the Market St. bus I thought I saw you
A shade toothless leaning in a phone booth
Munching on a piece of bread
And smiling at the same time
Perhaps reading a bit of inspired graffiti
The last time I saw you you were dealing
Had a cupboard full of whiskey gin & wine
You'd given someone a birthday party
Everyone showed up so wasted on speed or smack
        Nothing got eaten or drank
        The cake still intact & stale
You drifted over to the box & stood there
        An old Sonny Criss record
One hand on your chin
Trying to figure out if the record was skipping
Or was Sonny bearing down on a really fine riff
Seeing how close he could come
On the ride over to score some speed

You told the recent life story of Sweet William
How he'd had the back of his head shot off
And when he arrived the morgue
Attendant noticed the carotid artery still pumping
                              shipped him upstairs to the hospital
You paused & added, "I always said
It'd take a sharpshooter to hit his brain"
                    As you laid on the bed
                    Your pants around your ankles
                    A fan of poetry books around your head
Your lady Sharon leaning over your legs
Probing for a vein in the back of your knee
                    Your face bliss
Even though you hadn't had your shot yet
                    The ugliness of your legs
                    Tenderness of the scene
I think that's all you ever really wanted
                    Not jails pain or death

                         *

Good News Bad News

after Apollinaire
in memory of Ted Berrigan

An old-fashioned sketchbook
With plenty of young women
Old wine the refined taste
Turns to restoring youth

Here the joy also heard
In the soft early songs
And this charm still enough
To save the new for an aged brain

To have old books past friends
Enjoy the ripe days Autumn
Here all the pleasures except
The one which always astonishes us

The one we call love
For this alone the world breathes
By this everyone knows the way out
The way in night & day

To live and die
Good news bad news

❉

Persephone

Just for a moment on the first day
while Lani was at the store
and when I was standing in front
          of my bookcase
I knew I was alone and my daughter gone

Who would have thought? I thought
eighteen years and Persephone's flown to Paris

And I turned to my books, & those
                    of favorite authors,
where there are words
for my condition, and several others,
and as I turned the huge
          shelves of unwritten books
                    that will be hers
revolved as I did, & remained behind
                    my back unseen

❉

JOEL DAILEY

Joie de Vivre

No citizen is melancholy
any longer.
Especially now, in these the 1980s,
latter half
of the 20th Century
where bread
has been a faithful companion
to much of humankind,
replacing the dog
in magnitude.
Man's best friend has become
a loaf of bread.
In the moment of this realization
let us fill
our lungs with the disappearing breath
of the household dog.
Inhale now.

*

Known

Sodden with drink
he returns
to return the carriage

Camel in ashtray
says Hello
Poetry waves Goodbye

weaves through the dark
over
the hills

When that butt
goes out
the World ends, O.K.?

*

Good Night

Good night, my table & chairs!
I own you, you know.
Buenas noches, Dodge in the driveway!
Until we meet & drive downtown together
    again!
Remember, I've pumped millions into you!
Bed, you cost me plenty, too; are you
    ready to do your dream stuff?
No more foolish nightmares!
Aufwiedersehen, my highly polished wood
    floors,
My darling house among houses!

*

Everyone in the World

Everyone in the world wakes tomorrow
refreshed and peaceful
as a landscape waiting to embrace the sun.

Everyone in the world is well-fed,
well mannered and equally well-heeled.
Disease, poverty, hate, ignorance,
greed, jealousy, war, famine, insanity,
have all flown like horrible vultures
from the World Vocabulary.

Everyone in the world, every child,
parent, aunt, uncle, grandparent,
every shoe salesman, policeman, secretary,
hot dog vender, check-out clerk, every
street sweeper, every man and woman,
possesses Happiness the very size
of the World and holds it in their hands.

Whatever everyone in the world desires,
it is instantly theirs, be it
unlimited quantities of perfume, sex, fun,
mountain ranges, swimming pools,
beauty, food, flowers, sun, travel or tissues.

And when everyone in the world
has all they could ever want or even
find the time to ask for, then
everyone in the world climbs into bed,
falls asleep and, while dreaming of tomorrow,
wakes to that perfect day.

✳

Meanwhile

in tribute to Frank O'Hara

In Mike's Diner the other day
I was reminded of you.
Deac & I strolled
in the door to find the long lunch
counter crowded
with famished souls

all eagerly scanning the menu
as if it were a book.
& it was: your Collected Poems!
Mike greeted us.
We looked at your book,
Frank, & ordered two hamburgers

& two malteds. Mike,
in a few minutes, delivered
our lunches, leaned over
the counter in his very white uniform
& said he truly enjoys
your poems & that, Collected

& bound, they made a great
menu for his Diner.
We agreed. Mike was right:
plenty of lunches
& dinners, not to mention
breakfasts & snacks—

& all in one volume too!
As we paid at the register, Mike
told us, "Thanks & stop
by again. I never
realized that poetry could be
so handy." We told Mike

that poetry always was
& always will be
as long as we live.

*

Revving Up La Rêve

Oh my Plutonian restaurateur!
Has anyone seen
my misplaced Mirth Packets?
Gross & engrossed
by any given mirror
affording a view
of the past, I
yearn for the bulging
brown lunchbags of my youth!
Nights I dream
mid-space collisions,
radar systems out
of whack & my
garbage scowl ship
never again caressing
the dimpled knees
of dawn on some
nameless, blameless planet. . .
I am in desperate
pursuit of the perfect,

seamless hotdog
& to the Universe's arse,
a deli cul-de-sac,
I will proceed!
Oh what malarkey!
Suture yourself!
Possessed by Errata,
victim of bad posture
& big ears, spirit
infiltrated by feelings
decidedly other
than boogie,
I flip tiny levers.
& Time minces on!
Every morning I slap
myself into
Consciousness.
Propelled through the days,
engine driven,
tres retrorocketed,
I dream of
The New Now,
nebulous, nomadic.

*

JEROME SALA

The Party

We see lots of people at the party.
There is a guy who deals heroin for the American Nazi Party.
There are two people shooting up on a bare wooden stage that
    begs for a beat-up piano.
There is our old motorcycle friend who calls us "professor" and
    says he'll fix us up with the "outfit" if we ever go to prison.
There is a girl they call "Melanie Smellanie" who knew us
    years ago and wants a copy of our book *Spaz Attack*: we don't
    think we can place her.
There is a smallish girl who dyed her hair from blond to black
    and used to look young, twiggy and pretty, but now
    looks old, gypsy and junkie.
She asks us did we see our old little blond friend who hates us
    now but is a little magical.
Yes, we agree, he is a little magical, but we forgot about that
    since we haven't seen him.
She says no you don't forget you never forget.
We say yes you do you do and she thumbs her nose at us.

Now we're away from the party, trying to live without
      ambition,
    but also without despair.
We think we succeed in this a little tonight as we walk around
    on the cool sidewalks we love,
Then in and back out of the hot bars we no longer like,
All the while picturing the blue stars looking down on us from
    Omar Khayyam's Bowl of Night,
Certain they are blue, without ever looking up at the sky.

*

Mother's Day

my mother punches my father today
                    at dinner in Greek-town
          he laughs
                    I hope I honor them
      the POLACKS!
                    like me they've got SOLIDARITY
      and the Virgin Mary
                    who make us chic now
      flashing the victory sign
                    at the big red stars
      we only salute the Vatican!
                    I'M A PAPIST
bring back the Holy Roman Empire
                    run by Polacks
      you Russians at our borders
                    watch out
          before you end the world
                    you've got my mother to answer to
my bad-ass father will kick your ass
                    my younger brother's in the Air Force
          making nukes for your
                    heretical heads
my older brother lifting weights
                    in Berwyn, having kids
          for the new Polish Army
                    my man Stan starting a band
      called TARGET MOSCOW
                    and ALL the mothers in the world today
          hiding tactical weapons
                    in their babushkas!

                    *

"The Ballad of Helmut Franze"

From "The Uncollected Poems of Ezra Pound"

Hitler courts in bombed Berlin
   Sipping Dubonnet:
"O where shall I find a young blond boy
   To man my ship of state?"

From the crowd crawls crippled Goebbels,
   And kisses the fuehrer's boots:
"Helmut Franze is the fairest lad
   To captain the German youth."

The fuehrer writes an edict
   And signs it in his blood
Delivered via Luftwaffe to Franze
   Asleep by the Danube's flood.

The first line on blond blood's purity
   Gives Helmut cause to smile
But the next line states the fuehrer's will
   and mists his teutonic eyes:

"O why has our father chosen me
   (I am not yet a man)
To march in brown, throughout the towns
   And save the fatherland?

Awake! Awake! My little brothers
   Our march begins today!"
"O say it's not true, good comrade Franze
   The communists are at bay.

Last midnight I saw eclipse
   Swallow the new moon's light—

A storm's at hand, good comrade Franze
  We'll perish in its blight!"

O our youth brigade was handsome
  But couldn't stem the red horde's tide
And soon after battle started
  Was captured by the other side.

O long long will his mother sip
  Swastika teacup in hand
Before her poor son Helmut
  Returns down the Autobahn.

O long long will his mother watch
  The new nation from a movie seat
Before Helmut Franze ever heads for home
  With victory in his teeth.

For across the wall lies East Berlin
  Just 30 kilometers away
And there the traitor Helmut lives
  A communist today.

*

At the Treatment Center

Everyday, Dietrich teaches a Mambo class of hillbilly patients.
Everyday, the hillbillies smile at Dietrich and push back their
  white hair.
Everyday, Dietrich's plum nylons whizz when she kicks
  and dances.
Everyday, the hillbillies mambo in their hospital gowns and
  ID bracelets.

Every night, Dietrich's corset lies under the pool table like an unused doberman.

Every night, the hillbillies sleep in their ward with open minds on the Mambo.

This therapy works with amazing success.

*

JIM GUSTAFSON

The Idea of San Francisco

Pretty white city. Precious white city.
Pretty precious white city.
The meaningful nod, the condescending but gentle smile,
crab meat under the fingernails,
city of pastel euphoria.
San Francisco is the Jose Cuervo School of Workin' It Out,
the home turf of the celestial lightweight,
the demand to finish what you start,
Swedish, Norwegian, Danish what you start.
Breezin' along with the breeze, as it were,
or what to do after outlasting
the going-home-to-die syndrome.
Plenty.
Steal books from City Lights, if they
have any, drink coffee at Malvina's
until your hands tremble like the wings of cheap jets,
call up A. or S. or G. and say
"Let's go look for some girls!"
call up G. or S. or A. and say
"Let's go look for some boys!",
take acid in the park and wait for the mounted police
to ride out of the bushes.
See the hippie run. Run hippie run.
City of many stances, of many hills, thirty-two,
home of the Tony Bennett Heart Depository,
breeding ground of the ravaged and the outraged,

city that swears in languages it doesn't speak,
city with one shoe on and one shoe off,
city you can thumb through like a coloring book
of basic evasion, city without pity,
city that dances the fluorescent cha cha
on the ballroom floor of zany consciousness.
Groovy white city. Nifty white city,
city that wears bridges as antlers,
that wants to be a book but can't decide which one,
temperate and mellow, anemic and perverse,
city that constantly squirms
but never screams.

*

The Idea of Detroit

Detroit just sits there
like the head of a large dog on a serving platter.
It lurks in the middle of a continent,
or passes itself off as a civilization
at the end of a rope.
The lumpiness of the skyline
is the lumpiness of a sheet stretched over
what's left of a tender young body.
Detroit groans and oppresses.
It amounts to Saturday night at the slaughter house,
and Sunday morning in bed
with a bag of bagels and the Special Obituary Supplement.
Air the color of brown Necco wafers,
a taste like the floor of an adult movie theater,
the movement through the streets
that of a legless, wingless, pigeon.
Detroit means lovers buying matching guns,
visitors taken on tours of the foundries,

children being born with all their teeth,
a deep scarlet kind of fear.
It breeds a unique bitterness,
one that leaves deep gashes in the tongue,
that doesn't answer telephones or letters,
that carves notches in everything,
that illustrate the difference between
"rise up singin'" and "sit down and shut your face".
It forms a special fondness for uncooked bacon,
for the smell of parking lots,
for police sirens as opposed to ambulance sirens,
for honest people who move their heads
whenever they move their eyes.
Detroit is a greasy enchilada
smeared across the face of a dilemma,
the sanctuary of the living dead,
the home of the Anywhere-But-Here travel agency,
the outhouse at the end of the rainbow.
Detroit just sits there
drinking can after can of Dupe beer,
checking the locks on the windows,
sighing deeply, knowing that nothing
can save it now.

*

Ambitious

Start to think of progress
in terms of not having made any.
It has been five years and the hero's tongue
is still lost under the wallpaper.
He doesn't look for it anymore.
He sits there and drinks vegetable juices
through a straw, apparently satisfied
that it's somewhere in the room.

Every year the earth gets smaller,
two or three inches at the equator,
but at the same time slightly heavier.
It is the aliens that sneak into the world
as birthday candles that refuse to go out;
that extra light accounting
for the additional weight.
Things become odd without becoming complicated.
Mythologies are invented to let the elders
be elders while they're still young
then lapse into obscurity.
The senses sway like a house trailer
crowded with hungry parrots.
The hero grows a hump and wants
to start an orchid farm on it:
At the time it seems
like a good idea.

*

Nervous Miracles

These emotional dive-bombers
sortie into our lives about as welcome
as a toilet brush in the quiche lorraine.
We seem to have hearts like suitcases
and minds like watertowers
and the annoying habit of constantly
being caught in dilemmas, each as hopeless
as politicians too ugly to murder
or books too wonderful to read.
We lay side by side in the terminal ward
each assuring the other "trust me,
I've been through this before".
It's like being a canary caged

in a double helix:
Nothing you do matters *or* makes sense.
Occasionally we get lucky,
or are visited by one of the nervous miracles.
We're insanely hungry when
a deadly but delicious predator
collapses at our feet.
If the instincts are right,
the sweetest meat should be
around the claws.

❖

The Dance

Oh the dances we have done!

The Ballet Diabolique,
                    The Wonderland One-Step,
The Dipso Calypso,
                    The Funky Rampage,
The Continental Drift,
                    The Chainsaw Samba,
The Deep Midnight Wiggle, Rant, and Stomp,
                    The Last Waltz,
                              The Voodoo Chicken. .

Oh we've done our share
of fancy struttin' and high kickin'!

We danced at the head
                    of the Festival of Pain Parade,
in small private offices
                    adjacent to the Grand Ballroom,
on stages and altars,

on the faces of enemies,
and the toes of our sweeties.
We've danced
at hoedowns in the Heartlands,
after funerals
in the Funzone,
off the end of piers with queers,
on the roofs
of moving cars,
in mirrors,
into walls.

Everywhere we went . . and we went everywhere
we danced.
The more we danced
the more we needed to dance.

To invent new steps,
to jump higher,
spin faster,
to impress our wreckless friends
with our wanton abandon
as the ruby dawn encroached
and the blood seeped
from our tattered shoes.

We danced to quiet the angry spirits,
to make the dope plants
want to grow
green and sweet and tall,
danced
The Lethargy Liturgy Dance,
The Victory Thru Vulnerability Dance,
danced
the I'm-Too-Old-To-Dance Dance,
danced
and lived

and felt better
            and wanted to dance   some more.

The orchestra had gone home
                        so we danced to the music
in our heads,
            danced to the throbbing
                        of our thumbs,
danced to the trickle
            of sweat
                        running down our cleavage,
danced ourselves delirious,
                        horizontal bopped
toward frenzied euphoria,
                        danced in our sleep
then threw off the sheets,
                        danced into the streets
beckoning the other dancers,
                        come dance with us,
and they did
            and we all danced.

Danced The Final Liberation Shuffle,
                        The-Box-In-One-
Polka-Around-The-Sun,
                        The Full Throttle Grovel Dance.
Danced
      until the cows came home
                        and left
                              appalled.

We danced to keep from dreaming,
                        danced to keep from dying
but mostly
            we just danced.

*

No Money in Art

You can be a dancing brontosaurus
in the Glimmer Twins chorus,
a terrorist, a therapist,
an expert on the clitoris,
go back to barter, protect Jimmy Carter,
write rubber rain checks,
run an obnoxious discotheque,
sell meat thermometers, metric odometers,
snowmobiles to Eskimos,
leave marks that don't show!
You can preach self-reliance,
form an East-West alliance,
force strict compliance,
cure Herpes Simplex,
be a stooge for the complex,
get an MBA and an MFA take some MDA
and be MIA in the USA!
You can be a security advisor,
a market analyzer, a human breathalyzer,
some sweet thang's protector,
a short arms inspector,
a radiation leak detector,
a Soviet defector!
You can forewarn of the apocalypse,
make burgers out of beeflips,
do talk shows, trade quips,
one, two, shape those hips!
Be a military advisor to El Salvador,
believe in a winnable nuclear war,
collect empties in the Cass Corridor!
You can join the CIA, get on MTV,
tell the little Gs & Bs how it's got to be.
Get rich in the struggle,
find something new to smuggle,

be a liar, a conniver,
a Tupelo truckdriver,
get real behind a laser,
locate a real and present danger,
be a major deal arranger,
oh it gets stranger and stranger!
    But I gotta tell you Honey,
    don't let it break your heart,
    but there ain't no money, Honey!
    No Money in Art!

❋

DARRELL GRAY

The 20th Century

after Bartusek

We photographed everything
we could see.
The click
of the release aroused our attention
from sleep.
Children turned their smiles
into meadows,
doorsteps,
birds.
The mothers occupied themselves
with distant emotions.
It was hot.
Strawberries hung red
and hot.
Suddenly summer failed
to resemble our longing . . .
the day dozed off
into a deep, sky-like sleep.
But since there was in fact no sky
we turned to vegetables
for reassurance, only to find
our own bodies.
Whole cities exposed their surfaces
to our lenses.
You see, we took snapshots
as we went.
Truth is the negative

we carry,
exposed to the polished strangeness,
asleep or awake.

❊

Moving

There comes the time
    moving its house,
the yard and cat
    that can't come back.

The dark was big. The car
    went through,
And what they thought
    they thought they knew—

the yard, the house,
    the car, the cat.
Goodbye, goodbye. It
    seemed so real.

❊

Foreplay of the Alphabet

I am the poet who waits
for the alphabet to move.
For this, my readers scorn me—
friends walk away confused.

How can I explain that all I want
is very little—so little
that all one can see
are sparks
shooting off the page—
just sparks:
    no metaphors,

          no symbols,
              no linebreaks designed to expose
              how everything flows . . .

   I don't want to say
   that if God were to come
   to me and say, 'Darrell,
   your poetry is bad, in fact
   downright
              flat,'
   I would take his criticism
   lightly.

   God, after all,
   is a concrete poet
   whose theory is
   the subject and object
   should get together
   more often.

                        *

Ode to Food

All day I have been dreaming of a dazzling stew,
and now it is time for dinner.
Oh food! how casually and yet punctually you arrive,
providing a focus, from out of nowhere, for the table.
My mind is ambushed by the leafy hearts of lettuce,
red globes of radishes
and tempting tendrils of celery
all tossed together in one miraculous
Creation—an organic medley beyond
mere human words!
How great is the pig, the cow, even the rudimentary chicken—
how fleeting the fish, that comes to our table but once.
How the abalone steams! How the lamb offers up
its eternal recurrence, succulent
and lean as the first supper.

Great plates and pots and skillets—
instruments of human sustenance, polished
and hung in rows, or lined up on long counters, waiting!
My mouth waters with the thought—the salt
smuggled in cells as in the holds of ships
setting sail from distant islands.
Fruits, how Cezanne loved you—and all those loaves
of bread broken open, glazed and translucent
in the paintings of English Masters.
Yes, food, you are the gateway to the insatiable
carnality of destiny, the inexhaustible angel
whose innocence sweetens the tongue,
and brightens the spirit.
How many apples have I bitten to their pungent core,
how many oranges peeled and devoured, segment by segment.
How many eggs (hardboiled, softboiled, scrambled), indoors
or at picnics have I unconsciously eaten!
All those grapes, those pancakes, syrup usurped
from tall stalks that grew up with the wind. . .
Asleep I often dream of melon-shaped planets,
gardens of light whose tendrils envelop the stars.
God is a farmer there, a gatherer
of honey (the bees' memory) and planter
of the a priori legumes of the soul.
Oh Hunger, you are hereby banished! Forever be gone!
Leave our planet to the perpetual music of mandibles—
the Irish do not need you, nor do the Chinese,
making lives miserable in your maddening vaporous wake!
Hunger, I banish you to the Dead Sea,
and the whitest lakes of the moon.
For now it is time to eat:
the fragrance of finitude flows from the kitchen door,
winds in little whisps around the lamps and tables,
almost a voice. The nose responds: the ears and eyes
join in. It says with its unnameable
and fleeting presence: I am the light of the body,
Come into me, and I will make you full.

*

BILL ZAVATSKY

The Ex-Poet

Wondering is a typical pastime of the leisure class
So Mao says,
The wondering about other minds
The wondering if the exterior world exists.

So:
I am reading *The Dialectics of Growing Peanuts*
and another useful book
The Dialectics of Bus-Driving,
the first written
by the successful director
of a North China peanut farm,
the second by Shanghai's
most decorated public servant.

So I won't lag behind
the development of objective reality.
The secret police.

Comrade, I urge you to do the same.
Be like our leader:
Think of the peanut field
shaking in warm July winds.
Begin to construct in your mind
a system of public transportation
flawless as a scientifically-grown peanut!
These are the important things in life,
not the shriveled peanut of philosophy. . .

Without direction the daydream
may be likened to a man who plants peanuts
under the seats of city buses—
and that is a madman!

No more time to compare the wind!
Take the imagination away from the water!
I personally wasted most of my life
scribbling about a woman I lost,
living in a future where we'd meet
one day by chance, the past
crushing the present of my pitiful life!

Puh!
Now all I'm interested in is how effectively I can cut this
    board
in two pieces: the philosophy
of the saw, the theory of the nail
that holds my world in place.

*

Testament

A lot of times I've thought about suicide
No kidding
but then I worried about who'd find the mess
poor loving wife mangled with grief
pussycats climbing the walls, never the same
neurotic friend passing by who "just dropped in"
Ha! Some surprise!
I thought about who'd have to clean "it" up
blood all over typewriter keys
hair smeared to windowshades, 1/2 tongue in teacup
other tongue fragment drooling among Ko-Rec-Type

brain dangling outside in tree like broken glider
smashed by high velocity futility
eyeball discovered months later clogging vacuum cleaner. . .

I've pondered my chances for a mythology. . .
Too silly a life for Sylvia Plath-type gothic hubbub
Serious enough not to merit *profundo* Ogden Nash
    requiem
No exciting alter ego, no zippy pennames
little published   barely known
oddball to famous critics
shining dumbbell even to closest friends

. . . a skeleton of a poet
big plans   bigdeal blueprints scribbled in hot air. . .

Then suddenly it hit me
how
in a magnanimous gesture toward the future
I could will my scrap-flashes of genius
those whiffs of the eternal fracturing light
that I scribbled madly on pads and envelopes and
    matchbook covers
bequeath them to some other struggling mind
heavy on the willpower
Somebody who can fit these bits and pieces together
into great masterpieces of literature
after I blow my brains out

What about
"Slit open the wind and let me kiss my breath"
(one of my better lines, I think)?
Or how about one of my best titles
"Moonlight and Spies"
—to which I never could attach
the weird faces of words.

Then there's my one-word poem masterpiece
(unjustly neglected, I feel):
"pinosceros."

Yes
maybe some tender policeman-poet
faking a timesheet this very moment
to steal time to write a poem
could do with a helping hand. . .

And that great looker
in the giant shoes,
lipstick blazing around her smile
like an arsonist?

Or that popeyed anarchist there,
or that brilliant ten year old?

Imagine someone sad and crushed
armed with my bequest
expressing all the madness of the world
for free!

Yes
some goofy genius
maybe right now lurking in my old home town
bumping into a parking meter
stunned
my lawyer's letter trembling in his hands,
strong new glasses on. . .

A mind who at last will write my Zavatsky-Iliads. . .

Zavatsky-Iliads
Hmmmmm. . .

Just a minute while I write that down!

*

Bald

In the mirror it's plain to see:
Soon I'll be bald, like the two faceless men
Living side by side in the word "soon."
Left profile crowding mirror, I can still pretend
It isn't happening. Enough tangled skeins
Of hair to hide the gleam. But from the right,
Where the wave lifts, I don't have to push my face
Close, to see it winking at me—
The mysterious island of my skull,
The dinky coastline of my baby head
Swimming back to me at last.
Through the pitiful shrubbery
That dots the beach (I mean my
Miserable hairs), it glints. Soon I'll crawl ashore
Where all uncles live, the ones who never
Had any hair, their clown cannibal heads
Hilarious in photographs, glaring like
Chromosomes from dresser picture frames
The way they always did when I and my cousins
Stopped short in a game of tag to stare at them
Trapped under glass in their dumb grown-up world,
A phrenology of how I'd never be. Then
Two years ago I saw my head in a three-way mirror
Buying a coat: a pink sliver of skin
At the back of my part. The overhead lighting
Shrivelling my scalp, scorching my silk purse
To a sow's ass. Soon the hairs in the sink
Reached out their arms and wailed to me.
Soon the moonlight with its chilly hands
Seized my cranium, taking measurements.
Even my wife kept quiet. I was the last to know.
Yes, I'm drifting closer. Closer
To where I'll live out my days

Training to be ever more the skeleton
That's taking over my body pore by pore.
Hair by hair its fingerbone scissors snip me
Away, I who in the Sixties fell in love
With my own hair! Who swooned among battalions of
        Narcissuses
Over the ripples our long tresses made in that mirror
Of our generation, the President's face!
I who have always known
that Death is a haircut!
Walking the streets I pause to study my scalp
In a butcher shop window where it hangs
Reflected beside the other meat.
Under my breath I sing the song I'm learning
That goes, "Bald is anonymous . . . bald is goodbye."
I will not grow the hair above my ear
Until it's ten feet long, and drape it suavely
Over the empty parking lot atop my head
Where the forest used to loom, and plaster it down
With goo. No, I don't want a toupee
To fall in my soup, or a hair transplant
Driven into my brain with giant needles!
I shoo away the mysterious weave
Spun from the dead hair of unfortunate ones,
Rich only in what grows from their head.
I reject the compensatory beard—I refuse
To live my life upside down!
I prepare myself to receive the litanies
Chanted by the kids as I enter the classroom:
"Chrome dome, marble head, baldy bean, skin head,
Bowling ball brain, reflector head, bubble top."
I urge them on in the making of metaphor!
I am content to merge with the reflection
Of every bald barber who ever adjusted my head.
I am enchanted, so late, to be becoming

Someone else—the face in the mirror that,
by the time I claim it, won't even look like me.
I am thrilled to realize that the scythe
Of the grim reaper is nothing more
Than a cheap plastic comb
You can buy in any drugstore,
And even its teeth fall out.

*

STEVE KOWIT

Hate Mail

I got a letter from an old acquaintance in New York
asking me to send some of my prose poems
to her literary magazine, *Unhinged.*
I should have known better.
In the old days she'd fluttered about
the coffee houses baring her long teeth.
We'd smile up politely & cover our throats.
But time makes you forget & ambition got the better of me
& a week later I got my poems back with a terse note:
Sorry, but this third-rate pornographic crap isn't for us.
& may I point out it is presumptuous of you
not to have enclosed a self-addressed stamped envelope.
Just who in hell does little Stevie Kowit think he is?
I was nonplussed.
I sent a stamp back with a note explaining
that I hadn't thought I was submitting to her magazine
so much as answering her letter.
I received a blistering reply:
Who was I kidding? What I had sent was a submission
to *Unhinged,* pure & simple.
In passing she referred to me as juvenile,
adolescent, immature, a sniveling brat, an infant
& a little baby—
truly the letter of a raving lunatic.
I suppose it would have been best to have ignored it,
forget the whole thing,
but that little Stevie Kowit business started eating at me
so I dropped a one-liner in an envelope & sent if off:
Dear C, you are a ca-ca pee-pee head.

*

It Was Your Song

I saw her once, briefly,
in the park
among the folk musicians
twenty years ago—
a barefoot child of twelve
or thirteen
in a light serape
& the faded, skintight levis
of the era. I recall
exactly how she stood there
one foot on the rise
of the fountain
finger-picking that guitar
& singing
in the most alluring
& delicious voice,
& as she sang she'd
flick her hair
behind one shoulder
in a gesture that meant nothing,
yet I stood there
stunned.
One of those exquisite
creatures of the Village
who would hang around
Rienzi's & Folk City,
haunting all the coffee houses
of MacDougal Street,
that child
has haunted my life
for twenty years.
Forgive me.
I am myself reticent
to speak of it,
this embarrassing infatuation

for a young girl,
seen once, briefly,
decades back,
as I hurried thru the park.
But there it is,
& I have written this
that I might linger at her side
a moment longer,
& to praise the Alexandrian,
Cavafy, that devotee
of beautiful boys,
& shameless rhapsodist
of the ephemeral encounter.
Cavafy, it was your song
from which I borrowed
both the manner & the courage.

*

A Swell Idea

One of these days
while demonstrating the use
of the possessive pronoun
preceding the gerund
I'll tell her a little joke,
grow playful,
stroke the soft hairs
on the back of Melanie's neck
then slip my hand
over her breast.
Just as I've dreamed!
She'll groan.
She'll giggle & put
her hand over mine.
She'll love it!

If not, what have I lost?
If she screams
& the others rush in
I'll deny everything.
I'll stand there
shaking my head,
"She's crazy she's
making it up she
practically forced me
for chrissake I'm
sick I'm a sick man
I need help
Help me!"
I'll cry out
in a hoarse,
broken voice
& slip to my knees
& bury my face in my hands.

✳

Renewal

One of those lubricious teenage latin beauties,
a sloe-eyed fox
with a small cross like a grave
between her breasts
gave up her seat on the S bus,
oozed thru the mob,
& began rubbing it off against my leg.
& not discreetly, either—
she absolutely abandoned herself!
I stared straight ahead,
afraid to move,
hardly believing it,

but managed, nevertheless,
to work my free hand
down to where I felt it
would do us both the most good.
The girl went crazy.
We both did.
We must have blazed away for 40 minutes,
all the way to 16th & Biscayne.
I got home hours later,
shaken but whistling—
like a man whose life has been renewed
by a miracle:
an ineradicable smirk on my face
& above my head
a halo clanging like a trash can lid.

When he pressed his lips to my mouth
the knot fell open of itself.
When he pressed them to my throat
the dress slipped to my feet.
So much I know—but
when his lips touched my breast
everything, I swear,
down to his very name,
because so much confused
that I am still,
dear friends,
unable to recount
(as much as I would care to)
what delights
were next bestowed upon me
& by whom.

after Vikatanitambā

That smudge of mascara by your mouth
& the stench of perfume
clinging to your hair
speak eloquently
O my beloved. Therefore
do not waste your breath
& put me off with silly lies.
What of it—
you had a night out on the town
with some rouged midinette
with pretty curls
& caught up on all the latest
subtleties of love-making.
Do you think I begrudge you that pleasure?
We are not children.
As for the girl, I envy
the loveliness & grace
that must have held you captive
& salute the good luck she had
to have used her night
to such advantage.
But please, O my dearest,
do not, in some attack
of misguided remorse,
blurt out her name—
for having heard it
I will have no recourse
but to find the little
bitch & scratch her eyes out.

after Vidyāpati

✻

ALEX KUO

Sheltering the Same Needs

this late in our century
a hot meal, warm clothes
someplace to sleep, is all

so many crammed into already-
crammed housing with Aunt Jo

lives edged-out by downtown
gentrification, someone always there
counting the rising index points

pretty soon they wear out their
welcome and are out on the streets

selling the Christmas tree
won in a Salvation Army drawing
"I don't feel it anymore"

eviction has replaced fire
as the most direct cause of homelessness

except maybe some brother-and-sister pair
whose background is hazy
no roots archived in someone's photo

UNDELIVERABLE MAILS
DEAD LETTER BRANCH
PCC-390 MAIN STREET ROOM 354
S.F. CA. 94105-9502

eyes always glossed bitter
astonished, remembering the body
we resemble most, call nothing ours

the Cellophane Lady lived and died
just one block from her daughter's apartment

"they can do anything to me"
our one prayer, improbable in the nearest
quarter-mile, killing us with all we've got

*

Turning On Daytime TV

for Leslie

1

Instant acts
Unrehearsed scenes
      of man sleeping with his woman
        while reading a script on his side
           in black & white indoors.

2

When the winds sweep down
      into the plains from the mountains

some 30 yrs. ago

& we begin counting

       staring at Manzanar California
       where we find 10,000
before we move to Minidoka Idaho
       where we get another 10,000

all the way until we reach 110,168
before we start all over again
       going for broke on TV

& remember someone once saying
       we had to stand in line for everything
          even for the c & w music
          stationed around the camps

we know we must have bumped into each other
       mountains apart

while we screamed
each time we died.

3

And a thousand times later
       we don't even see the cottonwoods
          on TV anymore

only the exhausted characters
       & their desperate lives
          pushed to their edges
       being moved about
          deeper into silver
just like our lives, we are told.

4

I know that you are watching it today
            just as I am:

are we watching
            their elaborations serials apart

but writing the same screaming story?

5

If you'll remember me
            when you die

the trees outside will take
            the warm winds

the springs will fill
            the rivers

                        & tonight

we'll both stand in line
            counting the coyotes howling in the hills
                        mountains apart.

*

Words Most Often Mispronouncd in Poetry

In bars 21 and 23 of the *Aria* to his "Goldberg Variations,"
J.S. Bach designated a clear three-note ascending slide ornamenta-
tion, from the German *Schleifer*, not anticipating that centuries
later pianists would be reproducing them with mortal narcissism.

———————

How the desire to fall into your lover's arms must be insolent without the threat of loss.

It's leaning toward pulse, in even sequences and held at bloodpoint for just a moment to let light in before the letting go, descending in either direction but end at the beginning of the same note turned upside down. You have never been this way before, baby.

DEFINITION

I have changed my mind. In my mouth are words that can walk right into this poem and keep an eye on you.

Do you like these things? Do you wish them? That yellow lamp that lets in the light, this Hasselblad that's seen World War II, or the woman with the mouth of her body open standing by the piano, car keys in hand? She's 33, a violinist who's never killed anyone or taught high school, who last appeared in *Tender is the Night*. Does she fit your needs? You can call her anything you want, except Desperate Innocence.

There, stand closer to her while I snap a picture of the two of you while there's still enough light.

Whatever happens, I am ready.

*

A Chinaman's Chance

Shanghai, 1945

When the bombs dropped on us at the end of the war
No one knew which side did it. We were under
Blankets, beds, that inside table, even chairs

Later when I walked out of the dropzone, I counted
The steps that were not mapped at the beginning
Wanting everyone to have the same, necessary things

Hundreds were queued up on every street corner
For airdropped powdered milk, chocolate, condoms
By the same planes that dropped the bombs the night before

If the truth be known, I had to kill to get away
Lucky, as luck would have it, I wasn't born
In the 18th century: Mozart loved slurs then

For heroes now, I retain Clemente, Gould, my two sons
And what the wind leaves: They have been here
All this time nearer my life, nearer my starfield

For direction, I call on the far points
That insist at intervals without explanation
That left with me in the last, unmarked C-46

Like the last flight out of Casablanca in 1940
In the fog and at gunpoint, just like that
Shutting out of a life, leaping out past the finish

Do not mistake me or look for me in another meaning
Where I won't be found. In a sense we have all survived
Our words depend on it, with each chance

*

CHUCK WACHTEL

A Sirventes Against the Management of the Mammoth Supermarket in Toulouse

*I have made a sirventes against the city of Toulouse
and it cost me plenty of garlic*
Paul Blackburn

The Associated Press called it
a bargain hunter's dream
come true

when the 40 cashiers of
the Mammoth Supermarket
staged
a wildcat-strike

allowing customers to
walk out
without paying

                Word
spread quickly

within minutes shoppers
carted off 30,000 dollars worth
of groceries

while the manager pleaded
with them to abandon
their carts

Officials could not
understand
how so many people learned
of the situation in
so short a time

        There are some
situations
the French understand
very quickly one
of the cashiers
said

*

A Paragraph Made Up of
Seven Sentences Which Have
Entered My Memory Via Hearing Them
or Reading Them and Have Each
Left an Impression There Like the
Slender Scar Left by a Salamander
In a Piece of Rapidly Cooling
Igneous Rock

for Brian Breger

Gentlemen, which of these three vegetables: tomatoes, pump-
kins, or squash, will your wives say most represents the part of
their anatomy that has come to sag the most since your wedding

night. There was no blood or anything but when I got there she was turning blue. It's forty-eight WABC degrees. We control the horizontal. Bachelor number three is a sales manager who collects Disney memorabilia. Missing coed found slain. All this in Encyclopedia Britannica 111: American Indians, Louis "Satchmo" Armstrong, The Reproductive System, Poisonous Animals and Plants, Atomic Energy, The Circus, Abominable Snowman, Napoleon and More. . .

✻

A Horror Story
Written For The Cover
Of A Matchbook

for Ted Greenwald

In the dark Naomi
mistook a shard of
broken light bulb
for her contact lens.

✻

The Answer

I always wondered why
a pizza cutter, sharp
enough to leave deep scratches
in the surface of a pie tray

never cuts through the bottom
of a take-out box, so I asked
the guy in Mike's Pizza
on First Avenue who told me

that when you cut it
in the box you never press
as hard

*

DAVID HILTON

The Melmac Year

Then it was still called hard rubber,
machined, grainy striations
whorled like giant thumbs, created
I believed in the atom smasher—
the modern homemaker's dinnerware.
Even new, it seemed worn, filmed
with a paleo-plastic dust,
but stronger than iron or stone,
guaranteed to last lifetimes,
another great breakthrough
thanks to World War Two.

So my mother kept working
toward her service for twelve,
60 unbreakable pieces to earn:
amassing stacks of Rinso boxtops
and Philip Morris buy-em-by-the-carton bonus coupons,
solving (I helped) the acrostics in the Oakland *Tribune*,
winning canasta tourneys and hula-hula contests,
selling jewelry door to door (as I held steady the
        gaudy dislays),
and bearing down to gct, almost every chance,
the Lucky Frame Gold Pin strike in the Ladies
Monday Dirty Laundry 650 handicap league.

Sometimes she'd make me go in Safeway
for the Melmac demonstrations.
I'd stand at the table, staring at my shoes,
thinking up fake names. I'd change my voice
and ask what I had to ask,
then meet her outside; wait, return—
claiming free prizes until they said don't come back.
Take any color, she told me.
Later she'd try to swap it for blue.

She never missed a Melmac night.
Church bazaars, movie palaces, roller rinks,
bingo emporiums, and pee-wee golf
grand openings, the long-awaited unveilings
of every latest make and model—
she was there. After dark in 1949
heaven became a spiring city of searchlights,
all looking for her. Any magnesium beam
might guide her to the El Dorado of blazing Melmac.

I don't think I ever knew
that you could simply buy it.

———————

At last my mother completed her set of Melmac.
San Lorenzo was here to stay.
The elm twig stuck in front
of each little slab rancher
finally rooted. The Admiral Nimitz freeway
had launched its slow course south toward us.
Lawns grew tall enough to burn
the straw-brown that we called golden.
No Negroes moved in, or Mexicans,
and no Okies that anybody knew of.
No one but America

could make an A-bomb. And one noon
an army surplus blimp sagged low
to celebrate the new, still unstriped
Village Parking Plaza, a vastness
of asphalt acres lifting, oozing,
curling at the edges—
so fresh a black
the blimp's shadow
sank beneath the tar.

The wives of San Lorenzo gazed upward.
Bright housedresses pressed against
the county sheriff's rope. The blimp
was idling over the Plaza's center,
more vibration than sound,
more heat than shape. Upon an X
made of shimmering tape stood a man
in a white suit waving pennants.
Suddenly his arms jerked downward
like a stricken dowser. A squadron
of seagulls scrambled. The man ran.
My mother let go my hand, pushed ahead
as the blimp's belly opened and the sky
turned into a crackled, then collapsing
dome of Melmac.

The ropes did not hold—
deputies fled as the wives
rushed to catch the Melmac.
Slices of pink and green and yellow
and my mother's blue
scudded down hard at them.
The cups hit first, thunking heads.
The bowls punched and gouged.
Plates and saucers slapped and cut.
Some women reached up, palms outward

in acceptance or prayer, as if the projectiles
would waft and settle into some perfect
vision of Melmac displayed in the finest homes.
They were the worst bloodied.
Some stumbled out crying,
hair and dresses ruined,
dazedly clutching maybe a cup.
Then my mother emerged, staggering, smiling,
with arms crossed, embracing
at least twenty tar-smeared pieces,
looking around for me for help.

The whole three miles home
(every house our house), my mother's shoes
thwacked off the sidewalk,
leaving black tracks.

So then she had it all, all
blue. High on her special shelf
cups gripped cups,
bowls brimmed tight with bowls,
saucers clicked into saucers, and
the plates—triuned for meat,
potatoes, and carrots or peas—
grasped together like vertebrae.

After the rare meals served upon Melmac,
I was the one who washed the dishes.
Alone at the sink, suds pinging, I loved
the simple solid sense of them.
I wanted thousands more, of every color,
to build towers climbing up
and out of the house.
Soaped, scrubbed, scraped,
scored, scarified, scarred if need be,
but *clean*—annealed in my care,
they locked, locked, locked
each into the other. Even when my mother
went behind her bedroom door,
I never knew so sure, so right a fit.

*

JACK COLLOM

Sidonie

I walked especially to the Brown Deer Grill
to visit Sidonie the butterfly-haired barmaid
opened the broken door of baubled deal

& sauntered in. Cow-Cow Silverblatt was
wringing opalescent rumbles from the
toy piano perched atop the bar. whaddlya

have? she asked, her eyes shrouded with cool
Flaubertian daily doings like some made-up city
just before Tarzan discovered it

wine, I grinned. later she brought it, & discovered
a bit of cork floating near the rim. oh oh, what's that?
that's all right, I quicklied, dot of earth

in the yellow sky of wine. no reply, I fumbled for the h.
uppmann in my shirt & glanced about the Brown Deer Grill,
    with pleasure. . .
here, said Sidonie, & proferred her ruby ring

to which I did press my cold cigarette, soon sucking
warm blue smoke that spoke of slow aromatic Anatolian
growth & the clash of scimitars

the evening sluiced by like the qualms of a would-be
assassin . . . goats & wraiths & even pickerels.
were dancing, splashing, all about but my eyes & feelings

became riveted
to the speck of cork that floated in my slightly lowered wine
    then
what if this

little thing is a great rough globe to someone
perhaps four-legged lurching weakly across its
jagged brown gobis, puzzled by a sweet intoxicating

scent, only to find as it barely hauls
itself over one last rough brown rock
a great soft mellow sea?—it gratefully

slips into the likely liquid, begins swimming
lazily under a night sky grammared by
giant light bulbs & evanescent smoky ways. . .

I lifted the glass & sipped—a horrible upheaval
of the yellow ocean, gravity spun, blood crashed, & then a
    mighty flow
down & down dark warmth—hell or heaven? it wondered

c'mon, said Sidonie, leading me by the hand to
her backroom alabaster-steaded rumbed, we've gotta get
that little critter out

*

Phone Number

when I was fifteen years of age
I stepped upon the slow-chapp'd stage
of formal labor. got a place
improving of Cook County's face
by cutting weeds & picking trash
up left by picnics quick & rash.
this work I did for Forest Preserve
District something; I did serve
two men as helper, one named Pesek,
one named something like it: Sebek.
there was a ranger, Callahan,
a lazy, lean-back, pipesmoke man,
who quoted poetry to me,
the following couplet, wild & free:
"The boy stood on the burning deck
eating peanuts by the peck."

Pesek & Sebek & I rode out
by 9 o'clock, with little doubt,
in District's wornout pickup truck
detritus of the woods to pluck
each day. we'd stop & drink a cup
of coffee or a sodapop up
along the way. we'd work a bunch
(about an hour), then have lunch,
a nice, long lunch among the stubs
of weeds we'd chopped, while watching flocks
of 'hoppers, work some more, then Cubs-
time, on Joe's radio, maybe Sox-,
depending on which team was home.
late afternoon we'd start to roam
"homeward," motors fixed & tools
cleaned up—we tried to 'bide by rules.

one day, at District, Eddie Buric
called some broad about some whoorish
assignation. first he chatted
with the maid, & then the fatted
calf herself, a dame of rings
& social fame in Western Springs.
this I gathered from the jokes
the men would mutter, envious pokes
at Eddie—he a Bohunk lean,
to screw a lady rich; I mean,
I wondered greatly at this stuff.
& then at home I had the guff
(since I had heard the number spoken)
to look through all the terse & broken
language of the phonebook for
the lady's name who was a "whore."
or was that Eddie? anyways
I found the name, & great amaze
filled my glowing teenage mind.
next day I blurted out my find
to Eddie, thinking he would bless
me for my clever doggedness.
he was my friend & very warm.
but now a sort of purple swarm
suffused his face at what I did;
the others cried, "he's just a kid!"
& slowly Eddie let his rage
die down—till on this page
some squiggle of it now appears
after an ice of thirty years.

it was a magic job I liked;
I used to get there on my bike.

*

PAUL HOOVER

Ode to the Protestant Poets

On, dour! Oh, Mayflower! But enough of that.
Air Step Fan Fare is a sign in a Loop shoe store.
It reminds me of Ensor, one of his titles,
but not Jesus Christ Enters Into Brussels—
I'll have to think of it later
or find it in an old notebook.
You see, I've been pretty poetic lately.
I've got to stop that or no one will talk to me.
Maxine's writing stories; they're pretty good, in fact,
and it's hard to be Wallace Stevens in 1980
with a treacherous farmboy heart:
"The barn is full of leaves, so why am I crying?"
and that sort of thing. Who said, by the way,
"In poetry one only desires an attractive mind at work"?
Probably Stevens again, though I'm beginning to think
I said it. The question is: am I attractive enough?
After all, I'm Protestant. Mirrors make me nervous,
insubstantial. How can I be attractive, you wonder,
when I always act so dignified?
Once I said "fuck" in a poem; that makes me
a little attractive (Dear Mom, I didn't mean a word).
There's my beautiful head on a chair,
propped on the usual ascot,
speaking to the class: "The assignment for next time
is the history of blue in seventeen lines."
I bet they think I'm rugged, but to tell the truth
I'm a sissy, splintery poet-boy

who's "very sensitive" and holds his heart a lot.
Yes, I'm "interested in philosophy,"
though I know next to nothing about it.
I prefer to think I thought everything up,
but I'm dumber than Aristotle, thicker than
Archimedean water. It was only this year
that I finally understood the parable of the cave.
I'd had it confused with Kafka's parable of the law,
where you stand at the door forever,
bullied into eternity by your own timidness.
But now I'm on the train, and we pass the Aragon
where Freddy Feelings is playing,
a Latin Rod McKuen, or "elegant young roughneck."
Describing the tornado, a guy in the paper says,
"It looked like a big blue mountain turned upside down."
You can tell he thought about it. I'd almost say
he thought the whole thing up.
Mostly I believe what I read in the papers,
Model Railroader, and *Popular Mechanics*.
Today, May 3, there's not much happening.
In Chicago a yellow dog leans from a window,
watching this train go by. I can see an elbow
drinking beer in Uptown. A child is dancing on a porch
and looking up at the sky. There's maybe a rat somewhere,
and a large empty ballpark with crisply snapping flags
is where the Cubs will play tomorrow,
stiff as nurses and slow as metaphysicians.

*

The School for Objects

The world begins with rough and smooth,
stone in mouth, spool in hand, their
difference in a dream, and how you differ

touching them, formless as the weather.
They wince to a single nod, are impotent
to speak in states of always being, deep
from edge to edge. Their anecdote's inert,
a calm voice saying calmer things.

Nothing happens, then it happens again,
like mica flecks on metal that make the building
shine. Call it ordinary brilliance.
A stone is not a spool, nor are "two stones
each other's monument." They're shifting
monuments, take no risks, are true.

*

Trumpet Voluntary

Like pianos advancing on ice, each moment's
slow enough. The later years are agile,
leaping in with a razor, angry about something.
What do objects think? They're thinking you in bed,
cope with your delight, and yet a graver solitude
does not exist in Hor Zagreb or Paris.
An eye in a blue fishbowl, you imitate the room.
Each song's unsigned, sideways and unsteady,

and while the neighborhood is pleasant
with its silly eternal flame and women embracing
on trains, you hover like a change of subject.
Call it dangling conversation, but dangling from what?
In a desert tent an 8×10 hangs from canvas walls.
It's the president of the country, scowling.

*

On History

"The murderer came down the chimney,
committed the foul deed and disappeared. . . ."
And it was beautiful outside.
The beautiful snow was falling,
heaping itself up in the clearing
where Anselm once kissed Clara.
The plowboy stops to ponder
his horse's shine and flicker
there in the warm stable.
It is good to be him, at such a time.
Imagine a castle. It will do for the scene,
maidens bending strangely at the knee,
leopards and deer together.
It is the only way we know to draw them,
everything skewed, flat-faced, wan.
A formal silence: the painting is drying
out on the line with the laundry.
One looks closely, as if history were really in it,
smoking elders assured in their power,
stupid-looking children.
Then something goes round in the head
like a hawk circling stuffed game,
a way also of conceiving events.
I.e., history is a bad painting
hanging on a clothesline.
The painter's children run around.
But consider also
the murderer's tracks in the snow,
their perfect calmness and alignment
approaching the awful house, and how,
sometimes later, they zig-zag crazily back
in no decided direction.

❊

Long History of the Short Poem

She dreamed they lived in Africa,
on a beautiful green savannah,
where they raised speckled apples
and owned a bright blue ladder.
Life was good and they were happy.
The following day, she knew,
they had to go on a trip
to buy some beautiful dirt,
the most beautiful dirt in the world!

This was a dream about money.

He dreamed he was lost in space,
floating around in a silver capsule,
and the name on his suit was Geezer.
Maybe he was old, the Geezer in Space or something.
He couldn't tell, since there wasn't a mirror,
just lots of fuzzy chrome.
All he could see was the tip of his nose,
which looked about the same.
The odd thing was, this music kept playing,
a black polka band or a white reggae group—
he couldn't tell the difference.
He also remembered thinking,
as he looked toward Saturn,
"If only I had a sister,
there would be nothing to fear."

This was a dream about courage.

She dreamed they owned an aquarium,
but in order to make it work
they had to put quarters in it,
like a Vibra-bed or TV set.

After they put one in,
the fish started moving again,
the water lights came on,
and the little mill in the corner,
with its plastic man in the doorway,
began to turn its wheel.

It was then, of course, they knew she was pregnant.

*

RODGER KAMENETZ

Pilpul

Rabbi, if a child is born with two heads
which head should wear the yarmulke
on which head the tefillin?
Some say the right head and some
say the left. All quote Torah.
Some say both heads, just in case.

But if a man is born with two heads
he is always confused. He never knows
on which head to wear the yarmulke.

Two heads and only two eyes.
He walks toward himself
in the old cemetery, where the rabbis
are buried. There seems to be some
disagreement: some are saying
we are dead; others, we are alive.
Some say both, all quote Torah.

*

Scraps

After he blacked out
backed over a gas main
cracked a fire hydrant

crashed into a window
crushed two parked cars
and nearly killed a dog

they took away his license.

And the family said why don't you two
move up there with him but we said
no we have our own life to live
so went down to Virginia.

And he said, How are you living there?
Grandpa, we have no running water
no bathroom, just an outhouse, no heat
we cut our own wood for fires.

And he said, I told your father not
to send you to Harvard.
Better you should have stayed at the state school.
Now your eyes are in the woods.

What do you mean, Grandpa?
but he just said,
They gave you everything
and you start from scraps.

———————

The Jews' history was huge and murky
no room for it anywhere in Europe.
If only the Jews could inherit Texas
it might be big enough to hold their past.

The Jews who went out West
wore cowboy hats
like Cousin Dan from Oklahoma
who showed up
at my grandfather's funeral

by uncanny instinct
in his cowboy hat and boots
and just sat in the living room
while we stared.

It is amazing how the land
will transform a man's face:
Cousin Dan looked part Cherokee
part fat cat oilman
(he sold buttons).
And he spoke with a twang,
the yarmulke kept falling off
his ten gallon head,
only a cowboy hat
would fit.

———————

Being Jewish is magnetic.
A polarity points us
in the same direction
just as all synagogues
have a praying wall facing east.
So that around a Jew, even if
he doesn't know he's a Jew,
there's a disturbance in the air,
something has cut across
his spiritual field,
someone is interfering
with the regular broadcast
to insert a special message.

Because what 5000 years
would sound like is
a lot of Jews killed
for no particular reason
over and over
in an insistent rhythm

that beats under ordinary time
sending shocks everywhere.
Any time a metaphor
gets out of hand
more Jews are killed
to restore the general complacency.

*

ALBERTO RIOS

Incident at Imuris

Mr. Aplinio Morales has reported this:
They were not after all
Watermelons, it was not the wild
Fruit patch they at first had thought;
In the manner of what moths do,
These were cocoons, as every child has
Picked up and squeezed,
But from in these came and they saw
Thousands of green-winged half moths,
Half moths, and not exactly butterflies,
Not exactly puppies—
A name for them did not exist here.
Half this and some of that,
What was familiar and what might be European.
And when the fruit rotted, or seemed to rot—
Almost all of them on the same day—
From out of each husk the beasts flew
Fat, equipped, at ease
So that they were not so much
Hungry as curious.
The watermelons had been generous homes.
These were not begging animals,
Not raccoons, nor rats,
Not second or third class;
These were the kind that if human
They would have worn dinner jackets
And sniffed, not at anything in particular,

Just as general commentary.
Animals who had time for tea.
Easily distracted and obviously educated
In some inexplicable manner,
The beasts of the watermelons left
The same day, after putting their heads
In windows, bored already
From chasing the horses
And drinking too much from the town well.

*

Juan Rulfo Moved Away

Tonight I am told
Juan Rulfo has died—
If such a thing is possible—
Tuesday last.
We've returned from a party
Watching Halley's comet,
And so should have known.
A heart attack. The way
The comet appeared
In the act itself of exploding,
Trying so hard to get somewhere
That something gets left:
In the cartoons
The way a creature runs so fast
It leaves its eyebrows behind.
A heart attack of the stars.
We have given medicine
          To our new son,
Almost eight weeks old this afternoon.
This boy trying to sleep now

Lying somewhere in between us
All, the sky, Juan Rulfo, my arms.
Juan Rulfo leaving so quickly
He did not pack bags.
I could not have guessed
He would be giving this boy room,
That he would leave as a lesson
The simple end of his book
Where a certain Mr. Paramo collapses
Into a pile of stones
Because he was a bad man.

*

Saints, and Their Care

Doña Gabriela made the front
        and biggest room of the house green
As a practical matter and in homage to
The fine framed picture of the painting
La Virgen de Guadalupe, and its coloration
        with which everyone is familiar
As she appeared to Juan Diego the Indian.
The white doilies on the green chairs furthermore
Made a pleasing contrast
With or without their having any inner knowledge
        of the presence of the picture in the room,
The doilies with their lace aspect
        looking like something one supposes
The Virgin must have worn, or desired to wear,
A color she wept from her eyes
Though the picture of the painting did not show it.
Green was her color, but white was her desire:
In her eyes, the way the pupils and irises
        were all business

But then all of the white to the sides
       being what she did in her leisure time
       after supper, after taking care of the dogs
       and having covered the parrot for sleep.
She was a saint, and this is their way,
       thought Doña Gabriela as she was finished
       with all of the pieces of the room.
To make one look only into the centers of their eyes.

*

BOB ROSENTHAL

Rude Awakenings

The man who sits on the bottom step
And sees the world as he did when toddling
Stands up still with the child eye
It will take time for this to grow up.
A seedling moment quietly dents his face
A wind of solid color pushes out the skin
The horseshoe spot ages the Autumn green
Before yellow and total waste.
There is no great disgrace for him than to be untoward
To the one he loves, and love is bitter refuge,
The truth peeks around the corner. He kicks
The trees in their yellow & orange dress.
He idles badly, a crank without a case,
To be remembered in love, a clear molting sensation.

*

Kissing Game

there is a coke bottle on the roof
with no one to spin it
filled with Florida sand
it is white and beige
with the sun striking the glass
it is a tint of green
it is a registered ® trademark

my middle name is Mark
and writing is my trade
tho not much my livelihood
and in truth I am a writer
of no ideas no things
nothing old or new
I bring no transcendent infusion
I do not write with my cock
I used to believe that it was someone
else who wrote my poems
I sat back unaccountable
but then my poems got better
so I figured it must be me
the great subjects are buried in the white
Floridian sand
and I must drink grit
just to see myself on a
bookshelf with a stiff spine
and black print declaring
a title and intention
and outrageous happening
it was Joe in *Great Expectations*
who declared the fun of reading
was to find your own name among
the words
speaking of words reminds me of writing
besides reading
reading reminds me of
taking a speed reading class
and learning that I needed glasses
now my glasses are like my names
I do not visualize them upon me
and even though I do think now
that I write these poems
I do not wear them like glasses
seeing all but them

or like a silent forgotten
middle Mark
there is a well-known trade
to get the words
then to get the words right
and then there is you
to give them all to
and you never were me
and you forever will be
the words and kisses
spinning the bottle

*

Pretty Vomit

see through four blocks
of see-through buildings
white smoke edging over
grey morning roofs
high rise pastel shades
balcon bacon and bar-b-que
helicopter trailing a seaplane
over the East River skyway
dogs collect in Tompkins
Square and yowl bark
Spring and smoke and
dissolution where grass
grows in isolation
blades separated by
caked building rubble
slipping into pretty vomit
St. Mark's Place
where the night before
twenty boys in
black leathers

lined the side of the bar
a row of black plastic bags
perforated leak red and yellow
gauze into the curb
bus stalls in the Avenue
the super emerges
from below the stoop
a bucket of steaming water
    slop   slop

*

Slightly Old

all of our machines need repair
the typewriter sticks
the amplifier changes volume of its own
the cassette machine died last year
the blender is starting to moan
a thought: I am getting old
In the World I'm slightly daft
I just got invited to my high school
        ten year reunion
for the last two years my ankles
        have popped and cracked
I can't even drink like I used to
only mothers look me over on the street
"Where are the masterpieces?" cries every cup of coffee
I am the former generation
      my hair is long
        I wear beads
Oh God, I gargle at night
        & feel like puking in the day
but "everything's going to be different"
If I can only make twenty-eight

*

Publishing 2001

it had to be a big book to be a whale
a bear, a city, or a song
as a moth is witness
smoothing out its antennae
   with silky legs
and then another sudden
    flutter barrage
on the wrong side of the screen

the screen is exhausting

or a man enlarged by sources
parting lips lest a part
paralyze

who is a man?
   the moth up and steps up
and says
  "Who's asking?"

the single chord the wild bar

*

The Eighties Becoming

it's day one of the end
oh sure there'll be plenty more
    warming days
cooling days but now in the beginning
of Primavera loss is global
even on East Eleven Street
jays and sparrows are singing

my yarning hands in the window
frightens the red head
but you say this is the end
OK the beginning of the end
                        how come?
Why now?   the Eighties has meant a tug-
of-war between lousy myth and cruddy war
the choice so nonexistent as
drive despair home like a second car in every garage
hard ain't it hard   to love one
who never will be true
the despair of the present can be erased
as simple as video tape
but before you can buy yr
integrated television video cassette stereo receiver intercom
before that comes to Radio Shack
it's time to look back
because looking forward is just messing
the gel on the lens
looking back through the horrors
history bathes us with
perhaps in that sanguine foreclosure the past
biting its own tail
a continuity in grim paradise
there must be a way to survive
the plush moment of the capitol
for my children will enter the world again
in the 90's

                                                I pray

to honestly follow them
for in my time all I have seen
are the ends   the beginnings
the middles and ends
                of ends
and enough has stood between
                the users and the other 95%

looking blank to the wall
we must hit it again and again
we must spill the blood of our vision
onto the corrugated
blockade that megabucks mulch into
even if I can be no more succinct than a mouse
gnawing a way under the floor
just for the right to crawl after my children

*

FRANK POLITE

Adman Into Toad

What's a toad *like*?
I mean, *image-wise*, what does the toad
project, resemble best?

Genius? Beauty? Soapflakes?
Whispering Sin as Milton saw it?
A Weird little bug world's circus tent?
Perhaps a slurp of something
turned inside-out, or better yet,
a threatened burp?

I think, image-wise, none of these really work.

So, O to be a toad!
To not be thought of *as*, not advertised above
my head, my load, my bed and board;
to sit slumped, flat-heeled in the sun,
to be, content to be
my own incredible imagery.

✳

The Japanese Consulate

I'm hurting a lot today.
O.K. I'm thirty, not a kid anymore
to pace about quoting *Tears from the depth
of some divine despair*, or adjusting
my face so as not to scare hell out of birds

that veer off anyway.

So, let's say I need
tighter control over my emotions, which
translates, Wider Escapes. I need (I know it)
wider escapes. Runways. . .

Maybe if I knew what's getting me down
I might . . . (Pain abounds with cliches, ever
notice that? Right down to essentials
always).
But, something must be done . . .

and so I have come to the Japanese Consulate.

I ask Information Papa-san
if any escaped?

He says, it was a religious act, perhaps
fanatical, that Kamikaze means
divine wind, that we must think of The Bomb
and forgive each other.

I tell Papa-san I agree
not to think of The Bomb. I ask again
if any escaped. He says, yes. One,

Pilot X, chickened over a battleship
at Subic Bay and was last seen racing west.
They figure the fink ran out of gas
and splashed somewhere mid-Pacific. I ask,

what are the chances he made it to Ohio, say
a 1943 summer day I'm taking my bike apart?
Startled look! You crazy, sick, or what?

I don't see it that way, O my Kamikaze heart.

✻

Empty at the Heart of Things

Sandy,

Hi, got your letter a few days ago.
Hey everyone needs to let off steam once
in awhile and I do my fair share.
I know your problem well and don't blame
you for letting loose at all.
And it does make you feel 100% better,
and I'm sure things have cooled
down a bit now anyhow.

Everything is pretty much the same here
as you last saw me a few days ago.
I went out and got a book and record
and now spend my time doing my 2
favorite things, reading and listening
to my favorite songs. I bought a
Donna Fargo album and Harold Robbins'
latest novel. It gives me a big

Lift to just sing along with my records.
It makes me feel less lonely. Bob
just isn't around all the time and I get
depressed. I like to think that
I'm the most important person in his life
but it isn't that way anymore. He's got
his friends and he likes to spend his time
with them. I guess if I had friends

my age it would be easier to accept.
But I don't have anyone now I can really
talk to and feel comfortable with.
It seems that most people just want

the latest gossip, and mostly that's you,
if you know what I mean. With the kids
I just can't pack up and go anywhere
I want. It's practically impossible, so

I just stick to my books and records
and radio. My biggest thrill is shopping
and walking around the mall. And then
afterwards I feel miserable and

kinda empty, you know. I guess because
I spent too much money. I say power
to ya if your getting back into religion.
Sometimes it really helps you feel

better about yourself and your problems.
Life isn't easy, and believing
something makes it liveable. I have my
religious feeling buried deep in my
heart because Bob laughs at my feelings
and point of view on anything and
everything. So if I feel something
I just keep it to myself.

Well, Bobby is crying and getting
cranky, so I better go. I hope things
are going smoothly for you now.
Kiss the baby for me and take care.
Write when you can. Love,

Sharon

(letter found Easter Sunday morning, Youngstown, Ohio, 1979)

✻

WILLIAM HATHAWAY

When I Was Dying

The dullest people I knew
gathered round my bed,
the ones who made me feel
stupid or ashamed when I
was living. My flustered
wife held my hand like a fish,
worried our children might
eat poorly at the neighbor lady's.
Outside the door I heard
the nurse with massive arms
send off students who learned
nothing from me, but came
anyway for final grade changes.
And while my mother's clergy-
man read aloud the governor's
telegram I died. What did
I care, bobbing off in dark
blue sea, under light blue sky?

*

Dear Wordsworth

I liked your poems "Michael," "We Are Seven,"
and "Idiot Boy" very much, even when
the teacher read them aloud and cried

and blew her nose. "Tintern Abbcy" is really neat,
though I don't understand it. I did a walk-
athon for March of Dimes once. I hate your poem
"Daffodils." Ha-ha, that's just a joke,
I just don't know better because of television.
Seriously, why did you become such a crusty,
old poo-poo? Professor Borck at the university
says you got tired of not being rich. My
dad says poor people are happy being poor
because God loves everyone—even poets. I
think it would be romantic to have a French
girlfriend and a dopefiend for a best friend.
I can hardly wait until my creepy sister
goes to college and I can have her room.
My best friend is Veralee Broussard and I can
talk about anything with her. I wish you
could tell me what it's like to be dead.
It would feel neat to lie in a cozy coffin
underneath the flowers and know everything
Really, you rot and go to heaven or hell.
Well, this is almost two hundred words, so
I have to go. Tomorrow we read Amy Lowell.
Mrs. Curtis says she smoked cigars!

※

The American Poet—"But Since It Came to Good . . ."

I knew a man who like us awoke alone
in the midst of his life, in a dark wood.
Always in his home there was wet stillness
of impending storm and a moist, rich smell
of fear wafted from the shadows of open doors.

His verse never advertised sick spirit like
my mean complaints I called "laments."
His wife was beautiful, kind and wise.
He was kind and wise. Indeed, all who wrote
knew his name, yet only the few friends
of his region knew the mute misery
of his table. Frankly, I thought his poems
dull. He seemed like an old world cabinet-
maker, persisting stubbornly in meticulous
craft—patiently squaring and leveling
by eye, desperately deaf to the roaring silence
of his cobwebbed shop. He did one thing
I particularly liked. He put out peanutbutter
crackers on a plate for the mice that lived
about his writing shed. They scampered freely
everywhere, leaving their droppings in his
books and work. I would have tried to pet
their soft, white bellies, but he just watched.
His red, cragged face cupped in his red hand,
one eye glittered behind splayed fingers with
melancholic reprieve. The other, severe and weary
under the great thatch of eyebrow stared
for hours at his little mice. In late Fall
a neighbor roofing this man's house fell
from that roof and broke his neck. The poet
found him twisted grotesquely in the gray
flowerbed, mouth agape and eyes staring.
If it had been me I would have babbled
manicly of nothing else for weeks until
my wife gagged me with a look and phrase.
But he said nothing, though the storm clouds
grew. Then one night over a meal of many
drinks he began to speak, and the things
he said were terrible. To you they will seem
mad, perhaps the banal clatter of our times,
but this man could think and talk—far too well

I think. He said it was his fault the man
was dead because he gave him a beer, but
that did not matter. He said he did not care
for any of our lives or deaths, we did not
matter. He wished Dante's hell was real,
but it was not and he hated our souls
which were not real. He wished everyone
was dead, except maybe Richard Nixon,
because we were boring and deserved to die.
He was one of my fathers and he said these
things to me. Now, living day by day
to keep sober, I put down my pencil
in the dead of night and cannot sleep.
Wired with coffee, my mind buzzing
with echoes I think of him, and of Hemingway's
story about the insomniac who thought
too well. The very first opiate of the people
is opium. I had lost sight of that simple truth
and so had my beloved teacher. Oh, don't be
smug, there are still circles in our modern
diagram of hell and a spot where each can wail.
Avarice, malice, cowardice—cruel, medieval
words that hiss too strong for our enfeebled
"solipsism" or "sick psyche." Insidious whispers
of authority so safely abstract we can accept
them eagerly. I do not want my sleeping wife
and children to die, but it will come to pass.
I need not die with a stinking liver, raving
in their faces. We will submit in dignity
with generous grief. Christ! In my mind's eye
I see those mice skittering back
night after night in the dusty plate.

✻

HARRISON FISHER

The Controls

George tells the story
of the blond acquaintance
who accidentally killed his mother
with a shotgun, and adds

that this same boy then killed
his father in a car accident
while the boy was driving
with only a learner's permit.

Martha describes George's first,
necessarily unpublished novel,
which is the story of this boy
and his fluke parenticides.

George *is* the boy. The Father
of Our Country. He needs only
the imaginary son to erase
a whole nuclear unit,

the Anti-Father who lives
out the sire he killed by
"killing" his own issue first.
For, just as birds are so

clearly lizards, the woman appears
heavy and painfully sentient,
the erect atom speeding up,
a quantum wish for a second leap.

Sorry: a second wish for a quantum
leap. Concentric charge redistributes.
The second wish requires a cancelling
third when the former brings a carrion son.

His heavy footsteps give way to
heavy knocks, the son who lived
his last in a machine. A
paw charges a palm. You can set

the controls to rise from a
houseboy to a stud. My last chance
at what I want most. What right now
do I want most in the world?

*

White Zombie

The morning's underplayed resistance
to the "dark night of the soul" syndrome
handles everything fondly in the murk
of nostalgic ontology, comprising a
catalogue of "This object first untied me
from the world. This object further untied me,
slackening the deeper, secondary bonds
secreted under the flesh. This object

untied me still more; perhaps there were no
fetters left to undo when it came into play.
And this object I have absolutely no
recollection of," wondering how
it inveigled its way into the room.

At the same time, the generic sun
announces its newest bird, bespeaking
the experimental oomph to unhinge
from a lazily-unfurling arc
still a better bird, that marblistic
burst, clear mental image, against
the lingering headache of sky.

✳

MAXINE CHERNOFF

A Name

Suppose your parents had called you Dirk. Wouldn't that be mo-
tive enough to commit a heinous crime, just as Judys always
become nurses and Brads, florists? After the act, your mom would
say, "He was always a good boy. Once on my birthday he gave me
one of those roses stuck in a glass ball. You know, the kind that
never gets soggy"—her Exhibit A. Exhibit B: a surprised corpse,
sharing a last moment of Dirk with the mortician. And Dad
would say, "Dirk once won a contest by spelling the work 'pyr-
rhic,' " and in his alcohol dream he sees the infant Dirk, all pink
and tinsel, signing his birth certificate with a knife. Still, Dirk
should have known better. He could tell you that antimony is
Panama's most important product. He remembered Vasco da
Gama and wished him well. Once he'd made a diorama of the all-
American boyhood: a little farm, cows the size of nails, cottonball
sheep, a corncob silo, but when he signed it Dirk, the crops were
blighted by bad faith. Too bad. And don't forget Exhibits C, D, E
. . . The stolen éclair, the zoo caper, the taunting of a certain Miss
W., who smelled of fried onions. It was his parents' fault. They
called him Dirk.

*

Breasts

If I were French, I'd write
about breasts, structuralist treatments
of breasts, deconstructionist breasts,
Gertrude Stein's breasts in Père Lachaise
under stately marble. Film noire breasts
no larger than olives, Edith Piaf's breasts
shadowed under a song, mad breasts raving
in the bird market on Sunday.
Tanguy breasts softening the landscape,
the politics of nipples (we're all equal).
A friend remembers nursing,
his twin a menacing blur. But wait,
we're in America, where breasts
were pointy until 1968. I once invented
a Busby Berkeley musical with naked women
underwater sitting at a counter
where David Bowie soda-jerked them
ice cream glaciers. It sounds so sexual
but had a Platonic airbrushed air.
Beckett calls them dugs, which makes me think
of potatoes, but who calls breasts potatoes?
Bolshoi dancers strap down their breasts
while practicing at the bar.
You guess they're thinking of sailing,
but probably it's bread, dinner,
and the *Igor Zlotik Show* (their
Phil Donahue). There's a photo of me
getting dressed where I'm surprised
by Paul and try to hide my breasts, and another
this year, posed on a pier, with my breasts
reflected in silver sunglasses. I blame
it on summer when flowers overcome gardens
and breasts point at the stars. Cats
have eight of them, and Colette tells

of a cat nursing its young while
being nursed by its mother. Imagine the scene
rendered human. And then there's the Russian
story about the woman . . . but wait,
they've turned the lights down, and Humphrey
Bogart is staring at Lauren Bacall's breasts
as if they might start speaking.

✻

How Lies Grow

The first time I lied to my baby, I told him that it was his face on
the baby food jar. The second time I lied to my baby, I told him
that he was the best baby in the world, that I hoped he'd never
leave me. Of course I want him to leave me someday. I don't want
him to become one of those fat shadows who live in their moth-
er's houses watching game shows all day. The third time I lied to
my baby I said, "Isn't she nice?" of the woman who'd caressed him
in his carriage. She was old and ugly and had a disease. The fourth
time I lied to my baby, I told him the truth, I thought. I told him
how he'd have to leave me someday or risk becoming a man in a
bow tie who eats macaroni on Fridays. I told him it was for the
best, but then I thought, I want him to live with me forever.
Someday he'll leave me: then what will I do?

✻

Utopia TV Store

Amid rows of tvs, screens blank as postcards from cemeteries, we
lose ourselves. And while we wait to have our sets repaired, we
discuss the owner's inventions: a shadow that never changes

length or width, a test pattern of pure memory, adapting through the ages of man.

Who says there are no heroes? We love the way he plunges his hand into sets, no regard for personal safety. It's those explosions no more frightening than weather reports from other cities that calm us.

Often customers who die leave their tvs in his care, he's told us with some tenderness. "Here's one that a widow left behind 10 years ago. Watching it's like washing clothes underwater. Total immersion. And let me tell you. It's better off than any of us. Inherited a Cadillac Seville, a houseboat, an empty lot. But does it need those things? Examine its console. Dark, smooth. Look at the antenna. No rigidity there, relaxed, wanting nothing."

"Of course it's happy here," we add, taking our usual cue. Yes, Utopia TV Store is always open. Even on Christmas Eve we're treated as guests. Mistletoe decking the sets. Perry Como beaming in on every capable tube as we focus our eyes on a pinpoint. Automatically tuning in and fading out, we listen to the steady CLICK CLICK, knowing we owe it our lives, more hazy and blurred with each day.

*

DAVID TRINIDAD

Monday, Monday

Radio's reality when
the hits just keep
happening: "I want
to kiss like lovers
do. . ." Why is it
I've always mistaken
these lyrics for my
true feelings? The
disc jockey says it's
spring and instantly
I'm filled with such
joy! Is it possible
that I'm experiencing
nature for the first
time? In the morning
the sun wakes me
and I am genuinely
moved, almost happy
to be alive. For a
couple of weeks it'd
been getting a little
bit brighter every
day. I wasn't aware
of this change until
the morning I noticed
the angle at which
the light hit your
GQ calendar, fully

accentuating the aus-
tere features of this
month's male model, as
I sat in the kitchen,
in your maroon robe,
and waited for my tea
to cool. I was thinking
about my feelings, about
how much I loved the sun
when I was a child and
how I loved the dark
as well, how thrilling
it was to lay in bed
on windy nights and
listen to the sound of
bushes and branches being
thrashed about outside.

Actually, that's what
I was thinking while
you were making the tea.
I was staring at the
calendar, at the smoke
from the tip of my
cigarette as it drifted
in the sunlight toward
the open window, when
you set the steaming
fifties-style cup in
front of me. Was it
at this point that
my manner changed?

Your gesture reminded
me of innumerable
mornings spent with

my parents in the pink
kitchen of my childhood.
I remembered my mother,
how she always wore her
gaudy floral bathrobe
and shuffled about in
her bedroom slippers as
she dutifully served us
breakfast. My father
sat alone at one end
of the table, his stern
face all but hidden
behind the front page
of the *Los Angeles Times*.
They seldom spoke. I
felt the tension between
them, watched with sleep-
filled eyes as he gave
her the obligatory kiss
on the cheek, then
clicked his briefcase
shut and, without a word,
walked out the door.

As I was getting dressed,
you grabbed me, kissed
me on the lips, said
something romantic.
I left your apartment
feeling confused, got
on the freeway and
inched my way through
the bumper-to-bumper
traffic. I was confused
about sex, about the
unexpected ambivalence
which, the night before,

prompted my hesitancy
and nonchalant attitude:
"It's late," I said,
"Let's just sleep."
The cars ahead of me
wouldn't budge. I
turned on the radio and
started changing stations.
I was afraid I would
always be that anxious,
that self-obsessed, that
I might never to able
to handle a mature
relationship. Stuck on
the freeway like that,
I was tempted to get
into it, the pain and
the drama, but the mood
soon passed. (After
all, it *is* spring.)
At last, traffic picked
up and I enjoyed the
rest of the drive, kept
the radio on all
the way to work and
listened to all those
songs, though I finally
realized those songs
were no longer my feelings.

✻

Meet the Supremes

When Petula Clark sang "Downtown," I wished I
could go there with her. I wanted to be free
to have fun and fall in love, but from suburbia
the city appeared more distant and dangerous
than it actually was. I withdrew and stayed
in my room, listened to Jackie DeShannon sing
"What The World Needs Now Is Love." I agreed,
but being somewhat morose considered the song
a hopeless plea. I listened to Skeeter Davis'
"The End Of The World" and decided that was
what it would be when I broke up with my first
boyfriend. My head spun as fast as the singles
I saved pennies to buy: "It's My Party," "Give
Him A Great Big Kiss," "(I Want To Be) Bobby's
Girl," "My Guy"—the list goes on. At the age
of ten, I rushed to the record store to get
"Little" Peggy March's smash hit, "I Will Follow
Him." An extreme example of lovesick devotion,
it held down the top spot on the charts for
several weeks in the spring of 1963. "Chapel
Of Love" came out the following year and was
my favorite song for a long time. The girls
who recorded it, The Dixie Cups, originally
called themselves Little Miss & The Muffets.
They cut three hits in quick succession, then
disappeared. I remember almost the exact moment
I heard "Johnny Angel" for the first time: it
came on the car radio while we were driving
down to Laguna Beach to visit some friends of
the family. In the back seat, I set the book I'd
been reading beside me and listened, completely
mesmerized by Shelley Fabares' dreamy, teenage
desire. Her sentimental lyrics continue to move
me (although not as intensely) to this day.

Throughout adolescence, no other song affected
me quite like that one.
On my transistor, I listened to the Top Twenty
countdown as, week after week, more girl singers
and groups
came and went than I could keep track of:

Darlene Love,
Brenda Lee,
Dee Dee Sharp,
Martha Reeves
& The Vandellas,
The Chantels,
The Shirelles,
The Marvelettes,
The Ronettes,
The Girlfriends,
The Rag Dolls,
The Cinderellas,
Alice Wonderland,
Annette, The
Beach-Nuts, Nancy
Sinatra, Little
Eva, Veronica,
The Pandoras,
Bonnie & The
Treasures,
The Murmaids,
Evie Sands,
The Pussycats,
The Patty Cakes,
The Trans-Sisters,
The Pixies Three,
The Toys, The
Juliettes and
The Pirouettes,

The Charmettes,
The Powder Puffs,
Patti Lace &
The Petticoats,
The Rev-Lons,
The Ribbons,
The Fashions,
The Petites,
The Pin-Ups,
Cupcakes,
Chic-Lets,
Jelly Beans,
Cookies, Goodies,
Sherrys, Crystals,
Butterflys,
Bouquets,
Blue-Belles,
Honey Bees,
Dusty Springfield,
The Raindrops,
The Blossoms,
The Petals,
The Angels,
The Halos,
The Hearts,
The Flamettes,
The Goodnight
Kisses, The
Strangeloves,
and The Bitter
Sweets.

I was ecstatic when "He's So Fine" hit the #1 spot.
I couldn't get the lyrics out of my mind and continued
to hum "Doo-lang Doo-lang Doo-lang" long after
puberty ended, a kind of secret anthem. Although

The Chiffons tried to repeat their early success
with numerous singles, none did as well as their
first release. "Sweet Talkin' Guy" came close,
sweeping them back into the Top Ten for a short
time, but after that there were no more hits.
Lulu made her mark in the mid-sixties with "To Sir
    With Love,"
which I would put on in order to daydream about
my junior high algebra instructor. By then I was
a genuine introvert. I'd come home from school,
having been made fun of for carrying my textbooks
like a girl, and listen to song after song from
my ever-expanding record collection. In those
days, no one sounded sadder than The Shangri-Las.
Two pairs of sisters from Queens, they became famous
for their classic "death disc shocker," "Leader Of
    The Pack,"
and for their mod look. They were imitated (but
    never equalled)
by such groups as The Nu-Luvs and The Whyte Boots.
The Shangri-Las stayed on top for a couple of
years, then lost their foothold and split up.
Much later, they appeared on rock 'n' roll revival
shows, an even sadder act since Marge, the fourth
member of the band, had died of an accidental
drug overdose. I started smoking cigarettes around
this time, but wouldn't discover pills, marijuana
or alcohol until my final year of high school.
I loved Lesley Gore because she was always crying
and listened to "As Tears Go By" till the single had
so many scratches I couldn't play it anymore.
I preferred Marianne Faithful to The Beatles and
The Rolling Stones, was fascinated by the stories
about her heroin addiction and suicide attempt.
She's still around. So is Diana Ross. She made
it to superstardom alone, maintaining the success

she'd previously achieved as the lead singer of
The Supremes, one of the most popular girl groups
of all time. Their debut album was the first LP

I owned. Most of the songs on it were hits—
one would reach the top of the charts as another
hit the bottom. Little did I know, as I listened
to "Nothing But Heartaches" and "Where Did Our Love
Go," that nearly twenty years later I would hit
bottom in an unfurnished Hollywood single, drunk
and stoned and fed up, still spinning those same
old tunes. The friction that already existed
within The Supremes escalated in 1967 as Diana
Ross made plans for her solo career. The impending
split hit Florence the hardest. Rebelliously,
she gained weight and missed several performances,
and was finally told to leave the group. The pain
she experienced in the years that followed was
a far cry from the kind of anguish expressed
in The Supremes' greatest hits. Florence lost
the lawsuit she filed against Motown, failed at
a solo career of her own, went through a bitter
divorce, and ended up on welfare. In this classic
photograph of the group, however, Florence is
smiling. Against a black backdrop, she and Mary
look up at and frame Diana, who stands in profile
and raises her right hand, as if toward the future.
The girs' sequinned and tasselled gowns sparkle
as they strike dramatic poses among some Grecian
columns. Thus, The Supremes are captured forever
like this, in an unreal, silvery light. That
moment, they're in heaven. Then, at least for Flo,
begins the long and painful process of letting go.

*

JACK SKELLEY

TV Blooper Spotter

In this very special, final Mod Squad episode,
Marty, the brother of Pete's girlfriend,
and Pete's best friend, is sent to Vietnam
and accidentally killed while handling explosives.
It turns out that the company owned by
Marty's father produced these bombs—
hence the father feels guilty, suicidal,
and in the final scene tries to blow up
his factory to atone his guilt; but at
the last possible moment before he
blows everything apart, Pete pretends he
is the dead son, and the delirious man
is willing to believe. Pete guides the father
down into the center of a maze of pipes
and wires, and listens with compassion
until the father collapses in Pete's arms.
Pete feels suddenly powerful, in control;
and the world is blazing all around him. He takes
the old man's detonation device. He has a big plan.

*

To Marie Osmond

There you are again,
your crystal-perfect face
on the cover of the *Enquirer*.
It seems you're everywhere this Spring,
on more magazines than April has roses.
And yes, your series flopped, but you really are
more suited to the slit sequined dresses of NBC
than to *Family Circle* declarations of virginity.
Lips of a TV Venus should pucker, not pout.

And what a waste that the nine men you love,
hinted at in this week's *Star*, turn out
to be your father and eight brothers, that
the husband you dream of would be another perfect virgin.
Your daddy's Mormon domain is as barren
of life as his head is of hair; let *me* be your conquering
consort and you'll be a far richer heiress, when
the shadows of Utah's long Winter are fled,
and you stand alone on the Rockies, surveying
an ancient city of soft buildings, which transubstantiate
and interpenetrate in moon-aluminum evening, where warm
headlighted insects dance in circles, and golden
movie star men stand upright among beasts,
holding tokens of serpents, sunglasses, electric guitars.

Put aside your moral raiment and I
alone among them come forth to offer
a litany of ardor: my bride, my guide, my lady,
my baby, couch of wisdom, crystal meth
connection, green plastic garden pail,
ice-covered pencil sharpener,
brand-new house in white-hot flames,
bright-painted gate to beautiful things,
interlocking dancer's thighs of black diamonds,
mystical video disk unfolding precisely
like flowers, tree-lined La Cienega to Hollywood
in Autumn, angel of the air, arriving
in clean reception, woman made of cities,
intricately busy with her own construction.
Once we were the issue of chaos, Marie, asleep
in the snows of virtue; now we wake up to mutual delight,
as priests and presidents wither into indefinite night.

*

ART LANGE

Confirmation

Let's look
out the window
where there seems
to be a con-
frontation between
the swollen
sties considered
Chicago-style arch-
itecture (gauche)
and the ghostly
slow quiet
quick of slick
snow shed
by the heavens,
swirls of elegant
inertia inspired
by years of
speculation. It's
a scene too
shrewd to notate
precisely; some
sun loiters
between the blisters
of air barely
audible in the early
evening blight and,
after all, it's
still life

painting after
the manner of,
say, Fairfield
Porter (sort of); so
disheveled even
devils of
will won't find
a home here, riddled
with rationale,
like vaudeville.

*

History

Lots of empty
space. Otherwise
opaque, until
you find yourself
on a cook's
tour of another
civilization,
where the kleenex
chrysanthemum
is national
flower and principal
export. Yet we
find what's lost
in the local
lingo's translation
is nerve, pure
and simple. Who
knew that compulsive
pneumatic patois
bode bad blood,

belied the ghost
I became? After
lunch this life
wears thin, begins
to hesitantly shed
its skin under
scrutiny, haunts
the dark dozing
halls of our
private gallery
with the weight
of a minor key
Hockney. It's great,
but not for me.

*

Poem

Some who are uncertain compel me
toward small blue serge paintings or uncontrollable
satisfaction like an enraged
winter night of lights or darkness of a moment's
grace: resplendent though slight
and fortunate enough in thrall
to be launched into dreams like a waterfall
or a subtle attraction to a life
lived in a calligraphy of casual
haste: words which come shyly
into this shadowy nuance of place
and I recognize it like a friend's face
in the way Sartre says that Giacometti ". . . takes
the fat off space."

*

Le Tombeau de Frank O'Hara

What sky! and I remember suddenly
as the head jerks (left side, eyes open), then
looking out the window one spies Glazunov heard
at the bookstore old in the rusty sounds
of summer browns of Breughel fastidious and slow
footsteps in the Five Spot Orchestra Hall cigarettes
Strega cardigans cognac the New York Times
obituary's on love. Driven to various hypnotic
dives, the precise shape of quartets and symphonies
remain our mirror, solely because we
forgive so easily. And floating through a day
of concise movement like a solo clarinet hot and
asking "What does anyone have that we
don't?" eating March 21st lentil soup

*

CHRISTY SHEFFIELD SANFORD

The Romance of Citrus

(Sectional Version)

Oranges
(Jamaica)

A cloud of esters escapes as Elena splits an orange. She takes each half and on hands and knees scrubs rhythmic circles. She is cleaning the floor of her restaurant after closing. Her husband Eddie bought the oranges from the market woman who is his mistress. A baby cries in the background.

Lemons
(Atlantic City)

On TV the movie star, Susan Sarandon, cuts a lemon and rubs the flesh of the fruit over her bare breasts and arms. She stands at a sink in front of her window. Burt Lancaster watches from across the way. Now Eddie grins as I remove a lemon segment from the fridge and rub it over my pregnant belly.

Grapefruit
(Miami)

Eddie's redheaded lover arranges hors d'oeuvres, and as she rounds the kitchen counter with a tray he squeezes her black velvet bottom. "A fanny like ripe grapefruit," he says to his son, age 7. Rachel smiles, but a sudden impulse to slap Eddie's face frightens her. Then he grabs his bongos, dedicates a jazz improv to her and her cunt throbs.

Limes (New Orleans)	On the verandah Eddie and I check our plane tickets to Guadalajara. Beside purple bougainvilleas we sip Lime Rickeys under the stars. Gazing at the lime rind in his glass, Eddie tells me how after school he used to lick limes, sprinkled with sugar. He flinches when I say, "What we're doing is very dangerous."
Tangerines (Guadalajara)	Eddie puts my feet on his shoes and dances me about—like my father did when I was 8. My daddy taught me to foxtrot to Bob Eberle singing "My heart belongs to Tangerine." I held his waist; he held my shoulders just below the curls. "Eddie," I say, looking at the high cheekbones I love, "would you mind if I changed my name to Tangerine?"

*

Traveling Through Ports That Begin With "M"

(Seafood Medley)

Mobile 1930 (Shrimp)	Jack scrubs the smell of hemp and tar from his hands and weaves his way along the waterfront. He's picking up Pearl. She doesn't want to go. Sure, they were childhood sweethearts, but now she's a platinum blond selling her body to merchant marines and shrimpers. Finally, he visits "Seven Sisters" the conjure woman in Hogansville. She tells him to swab sweat from his right armpit, mix it with cologne and dab it on the desired lady. He has to hold Pearl down to do that. Later she says, "It was your desperation, not spells, that won me."

Maracaibo Sweat rolls down Jack's face as he climbs over a
1935 derrick. It's 82° and almost time for siesta. Schools
(Snapper) of yellow-tail snapper leave the ocean to dart in and
around the lake. Mosquitos thrive in spite of the fish.
At first, Jack's body is strong. Then malaria flattens
him. Beside a lone orange hibiscus, Pearl sets a chair.
She clips the hair of oil riggers and with her intimate
touch she earns enough to book passage on a coffee
boat to Marseilles. Her Uncle Leon de Lesseps has
offered his aid once they land.

Marseilles In a hospital near the quai, Jack tosses with an after-
1940 noon fever. A storm rumbles through the harbor.
(Octopus) Pearl's bedroom chandelier sways and tinkles in the
wind. In a dream she watches the light turn into an
octopus. Tentacles unfurl and squeeze her. She wakes
in Leon's sleepladen embrace. "Men's sex organs are so
much alike," she muses. Something she'd forgotten.
She pats his haunch, slips on her robe and walks into
the garden to plant basil and mint for Jack's tea. He's
almost well. Pearl considers joining the French Resis-
tance.

Manila Jack enters the city by crashing through a wall in a
1945 U.S. tank. He stays to help Filipinos clean up the rub-
(Shark) ble. Pearl didn't think she could have children, but
here she is suckling a war baby. With Jacqueline on her
hip she works for the Red Cross—bathing and barber-
ing the wounded. One day on the way home, she
swoons against a shop. The facade crumbles. She and
Jacqueline barely escape. Meanwhile Jack lends a hand
to a guy hoisting a catch and loses three fingers to a
requiem shark.

Mazatlan Glazed sailfish stud the wall of the yacht club. Jack
1950 finishes a Cuba libre and climbs aboard his sleek
(Sailfish) cruiser. A "billfishing" expert, he's taking out a couple

of rich Texans for a rodeo. Jacks tugs at his cap's bill with its scrambled eggs and secures a shirt-button over his tan stomach, protruding above bermudas. Nearby in his backyard, Jackie, now five, says, "Get back in there!" as she pokes at a scorpion in a jar. In the house Pearl stirs ice tea for Jack's dinner. She adds a sprig of mint and bruises the leaves lightly against the rim of the glass.

*

Dreams of Snakes, Chocolate and Men

Snake	On Captiva Island I sit on a ledge beside palmettos; a blue and green snake sticks its head through pine straw. I lift the reptile, thin as my ring finger, and it expands to a gray, puffy-cheeked, diamond-backed rattler the length of a bed. Trembling I sling the snake onto snapping twigs.
Chocolate Bar	Hmmm, my bittersweet addiction. A waiter serves me a dark, satiny chocolate bar, lumpy with peanuts like a Baby Ruth, but with a few bites missing. My teeth clamp on something hard. I try again. My jaws ache. I shove the confection off the table. The dessert plate breaks.
Snake, Chocolate Bar	A viper slithers over an inedible candy bar. I tear aside the skin, do a cross section on the bar— discover only a teleidoscope of rich designs. Even under the microscope candy looks alluring. Yet the surfaces within surfaces confound me.

Man, Snake, Chocolate Bar	A swarthy man wears a violet shirt and eats pink watermelon. A purple snake shifts in his black hair, slides across his chest, intertwines our legs. He peels a wrapper from his chocolate bar, munches the candy, passes it to me. I taste. "Theobroma—food of the gods," he whispers. A delicious spasm ripples through my pelvis.
Chocolate, Snakes, Man	Last night the chocolate factory exploded and burned. The smell of scorched chocolate permeated every room in my house. The lost luscious promises. In the surrounding woods some snakes fled underground; others died of smoke inhalation. And in the plant a man eating watermelon on his break perished.
Chocolate, Men, Snakes	Even now in the Orinoco basin, harvesters with machetes reap cacao pods for me. My brain still carries the chemicals chocolate and men trigger. All over the world men in violet shirts split watermelons and toast me with their juicy sections. Racers, whips, cobras and kings wait, ready to weave through all my dreams.

*

The Romance of Imprinting

(Cases of Bonding and Possession)

Animal Behavior	Newborn greylag geese follow anyone who moves. But mallards require sound. Some birds learn by sight, others . . . I jump in pond,

swim across; goslings shadow me everywhere. There must come a time when bonding . . . and we all become . . .

Environmental Art

The Oppenheims' (father and son) fingerprints photographed, enlarged, printed with hot tar on landscape. Adjacent grass inexplicably fertilized (NY, 1976). I long for you to include my thumb/index. Could you stamp my identity over part of your. . .

Popular Art

Tattoo located at 11 o'clock, edge of left breast. Two-inch rosy heart with your name needled in—a gold banner with "I belong to .." trailing off. A flowered border of crape myrtle. Each night as I try to sleep, I touch it, consider. . .

Poetry

Poet William Blake glued/gurued into soul of Allen Ginsberg (NY, 1948). Burroughs proposed this analogous to a kind of imprinting process. Allen attempts to loosen adhesives—unstick sunflowers and roses and saintly voices. I offer . . .

The Elements

Tree-like patterns and metal transfers seared into lightning victims' flesh. Scientifically unverifi. . . Bay of Armiro (1825) transfer of horseshoe print from mast to sailor's back. Parishioners in Wells, England (1595), marked with crosses. Numerous scattered. . .

*

Scattered Fog

*(Caresses and Bruises Received
in the Mist)*

1. Smoky bar in Matamoros. Blind date. We each have a Margarita. His with salt, mine without. He grasps my hand. Orgasm—a miracle, rare as one of those cases in which a human spontaneously combusts. My back is warm for him.

2. Fire starts in the peat bogs, spreads across a south Georgia pine forest. Five miles away we camp, make love in a haze. In the morning we see a fringe of black charred grass 50 ft. from our site. Smoke smells in our hair, on our clothes.

3. I pull on my boots while he twists up hairpin curves in the Smokies. "Heavy Fog, Next 5 mi." We begin our hike down the Appalachian trail; 30 min. later a car shoots over our path, blends into a waterfall. Diving repeatedly, we find only an empty '58 Impala.

4. We jet out of L.A., fly over the Peruvian Andes. Our plane enters clouds. We are unable to . . . visibility zero. Exiting the mist, our right wing almost grazes the mountain. He holds my hand. Tomorrow he will begin cataloguing over 1000 Quechua Indian words for potato.

5. After dinner I listen on the balcony to a baleful fog horn. A March houseparty in St. Simons. Our place is right on the ocean. Cloudy, rainy and I want him. We sleep separately in the same room. My breathing begins to follow his. I get up, masturbate in veiled moonlight.

*

SIMON SCHUCHAT

A Long & Happy Life

When I see the next century
Who of you will still be there,
Carrying on in the shadows
Beneath the towers, climbing a stair
That leads you to a quiet place
Where all remaining are together
In the happy sight of a single grin—
Yours, or mine, our special lever
To move what world will still exist
Around our softly aging limbs.
There our visible graces shall persist
In the wrinkled light of our skins.
Say if I will see you then,
Or if you'll be long buried
In some unshaven field of dirt
And your word will be carried
For the next twenty-four years
In a surreptitious mental pouch
As a kind of Unknown Soldier
Standing guard to prevent any harm
From those who answer in a bolder voice
The bigger questions of a warm
And passionate glance.
                              It is your choice
To continue to walk among the trees
And buildings of this busy island

Over many summers, many winters' freeze
And rain of all seasons, the turmoil
Of any blood and head.
                    I only ask
Because my solid hand foretells
I'm expected to be there to bask
In the rolling thunder of the bells
Which will invite us to further game
And I should like to know my company
From memory, by face and name,
Although no entertainments can be planned
And I will never read what's written
In another's solid hands.

*

Anti-Memoirs

In the way we made the world from a boat
We live in a world of imaginary spectacles
Like the way we can only see so far
But that's only one way to see, you see?
I saw the future and I worked for it
I'll grant its nice work if you can find it
If you've got the time—what time is it!
Where am I expected to be tonight?
What is there interesting that's happened?
I walk on A with Blondie in the sun
The deadline has come and went because
It got itself a little extension
Very handy, you see, to fix the walls for the maximum
Current, later you sell it to a special
Collection or did that man work all for free
Or didn't he notice the fishtank in the closet?
Remember where you got the tongue
        What do you want, to be a remainder?

Dummy in the waxworks Bateau Lavoir?
To whom nothing interesting ever happened:
He's really sharp, but it's like a knife
Where it's the handle that's sharp, not the blade
Nonetheless one wears shoes, want good ones, tied
With a double bind—bourgeois sociologist poet
Clever at redundancy, valorous in struggle
Against the biggest whitest sheet in Christendom
The poem gets blown by teeth and foliage
That is, it blows its cover and then people
Don't quite recall what it is they're thinking!
I think continually of those who are truly statuettes
Who, from the womb, dished up a soul and history
In colanders of leek when the garlic is done
He served his people and language like a salad
So pure it is mentioned he becomes a radish
Though some suspect he had a clever recipe
Suggesting how to come by the requisite saffron
He definitely listened to the usual AM broadcasts
You know: shake the hand, the hand falls off

*

TERENCE WINCH

Success Story

My clothes are perfectly contoured
to my body. My shoes and socks
fit just right. My cat is a delightful
intelligent animal. My apartment
is great. The right location,
cheap rent. I eat the best food.
My friends love me. I adore them.
My lover is terrific & beautiful.
The sun is shining. There are trees
even in the slums in Washington.
I have tons of money & a gorgeous
air conditioner. Great art hangs
on my wall. I live a spine tingling life
of delirious sex & intense happiness.

✻

Iron Eyes

You want my fingers spread
my legs pumping, my heart jumping
lying pretty on your bed
I wept thinking of you
I slept dreaming of you
C'mere, you said, get in my car
I was your automatic pilot

My veins popped out & I became
concise & now I'm thirty-eight
and I just want to stay sober
I held your head & kissed your eyes
in the oblique black & white
age of small details
Okay, you said, c'mon:
dominate the night for me

*

The Bells Are Ringing
for Me and Chagall

If you are involved in a fantasy relationship with someone
in which the sex is so good it's like a fantasy
and things happen between you that are
incredibly private and unmentionable that
you could never do with any one else ever again
so much so that you moan with pleasure in bed and can't
believe it's really happening and don't even
bother fantasizing about any one else or any
situation other than the one you're in, then you
are in very very serious trouble and good luck
to you. It won't last and when it ends, you'll
walk the floor and wear out your shoes.

If, on the other hand, you are involved with someone
with whom you have regular, decent sex
that feels good and normal, but that you
would never think about for a moment
when masturbating—which is by no means to put
it down—then the chances of *this* relationship lasting

a very long time, of the two of you growing old together,
are very good. But often this is simply not enough.
Or it *is* enough when what is wanted, unfortunately or not,
is more than enough.

✳

Comfortable Strangers

for Cesar Vallejo

In the morning I didn't know
what had happened. Things
seemed blurry to me and I felt
funny. She smiled.

Clothes hurt my skin.
I found it hard to think about abstractions.
I washed my eyes out.

I emptied you while
you slept, she said.
I know how to do it.
She was trying to scare me.

You're beautiful, I said.
Fuck you, she told me.
At breakfast I read the paper.
Everything tastes like licorice.

I enjoy being in the world,
but all I can think about is rhythm,
distance, houses, railway tracks, windows.
She sleeps next to me naked
in the dark, cool bedroom.

She tastes like licorice
and I like to go down on her.
I do not want to go to work today.
My legs ache & I feel lonely.

✻

The Them Decade

Hours and hours go by, traffic flows
smoothly through the arteries.
Buses discharge their passengers.

I stand in the middle of the bright day
posing next to the mailbox,
a glum expression on my face.
I wonder what Pete Rose is doing right now.

All I do is drink coffee and smoke.
I want to soak in a tub of ink
and become a masterpiece.
I am tired of the way cab drivers
whine in this city. I love the zone system.

The sun sets as the H-6 cruises
past the World Bank. I wonder
where Robert S. McNamara is right now.

At the Kennedy Center Fred Astaire
is honored. Ginger Rogers doesn't show up.
Mayor Barry's wife, Effi, is planning
to host a radio show.
Some people want a white chief of police,
some want a black one. Toby Thompson
flies through Cabin John becoming blonder,
sleeker, crazier. Bernard Welt is always
on the way to teach a class. Doug Lang
remains a mystery. I wonder where
Michael Denney is right now. Somewhere
in Baltimore telling a pointless story
with no end, but brilliant nonetheless.

Now it is dark. I watch the flags
fly on F Street. (Union Station
is beautiful at night.) I long
for something permanent.

*

Mysteries

All last night I kept speaking in this
archaic language, because I had been reading
Poe & thinking about him. I read "The Murders
in the Rue Morgue" which is supposedly the first
detective story. Who dun it? I wondered.
It turns out an orangutan was the murderer.
It looks to me like the detective story genre got off
to a pretty ridiculous start. I used to visit
Poe's house in the Bronx. I used to think,
God, Poe must have been a midget. Everything
was so small. Poe died in Baltimore and I can see why.

In Baltimore, all the people are very big and sincere.
During dinner last night, I told Doug and Susan
about "Murders in the Rue Morgue." I said I hadn't
finished it yet, but it looked like the murderer
was going to turn out to be an orangutan, unless
the plot took a surprising new twist. Then Doug
suggested that he and I collaborate
on a series of detective stories in which
the murderer is *always* an orangutan.

*

DENNIS COOPER

Being Aware

Men are drawn to my ass by
my death-trance blue eyes
and black hair, tiny outfit,
while my father is home with
a girl, moved by the things
I could never think clearly.

Men smudge me onto a bed,
drug me stupid, gossip and
photograph me till I'm famous
in alleys, like one of those
jerk offs who stare from
the porno I sort of admire.

I'm fifteen. Screwing means
more to the men than to me.
I daydream right through it
while money puts chills on
my arms, from this to that
grip. I was meant to be naked.

Hey, Dad, it's been like this
for decades. I was always
approached by your type, given
dollars for hours. I took a
deep breath, stripped and they
never forgot how I trembled.

It means tons to me. Aside
from the obvious heaven
when cumming, there's times
I'm with them that I'm happy
or know what the other guy
feels, which is progress.

Or, nights when I'm angry,
if in a man's arms moving
slowly to the quietest music—
his hands on my arms, in my
hands, in the small of my back
take me back before everything.

✳

Hustlers

for Jerry Patterson

Two beers screw my head up.
I lean back against a dark wall.
My long hair drifts in my eyes.
Let's say the moon makes a decision.
I land the corner legend surrounds.
I say more than I pretend to.
I prefer to be fucked to The Beatles.
I stand with the guys I resemble.
Jerry, Tom, Dick, Sam, Julian, Max, Timmy.
Guess which of those names is perfect.
We dream of a casual million.
We light our cigarettes gently.

I take what the night has to offer.
I roll a ripe peach from one wrist to the other.
I can't speak I'm so fucking stupid.
Our bodies are simply stupendous.
When we breathe, it takes us apart.
You know. You're inside us.

*

My Past

for Jim Stegmiller

is a short string of beautiful
boys or young men I admired,
dragged to bed, left in ruins
on corners with taxi fare home.
Another of friends who were
horny, who I could have slept
with but didn't because they
were ugly, insane or too much
like me to be sexy. We were
partners for sweeps of wild
parties, took dope till they felt
like museums which we
could pick-over for bodies
to idealize with caresses.
The sun rose slowly, I was
still huffing and toiling
with them, like a sculptor
attempting to get things just
right—finally collapsing
in bed with some smeared,
smelly torso before me, and

a powerful wish to be left
alone. Take you, for example,
who I found throwing-up in
the bathroom of some actor's
mansion and crowned my new
boyfriend. Your ass made me
nervous till I explored it.
Now I want to forget it. My
friends feel this way too.
I know them. We've been close
since before we were artists
working to leave haunted eyes
on our lovers. I've thrown
out hundreds like you, and
found only art can remain so
aloof in its make-up that I'll
stare endlessly into its eyes
like a kid with a microscope.
Once I was back when art chatted
just over my head, when I was
still glancing up the red swim
trunks of some boy who I think
was named Jimmy, and wondering
what could be out there, miles
from my hands. He was leaving
like you. Who knows where that
man and that feeling are now.

*

TOM DENT

Mississippi Mornings

for John Buffington

early early early
before the eternal basketball game
John meeting & greeting the peoples
getting together the latest
proposal
listening to Staple Singers
   dark woods in the house where Feather
lived & the picture of lean
Mississippi girl with hoe staring
somewhere the groan of tractor
chickens, the country green earth
smell memory of last night's gin
folly burned out by the new sun

soon everything moving & the
hustle is on
toward busy new
early early

✳

The Blue Light

Even while the blue light darts into his room
He is held captive by the sound of a leaf falling.

Charming he thinks to be laid away, for instance, in
    May
Among pure amber, impure purple of pansies
Exotic roots of tempestuous herbs;
These and others come out to play.

Soon his rain will dance
On the plastic surface of a still pond.
Somewhere else, another rain will slip through the
    airholes
Of a subway station to reliquify dried urine.

Now, his night.
Sharp lines melt into blurred shadows.
Trees whistle their secret tunes.
Held captive. Held captive.

Watch him stagger through night with the stars
In search of the blue light.

*

On Dreams and Mexican Songs

for any newspaperman

    The child is a Killer. He goes BOOM and someone falls. The
nighttime is a resting time, but it is time for BOOM BOOM too.
    Because in his mother's womb he can hear the steady drone of
blood, before explanations. He raises his shotgun to make the

other face look like hamburger meat: a miracle of conversion. He pulls the trigger because of the compulsion of dream, the environment of the city jungle, the code of honor, the . . . Ha! "Hoooey, hoooey, hoooey," okay, let's cut the foolishness out, i shouldn't be playing around with jokes, i shouldn't be singing Mexican songs— this is a newspaper story. Okay, *for no reason.*

He pulls the trigger, "four bullets went off/at two o'clock in the morning," the nighttime is a resting time, time is still, laggard, languished, it is, to be quaint, a time for echoes.

He pulling the trigger, the other boy's face becoming hamburger meat, it is the miracle of conversion, and you are the Victor if you can evoke the mystery of death that easily; an easy game to play. An old game. Only this is not face at all, let me describe for you the absence of eyes, the disappearance of nose, the conversion of mouth. . . . He is amazed, it is actually happening, blood oozing like the best red wine; no one should miss something like that. Then is fear, he drops the shotgun, runs around the block, are the police coming? Anyone hear the shots? Some glass from a storefront window shattered too. No time to think, must get away, let the song take over: "the gun went off/but I didn't kill him. . . ."

Now is the proper time for night, for those little unmentionables we all do, then release quickly as done: return to the scene, get the rifle, they might find my fingerprints on it.

The nighttime is a dreaming time, but somewhere a horrible mistake has been made: dream and reality have merged. Merged like a total eclipse to shroud his senses in umbraic darkness, blew out his fuse, but they'll pull away soon, an eclipse it don't last long.

Soon, like the sun getting himself up, all this will sift into dream again: dream gun, dream cowboy, dream night, dream moon, dream BOOM, dream deadboy and wine once more Gallo. And there in dream it will find its proper resting place, six feet under, with the headstone: *"beyond memory, but 'my luck will be your luck/ my death will be your death' "*

And all these dreams scattered over the universe like things, like its. We do not know what they are.

Shed no tears, that's the way it is.

✻

JEFF WRIGHT

Flesh Coupon

America, watch out!
The clocks will not hide
your malnutritious fat
people much longer.

We weren't sent here
merely to be great!
I must have more than
a photographic memory.

Call out the squadron
of dragoons who answers
for these absurd ideals
with the inviolate
jism of squandered dreams.

Here. I insist. I want
to pay them all back.

*

Stay Beautiful

for Kay Spurlock

Blond in gray & black & silver
You hold your end, a blue blowtorch
Arching into the end of a decade. I am
Honored to have served beside you
& be served on our complicit terrain.
We who ride shotgun on each other's
Motion-ridden rigs, are marooned
At desks & crochet needles, pleased to be
Desperate, white-hot & religiously naughty.
Here we open the door to our crazy amigos
& make love in the grizzled afternoons,
Screwed to the bed our eyelids flicker
Our tongues wag out—when we go out
To get ripped—some young lovers break in
& then we get ripped & then we get ripped

*

Industrial Size

Inside the processing complex
yawns are vacuum packed.

Carving my name
on your heart, my lips
utter the sweet nothings
I was born for.

Leaves along the gutter
bluster, caught fish, leap up.

The nights come after me
low & polished like limousines.

*

Higher Love

Blue roses ring the fire brigade.
Cathedrals on stilts
beg forgiveness
for their holy sins
of will power—
to reach higher—
to bring me
a higher love.

We danced 'til three
and then we
devoured the wee hours
bolting them in jaws
flapping like the ensign's
standard, red on blue.

Full moon bored through
Our Lady of Pompeii's stained glass.
Lead veins dissect panes,
blue roses ring the fire brigade.

So you are in my blood
even at low tide, bits
of shell chitter
as hissing foam resides.

Fragrant with whimsey,
nagged by struggle,
your bones dye black blocks
where none walk, windows dark.

We have used all the light
we could garner.
We have leapt over tall buildings
to earn ourselves and help others.

I have held open the door for you
    for so long
you have become the door.
I have held your heavy knocker
a cinder in the ashpit
    of my heart
that spits on night's
    conditioned surrender.

*

Sermon on the Mount

In the long night
as we held tight
my darling thing,
my fairest fiend,
the city slept,
sly robbers crept.
A waitress counted tips,
showgirls checked their lips.
A truck backfired.
A newborn cried.
A motorcycle thrummed
as the light changed.
The headnurse yawned
and doormen silent pawned
their dreams of being
rock n' roll singers
or driving Mercedes
with high heeled ladies
and watched tv—
their shift done.
Then I'll leave
you in your tower
and over the world
will a glow spread.

*

ROCHELLE KRAUT

My Makeup

on my cheeks I wear
the flush of two beers

on my eyes I use
the dark circles of sleepless nights
to great advantage

for lipstick
I wear my lips

*

We Laughed

my friend
we flirted
and we were so smart
we were witty
and we knew what we
were thinking
and we were surprised
by our own thoughts
and we laughed
and we laughed

*

No Regret

resenting all
who with charm and beauty
cultivate all that
I let go to weed

but I study the beauty
and know the names
of many of these
wild flowers

*

Sheep

I count my blessings
and fall asleep
before I finish

*

WILL BENNETT

Poor Movies

See how the language listens up this spring
of morning poverty. Across the alley
a couple is arguing in French. She says: "You have
no food. You have nothing to say here." Their child
plays with string hung out the window. The father's
bellow is so deep I can't understand.

Of all the air to feel this morning. Cool & lightly
empty. No hint of starvation for the insects or birds,
just a morning touched with floating ashes, to be flown
through The sun reaches through our one tree the same
way it would a whole forest, & lights the ground.
The couple have stopped fighting, the child has stopped
reaching from the window. A bell rings & the morning ends.
I should say goodnight to the morning as it shuts down
like a factory on those who watch it, unemployed
with no prospects for work.

*

Nod

Nod is like last time, and this time
in a minute restaurant, a pleasantly
small cage. Nod is a neutral movie
daringly illustrated in vanishing ink.
A rapidly souring ultimate privacy.
A kiss to myself, a nod to myself, yes.
A long yes and an imperceptible wave goodbye.
Slight smile, musical comedy practice of
the Orient. No one starves here, warmth of
indirect restaurant brightness.
I wave my arm like someone drowning;
achieve motion as a statue might,
by innuendo.

*

New Jersey

for Donald Evans

Up in the carbon, as you play postage,
hear traffic ambulance Rt. 73, the pipes heat
with a terrific shadow. Ask a question,
& the small answer is, "Other countries."

Water touching beaches is not enough.
The oily brushes are not far enough away
for the new answer, "Something terrible."
You were told where to go, but not how
or when to leave the room.

*

HENRY KANABUS

Accordance

'Certainties are arrived at only on foot.'
The darkening road permeates his right eye,
his left chatters like a tympany in which
lacewings are imprisoned. He sings to his
nurse. She has kept him in bed for over
a decade. Long since, he has ceased calling
her his muse. She brings him coffee and cake,
a small boat, and a fork to eat the fish
with some enchantment for the lake it had
crept in.

*

The Access

you've grown to fire
delicately

The archer (acquainted with brilliance)
inhabits a desperate vanity

Lace becomes an adjunct
to flame

An error in tribal delineations
places the magician
in the homes of the mad

It is pride not wealth
that traces disparate feathers

on the white arena
of his skin

Easy to see how starlight
becomes deadly
    when you walk with him.

*

The Scythe

The wind accounted for all
it had shattered
          (night-dancing
in lace prints of bone)

We confuse its wisdom
with the anger of cats - both

lay large upon the wheat

We realize the urgency and notify
the heliotrope

    It is waving its arms
in a thousand different parodies.

*

MICHAEL ANDRE

1,000 Illustrations
& A Complete Concordance

I spent my afternoon like my morning and that was good.
It's those afternoons that give me trouble.
It took me a while to decide I liked them.
Unusual are the pains that no one feels.

Elegiac are the moods of sunrise
Jesus gently pulls back his skin to show
his sacred heart
Michael gently pulls forward his skin to cover
his sacred bird
It's the lead pedal and the gold pedal of the bicycle

What's going to happen later in the day if already I've seen so
    much?
The operator swings his iron ball
elegantly
the walls just crumble

Though blood now dribbles from his mouth
unusual as from a toy
Gerard is poor but glamorous and not sorry.

I imagine I'm smarter than a psychiatrist.
I've too high an opinion of knowledge.
Things are just hanging out, like shirt tails.

I'm too sophisticated to have muscles.
I never resent a communication.

*

My Regrets

I send a rose with a card for myself
saying, sorry to say I'm here.

———————

Our cigarettes cross in the ashtray.
The lipstick on your Camel, my love,

is the shade of your cunt's lips too
radish. We match so, we too.

And so we withdraw, with regrets,
only way to do anything.

The senses of perception, like the sense of history,
dull: my left ear worsens, my eyes redden.

I'm dying piecemeal. You too my love your cunt
fragrant as the rose at dawn in spring etc.

*

STEVEN LAVOIE

Make Way

stopped to talk
not to resume the duties it curtailed
for many months

it left its buzzing
at ordinary harmony to the interferences
of common appliances

a few visits
in a string whose voices some
music allows

promises vistas ahead
whose distances are potential
monumentally remote

left with appetite
enough to wait it out for
something satisfactory

on the way
neither aging nor desire
makes enough time

*

In Mutual Time

The tearless oblivion in an expanse
of wasteful terror
$\qquad\qquad\qquad$ feast of senses
$\qquad\quad$ to
$\qquad\qquad\qquad\quad$ brimming with what
has been established as Ideal in the meantime

to fulfill even the minimum human
expectation we must grapple with
a compulsion to exult
$\qquad\qquad\qquad\qquad$ constructs of
the every day
$\qquad\qquad\qquad\qquad$ stand in
the way
$\qquad\qquad\qquad\qquad\quad$ Your days would be
ours in mutual time—what came before,
$\qquad\qquad$ a study not a real experience.

$\qquad\qquad\qquad\qquad\qquad$ Thresholds are
skipped. . .
$\qquad\qquad\quad$ the topology of the most familiar
terrain
$\qquad\quad$ is nothing like it was.

Arroyos burst forth with elixirs;
rugged canyons smooth into valleys
while shards reform their urn.

$\qquad\qquad\qquad$ *

Cloud Spots

Items riddle space,
having condensed through
a world of talk.
Its weaker physics allow
for spontaneous generation.

A kitchenette forms in
your mind. No unit is distinct.
It consists of table and chairs,
matching, a leaf goes
in the middle. The surface is
blank but for the settings.

Dots provide a texture
of fuzz, mass of blips,
until you back up to see
the bust of a great statesman.

Condensation allows for
recognition. Features develop.
Unique noses and unmistakable
thick lips.

The fog endows life
while you stagger through it,
landmarks forming to
guide you. Man
in this cloud spots
a common man. Where
nothing is familiar.

*

MICHAEL PALMER

View From an Apartment

(symmetrical poem)

The word "dream" is technical and means nothing
so we can use it
whenever we want
Max's dream has masks
and is lit from the side and the back
I did not dream this dream
but lay with eyes open instead
and the dancers were my friends
We have lived a life that lasted some time
Now we live another, liquid one
Our vestments are invisible
say the crows
Our lake is a secret
imperfectly kept
says the Ténébreuse
You must stay awake until this ends

*

Alogon

(a spiral for voice)

It is light and dark a book lay on the table beside the sun are moon and stars. Sometimes keys are forgotten and the door locks. Above his head is a row of stars and books suggesting the complexity of the art. A chart is being drawn. I would rather live here than in that city. Thank you is what he said. Thank you is what I'm sure she said. Forty children of the poor died. Another 5,960 will have died. The prediction has been made 308 times. Our bellies are swollen with food or the lack thereof. It is morning again. He looks through the drawer for his keys. The door locks behind him. The heart stands up and announces 'I have felt'. A goat is tethered in the shade, a horse approaches the fence. He listens to the ducts from an adjoining room. Begin she says and he begins. The lips and tongue form a yes or yet. If he has been chosen he wonders why. She applies the color with a small brush. A chart is being filled in. The sky has partially cleared. The south wall is missing. He asks for more water and it is brought. He examines the mirror. He searches for the mirror in the dark. Begin she says I have begun. He points toward the window and a building beyond. It's three or four o'clock. She notices the fountain. Inside it's growing dark. Can you remember all that or should I write it down. She moves from the chair toward the door. I have retained the use of legs and arms. Benches and clouds. Secret speech is forbidden in the park. There was no one in the park. He paces back and forth between the bed and the door. I don't know how to assess myself. My father lived here until he was born. A folio lies open to his right. I recognize nothing from before. This might or might not have been hers. All over the world they flower at once. That's mint and lemon that you smell. He cannot seem to recall. Open or opening to a page.

She draws the remains of a recognizable face.

The subject is seated opposite. A row of books suggests the art. I have little access to myself.

*

Notes for Echo Lake II

An eye remembers history by the pages of the house in flames, rolls forward like a rose, head to hip, recalling words by their accidents. An ear announces a vertical light without shadow, letters figured across the forehead and wrist, there are no vowels or nouns. Write to me soon I can say nothing more for now. He grew accustomed to the spells of dizziness. I can see about a foot beyond my outstretched arm. I gave up teaching long ago. He expected to die young as if he were immortal. There is a perfect architecture. He grew used to falling unexpectedly. My left eye is closed so I will read these sentences aloud. Mathematics is a minor category of music. The day ends this way each day until it ends. Words listen to the words until you hear them. The words form circles. Water transmits sound. The words cannot be spelled. The table was made of glass which decided to shatter. The dog had an unfortunate habit of farting when important guests were present. They made love by the fire while her husband slept. This mushroom is beautiful and has no name. Lake receives light. By stages you dismember the story. He explained that the word contained a silent *l*. They parted and he entered a cloud. The words do not form circles. I don't think I have a right to leave your letter unanswered. I would like to keep working. I think I see a new way out. The following are matters concerning me and the roof of my mouth. The letters combined into the word for silence. The song came in stanzas as is the manner of such songs. Those who then heard it laughed themselves to death. I was first and last among them. I fled in the direction of the invisible city. I wept before its walls. That night I invented the following dream. It is evening and my father and I are walking east toward Fifth Avenue on the street where we once lived. Every other building has been reduced to rubble as if by an aerial attack. The scene thus resembles those photographs of bombed cities I remember from childhood, except that the buildings remaining appear completely unharmed. Eventually we attempt to enter a favorite restaurant of his but realize that it is in a similar building on a parallel street one block north. We turn away and I wake, as always violently trembling. Once I saw the master of memory sleeping at his desk. Here I will insert the word 'real' to indicate a tree. She brushed against the decanter with her left arm, spilling its contents onto the tile floor. We woke at the same moment and looked up. Here I will insert the word 'red' to indicate a tree. Number imitates measure in a flowered dress. I learned to count to ten and back again. Her fingers sought the indicators at the base of his neck. The words disappeared as he read them. The leaves fell early. Snow caused our arms to fold. Of the seven million one-half have died. Speech seems a welcome impossibility, the room a congeries of useless objects mistaken for events. The song came in fragments as is the nature of such songs. I rose and departed by the far door, no longer able to see. I played among the rats by the river's edge, counted up the condoms and bottles and human limbs, then slept. Wednesday passed in tranquility. Merchants are building towers, each higher than the last. I shared breakfast with a cat, dinner with an owl. The mountain quivers on the surface of the lake. Your letters reach me at monthly intervals. The angle of the light has changed greatly this past week. I have learned to use my eyes and to distrust them. I am dependent on everything. Words gather into triangles and vertical lines. The sentences they form should not exist. Poems will sometimes overcome them, or else stones.

*

from "Baudelaire Series"

Words say, Mispell and Mispell your name
Words say, Leave this life

From the singer streams of color
but from you

a room within a smaller room
habits of opposite and alcove

Eros seated on a skull as on a throne
Words say, Timaeus you are time

A page is edging along a string
Never sleep never dream in this place

And altered words say
O is the color of this name

full of broken tones
silences we mean to cross one day

*

Desire was a quotation from someone.

Someone says, This this. Someone says, Is.

The tribe confronts a landscape of ice.

He says, I will see you in the parallel life.

She says, A miser has died from the cold; he spoke all
his sentences and meant no harm.

My voice is clipped, yours a pattern of dots.

Three unmailed have preceded this, a kind of illness.

Now I give you these lines without any marks, not even
a breeze

dumb words mangled by use

like reciting a lesson or the Lord's Prayer.

How lovely the unspeakable must be. You have only to say
it and it tells a story.

A few dead and a few missing

and the tribe to show you its tongue. It has only one.

*

She says, You are the negative—
Behind you an horizon in red
and the horizon a question
a mark in final red
your eyes are sealed against

She says, You do not know when

She says, You are counter
You are degrees only
and now in summer a mouthful of blood
and sutured nylon thread

You are professor of watery tablets
from moment to memory a swollen debt

She says, You cannot not hear this
Far less than a second will have passed

(Kootenay sonnet)

*

Barely anything to say, everything said. But you break,
as a hooded traveller, scattering images across the plain,
I among them and other I's. This prose, a

color sampler, is meant for you: *Voile bleu, Dame du Sud,
Bleu Medicis*, fifty dead on the tarmac, creases of the
hand. Is there still an outside, uncancelled as yet by
other

codes appearing in service to what

revolutionary pleasures, what floods
of a matrix in slow dissolve

there on the screen, where everything is named difference,
and is always the same for that reason, since you've watched
it many times before and counted the limbs?

Glides and rests.

Let's say a particular music, in profile.

Let's say mythological figures, freeze dried, who—once
immersed—emerge from their gelatin capsules: Syrinx,
Polyeidos, the Dioskuroi; Earth Diver, Frog and Moon,
        Mephisto.

They refuse you their stories, pour soot on you
                                    and into you.

And that other music, sort of gasped out now by the
        synthetron,
the instruments slightly more than real, if ontically pro-
blematic at best.

Or we might say just as you said, It's snowing in Paris,
which does not exist.

(A painting of that.)

Or the problem we began with, that words have no letters.

And that each of those letters has a distinctive shape.
Or shade. Impossible to remember.

✻

for C.E.

I have answers to all of your questions. My name is the word for
wall, my head is buried in that wall. When I leap over that wall I
think of my head, I can assure you. And into the garden: para-
dise—broken bottles, tractor tires, shattered adjectives (fragments
of a wall). The sky beyond on fire, this is true. The hills beyond a
glinting gold, also true. And you married to that clown, that ape,
that gribbling assassin of light. Your daughters will avenge you.
And into the garden: paradise—the soldiers, their rifles, their
boots, their eyes narrowed, searching for a lost head. Or a stolen
head? The head of a pornographer. There, I've said it. Pink nipples
grow hard as she brushes them with her lips. Moans can be heard
coming from poems—poems you, Senator, want desperately to
read but will not let yourself, since you are a citizen, proud and
erect. And out of the head laughter, tears, tiny bubbles of spit. It is
a head from another century, the last one or the next.

✻

MARILYN KITCHELL

Three

moon
     real
estate and scree cascading 9
                       leads
to the trap/
         live zoo/
              white fish
ecology of words—pica,
               the callous stripping spell-
bound print / snow's creep and fluttered
                        forehead;
         to my belly
             and my knees

             en route,
troy—closed on monday but for silver
spur of crazy eye'd hellos
fall over your left
        shoulder—
       it's so easy . . .
fall in love and fill your glass up,
      find another
            parking lot—
       another cup of light
reveals the seven bars
      (four in a row)

                                    across the tracks
i buried the forced out—this
                                    sunrise
                              Browning/milk
                    evaporated site;
the muddy road, puddle
strong coffee
                    grounds my thoughts to stay
up through the night i wandered
to this rotting
                    stump i kick apart
                    beside the river—
                    i (hear
rushing much too loud for sense to carry seed—
spit in a pool. . .
                          it floats above smooth
boulder
          till—the current trappings'
weight/will
                    pull it down in water—logged,
the steep pull
                    lances with their feathers;
                    still attached, i
                                    watch
inverted penta-hedron burn
its victims in suspension
as the bubbles rise. . .
                              on my new skin
a heritage? these
                    line's—
                                    age? privilege?
                                    a sordid ledge
wear gold drops shrivel from my fruit
twisting contortion; in the blaze
heat decomposes glare on stones
                                    i eat
                    the inner white
                              /

                                        curled membrane
tiny ants have crawled through / final dribble—
prism clear tinged faintly red

                            rolls on my surface,
                            sinks and disappears
in creviced oil. . .
as i leave i carry with me outer skins,
torn sheaves / this paper—

                        a necessity?
more easily degraded dermal flaking
i picked a copy of

                    outside—the magazine i read. . .
an odyssey of hermits

                    in the valley
                    dry/din
echoes the vast emptiness

                        i saw
the sleeping indian

                    departure
marks. . .
            an inter
                    rim of waiting
            for my voice
to catch
            a quality toward witch
i suppose i
            would, as pyre—

                        "in cold hell. . ."
                        feel flame;

                                    "in thicket"
                        sky splash—sun
with rain and wind
                        beyond the swamp, i swim
beneath the power lines—the swirl of green
so delicate
            /
            strong streaming from the rocks'

white water pools to where i look

                        back naked. . .

        on the edge, see my wet tracks
release
        dead wandering—
the wild wood
            cross my brow
                    sing golden eagle
and your name—a mar
                  mot tail chases a passage
through the talus;
(high cliff throne the common scavenger finds)
                trail so wide, we
(all three) choose our own
paths' question—
            weight. . .
            or wade the steps before the bridge
made easy crossing / north side
perfect arching curve
           /
            a fragile edge of 3
moist in my hand,
           i could go crazy
           on this shoreline
           staring at the polished spheres;
i tell myself that i must
keep the other
        free—
           a hand for holding
           balance or a heart
           in great profusion
here—the zero's no-sail sulphureminiscence
                thoughts. . .

            all you. . .

my sister scrambled through
the needles in a dream state
naked chested, kneed—
no breaks in darkness or the dew,

                witch raised

our shelter
       where i did not hear
her
       scratching . . . on the road,
a thought—absconded; or
        perhaps she was
an animal of large
         sorts waking me / my hair—
font shivered filaments that whispered
film of dawning / call of passing strange
birds . . . cormorant
         encounters coming in-
let tea, the shades in
         jested on the shore recall
         another coast,
another season
      all an other
         you—
an absence / lover i am
longing to be—
        tracing salt worn ligaments
to tend
    on's smooth
gouged blood pools of changed coursings
where the corpuscles are shimmering
a pause
     in foam. . .
i find a spoon,

my sisters find a shack, we
watch a star
      fish for a fallen piece of moon. . .

we stare through giants in deep
tide, my vision fades in settling
missed—
          the petroglyphs / our everywhere. . .
the paint
          brush red and yellow on
          the ledge—rough texture /
almost peaks / the cracks of looking
very breakable—
                    slime

                         green

                              drips from the inner
                              surface of the hole in
wall bare
          back hangs
                    shreds of passage. . .

                    shoulder cape
a man—side to
the surf
          face stoic
          folded arms—a totem table
"we could wade through at a lower ebb. . ."

          "perhaps
the fog will soon be lifting
                    from this spot. . ."
the body is inside
                    the tree hosting
external shelf of white
                         encasement—
spore producing only for one year
                              the flower
fragrance drifts—
                    a species of the lupine
and the fox's poison
          /

                              glove waves. . .
        to a screeching
                              leda neck—long black distracts
        my gaze
                    between eroded thumbprints

i grow weary. . .
you are hot, take off
                    your shirt / the rocks
                    begin to crumble underneath

                                                            my feet
unsure of their momentum—
lava growing
green deceptive slippery
                    /
                              the color of the sound. . .

wet flutes—pan covering
green slime lochs oar
a deeper sound than passed

                              above the title edge. . .
we lay our tarp between logs—

                              burrowed home of sow
bugs—we move unlike
                    /
                    lines of vertebrae
smooth interlocking arms that catch my run
                    through
                              matchstick sculpture
                              sleeping graveyard. . .

some limbs raw with red—

                              the new arrivals
here,
the sand warm is memorial of farther south;

and farther north,

wearing a fishbone in my hair
i smell of fish—

watch

travelers . . . they journey to our starting point,
all destination—
tent pitch shaking
sand moves
at my feet
i think. . .
to sleep inside
the hollow of a bone. . .

✲

GEORGE-THÉRÈSE DICKENSON

from "Transducing"

> *You stand between the cedars and the green spruces,*
> *brilliantly naked.*
> Amy Lowell, *Pictures of the Floating World*

Astigmatic rendering. Introspect nor take relinquish of. The two in the broad beams similarly from across the settlements or as if generations. One happens tersely. Interjections taking the place of other banished items.

When I returned years later, his arm was still raised. Waste disposal has become a major issue. Polite restrictions discourage consider. Slush fund and dwindling. Time to look for the next big marker on the road.

All point whereof. Jobs seem all pretty much the same. But in the subsensuous realm they keep you from. Basic chunks excised. Messy, the edges compound in a drifty sort of way into everything you try to go to bed with.

A sudden religion. Old Harken myths.

For *instance*. Epitomes. Examples shut doors all over the world. "As such and such would say" subbing for "Your knishes are gray." Suggestions don't seem to be working. Everything becomes an insult in the tousled hospital of your hair.

Envelope. As either. Though reification more apparent in the active case. He to her a little seed case. The job becomes her.

As opposed to a person who "happens also to." Meanwhile continues as the paint is slapped onto the peach rooms. Sexual engross. So exhausted from looking, he couldn't get it up. Everything goes on as a diorama. Satisfact to the point of willfully remaining overtime.

Excumbers. Histoires in the meadows. Rebellion gives way to discipline stage in which they cannot stop. Sight risk to both parties. Encompassing is complete when the concept of "leisure" is reinvented internally. Luxurious oats speckle the film where Jeneifa under a logger whittles.

Contractual absorption. Amortization of face. Terrified she'd no one to dance with. Figuring angles with his pectorals.

Climactics, asbestos garb for the little man, mack, muddle, plangent both ways traduce built in. Instrument or issuings therefrom reappearing in another form, piper pips, rectangled infinite 1's on itself in the shape of a nautilus. Rarely given and always taken back. Small clicks and whirrings pleach the atrium.

Toolings up rapidly outdate themselves. Other countries pull, vanquished, ahead—"our" helpful couch.

It was degenerating. I wouldn't recognize it if I saw it. Almost as though from another planet, though we have big words for it and go by them.

Little fires are spaced along the path. The big ones divert as revolving headlines. The small ones keep us warm and we are grateful. Especially now that the lacunae are longer. Old theories of seem to work again. At least for now.

*

GEOFFREY YOUNG

Rocks and Deals

"as long as this wet pitch contorts"

1
Funny you should mention the beach. Was it 1978?
　　The first I HATE WOODY ALLEN t-shirts hit
The Berkeley streets. Though this thus doesn't mean
　　That there, else I'm reading wrong. I have
To be in Sausalito for a shoot. Everything seems more
　　Alive since we were thrown from our bed in the
Earthquake. Ellsberg says for the first time he thinks
　　We freeze folks are in the majority. Hey,
You dropped your sweater, excuse me, hello, you dropped
　　Your sweater. But do you care what Butterick
Paid for Olson's passport? We either do or do not
　　Live in a world where only poets read poetry.
The aim, simply said, is to teach the children to breathe.
　　Or was it a dream? I saw the zen master tap
Wallace Stevens on the head and say, "Aqui esta la cabeza."
　　Throw followers a fresh scent, *aus der Hose malen.*
Art is where vanity really counts you out, but the *pipe*
　　Here is always and intractably "pipe." Sketches
Of thumbnails, of shell limpidity. I'm about to place
　　My bet on the last years of the XXth Century.
My name is March Goodwin. I live at 1725 Ashland,
　　Just down the street from a carwash. Traffic
Never bothers me because I'm learning Italian by tape.
　　Except for palmtrees, we're all really in the same

Place. Look for the sky. Now let's make our way through
    This crowd, let's pick out each digressing thing.
Let's make the poem say the reader's eye is a new museum.
    And add that when Miles hired Wayne they cut ESP?
It was better than TV and you could read at the same time.
    Now poetry's pious servants genuflect before
The world's mortal remains, crania with mandibles and
    dentition
    Still intact tearing sound from the tiniest letters,
While WEST is Venus at 9:15. Of course you should have
    An encore if the situation calls for it. No use
Being thin on a windy day. Poets exist to heave the species
    In the hammer throw, if the most productive thing
You can place on the land is a hand's shadow writing
    In a notebook. I misunderstand doors
If I only knock. A chair creaks at the table, but who's
    Sitting pretty? Is there an artist out there
Would stitch the San Andreas Fault together to stretch
    New voices past the house? Delacroix's first
Engraving was born on the base of a copper saucepan.
    A caudal goes into the base of the tailbone,
An epidermal higher up the spine. Thus it is she not he
    Has the baby. It's hush hush time, looking at your
Newborn, looking back at you. The intelligent thing.

    2
Though next to me she lies, a rock, of ages, we are not
    Merely born to suggest that light years pass,
Nor raised like shrewd ornaments to be placed on a page.
    What to put here and what to put there, and how
To make it go with what is already here: a sizzling wok.
    Then it was night, it was Eagle Rock, it was aluminum
Chairs on his front porch. Suddenly he turned "Deborah"
    Up loud, and said, "Artifice is what the dead
So adroitly practiced." One day mobile, active, radiating
    Health, the streets so filled with shiny bodies
You begin to look for chocolate bits in the trailmix, and the
    next

They won't even let you wear jogging shoes just to watch.
Feelings end when they're felt, time keeps starting back up.
    A hand's friend is open. Or does the wheel mislead
This conversation, while we slip, we waver, we check each
        other
    Out, imagining a living wage? For there to be a sign,
There must be an agreement: Two goes into one 'bout half the
        time.
    We are mock idiom predators, speaking separate
Languages. Still I dub the stills with motley aperçus: "The man
    In that photograph is screaming." "The proper use of
The poetic faculty is to graduate." "It's a question of voices,
    Of voices to keep voicing, of checks with your new name
On them." Perfect pitch—no pitch-pipe necessary. Who
    Do you know? An enigma's only enigmatic if it remains so.
And cancer? She was the view, in this case, a close up.
    The lens, a zoom. Heart, the same. From your outside life
To your inside life, is written. Perhaps it is time to become just
    A little indifferent here, to learn caution, or better
Still, to look away, *to go away*. Now I'm back to let you know
    I can really shake 'em down. Watch me now, hey!
Mashed potatoes! But what can't be forgotten is the
        unnameable,
    Like slate, a great rock to draw on. The road was
In his head, his eyes were on the driving. I run into a wall.
    It puts me back on the right track. I am being watched,
It's the meaning of the sentence. Talk writes to speech,
    Says divide me up. Then this living hand, now warm
And capable, reaches into the hamper for the dirty clothes.
    (There are only as many hours as you put in.) And
If we haven't mentioned your flight it's because we don't
    Have the blackhole located yet. (Then his devices
Began to show through.) Equate me with him who exists,
    No matter how, with him whose story this story the brief
Ambition to be, is. Never lose the thread because it isn't one.
    But if the dead could write, would we bother to?

*

ALAN BERNHEIMER

Portrait Of A Man

Your face fills the sky
like a windmill
with the look of living certainty
and a smile dissolved by air

You sit on your shoulders

We see hair, mouth
the nose on your facc
and the light brown
light in your brown
fifteenth century eyes
one looking inside
the other ahead

You wear black
the color of the universe
and the blue sky is white in back

What we don't know
is what you are about to say

*

Specimen Of An Induction To A Poem

Nature especially abhors the smell of vacuums
While the spiritual
        cottager frescoes
                his crystal ball

Weak weather for a length of time

Images harbor messy affinities
Like doctors we're used to it

Once thaws gradually decline
Spring leaves trees green

Demonstrates words used as words
One breath of air
            the next of smoke

But the picture doesn't recognize me

A unit of general signal should alter fate

Your furniture is six days old
And sleep has absorbed falsehood

Resting objects
            different as eggs
Shadow thoughts

Botanical calm slips from stills

*

Word Of Art

First a flicker of telepathy
Then screw le mot juste
Carefully into its socket
So the electricity doesn't spill.

Act natural.
It isn't all honey for people with learning
And don't make excuses for rock.

Eye on curve, hand on lever, things on mind,
The rest of the subjects refer to you.

Words make wide open spaces.

Dissolve to perpetual motion
With time off for behavior.

The body likes its relations
Embroidering inventions
To say anything:

This music is not of my choosing.
The enormous seaminess throws a textbook punch.
But it wasn't the stars that thrilled me.

*

Passing Strange

Blunt good looks cut out day
patterned after strides through nerve

No accident the sky clouds
figure is envelope blue

dovetails with appetite
It sounds like it

Weather is personal equation
and existing light jolts small fortune
by weight of characteristic

What I think I hear are words
lost in plain sight
though details feel passing fancy
with binocular relief

Material needs a life of fact
to make a spectacle of
one of these days

✳

KIT ROBINSON

It's A

I go in
really reading
and the girl at the counter
forgets to charge
"Kit"
w/ black shoes
& lack of color's
interesting or
absorbing light
looking up from
under your hat
and nothing is said
it's a minor pleasure
over a major pain
little enough
without much to do
about how to improve
hanging in on your
honor not hurt or
nervous after
all that
might be made light of
in light of fine error
approximation's walk a
round, hip to swagger under
sky as one
day like any (I is
the) other

'our man'
its place
to sleep in
a rush, bring
us up to our
best recollection's
opposite number
on a ordinary day

*

In the Orpheum Building

Single story two bedroom dwelling across from
Parts unknown and won't be back and hesitates
To hand over that strongbox. The men were very
Nice and sunny down there and we have everything
Sorted out with all the lights on all night

Representatives stationed at regular intervals
Publish twice weekly (Wednesday and Friday)
Couldn't be better, on the quarter, stop on a
Stretch. After the tone there's a hiatus of
Ten years. Probable link to shadow play

"I'm going to City Hall." What's going on over
Night coach service to points east including
Everything you are, no greater love, all the
Staggered elements piggybacking on a trace
Call of the transport board, the yield

Glowing, and we're planning a trip up north
Happenstance. I guess you could say a
More relaxed way of fastening onto sound seams
As sensible strands· part, might shed light
Hey, how many people do you realize go by

In a day when jazz would be better as a girl's name
"Now I have to re-check his work." What's in
Back to bowling flower bunches in the slides
Has hands and bells out over a body of water
Maybe's both ways, be simpler catching a bucket

❊

Up Early

for Lyn Hejinian

the tenor of your madness
leads me to believe
along lines of force
the commencement signals an end
from which to disembark
on a journey to three islands
the island of early morning
the island of the little pipe
and the island where the rubber meets the road
as I have been telling you
and a steady hum reaches our ears
along lines of force
                    10/14/86

how do I live? by swinging
from cliché to cliché the way an elephant
steps from lily pad to lily pad
in the sky
the letter M in your meaning
splits the face I know
middle-of-the-road politics
posing as objectivity
until each quick and simple thing

folds beneath the unassailable
weight of stars
from which so much sense has been derived
10/24/86

I have also reversed the sky and field
stood old Marx on his head
and leaned into the rusty light
the rhetoric seems to slide away from the car
portrait or landscape
your may not notarize your own signature
even before a full-length mirror
and I can't speak for your experience of this
but as for myself
and access to letters opens the possible
clasped tight in change
but I turn and imitate your tremendous seeming
12/12/86

the fog is not an institution
its shadow on the road
you can play it several ways
undo the principle concavity
to divulge air of its secret sponginess
repeatedly
while aspirins click in the night cafeteria
U. S. of A. crashes from the sidewalk
rooftop publishing
away with all dots
until evidence of a blind is felt
matter having crossed the street
2/4/87

I've ramped the stops and tossed the cold off hand by hand
to notarize interrogatories on the crack of done
pitched hostile licensees about in a boat half-caulked with
   slime
when only unauthorized returns poured into the regional fan

dealt rhetoric a blow-by-blow
recorded each interruption
and stocked my daintiness with full sore billions
in an amalgam of rash hacks
but the bone has two nodes
and still I wonder
stone holding song-ends apart
breaches the terrible haughtiness alive in a shell of mass
                                        2/20/87

there are reasons reason doesn't even use
the instant an integer bursts upon the scene
a flight of clocks passes over the trees
a brother stands in a cool forest
high winds take great boughs
apart and plant them between periods
time collapses into glove compartment
some have time on hands
others are pressed for it
either way there's a jolt
translate image and anecdote
Gogol boots
                                        2/23-87

regards from treasure traffic island
nerves thaw on address from too many branches
the cold at hand tips the scale in our father
smoking touch of tobacco to feel the morning light
sky the damp and crumpled image of a hat
words down lanes, a handful of starry ideas
rhythm, repetition, variation, somnambulance
what is this error that runs through the speaking text?
a line of thought goes straight to the heart of matter
extension prevails on essence to flesh out a form
rain glances off dots that divide the lanes
that contain the flow that issues from consummate waking
                                        3/5/87

*

Archangel

Air arcs overhead.
Light gets in
through rectangular holes.
Imagine customs reduced
to a bit-sized
grid. Locked into
habit, the daily
passengers drive the
self to work
for more craziness
in industry. Foreign
shores tremble in
light of great
heat. Beef sources
are more obscure
than any writing.

I'm sitting here
watching this chair-back
revolve behind a
desk. I'm sitting
here thinking just
how otherwise to
conduct my affairs.
I'm superficially repeating
patterns from memory
onto the wallpaper
that is this
world. Across the
gulf, a mess
of flowered bodies
lies past aching.
The insulation I
feel is made

of money and
the ability to
control lives. I'm
simply put. But
I can wrinkle.

Voices delight in
sporadic dislocations,
touching
the key points
on a map
of crudely rendered
deletions. Happy as
a baby tire
hugging the blacktop,
a man in
the neck of
a woods discloses
ties to a
woman in shoes
and a bright
idea, glad to
be out of
luck and onto
the main drag
where work clocks
the body for
seed and life
hangs by an
arm of the
sky. Talk covers
the tracks made
of every bed
ever slept in.

In my solitude
I have occasion

to get to
know a lot
of great people.
We clown around
in an arbitrary
way for about
two thousand years.
Then it's time
to get back
to work. Refreshed
and invigorated, we
plunge headlong into
an increasingly complex
series of problems.
There's no way
we're going to
finish in time.
But it's ok.
The machine that
keeps track of
all this is
out of order.

Curved air, high
windows, heavy traffic,
light industry, foreign
investment, local suffering:
color by numbers.
Something that one
ought to do
or must do
is an office.
The camera pans
a drifting fragment
of the flat

thin ice that
forms in bays
along the shore.
Complete days reach
harmonic proportions, narrowly
entering the flood.

*

LYN HEJINIAN

Redo, 1–5

1.

Agreement swerves
a sonnet to the consonants.
Sparrows. As a wind
blows over the twigs of a rough nest
entered by a bird that impales

a vowel on its beak.
When unable to think of two things
unless we think twice, the rower
in the water jerks to travel. Her autobiography
is ninety percent picaresque.

While thus moralizing all we have done
is shout
the name of someone we know.
In the intellectual water the rattling sweaters
and the fluffy rocks seem to be wheezing

in the wind. As a child
so simple with sincerity I found it unbearable
to have friends while inhibited with sympathy
I had them. Some were a) aggressive
and beloved, b) consistently contradictory

or c) casual & splay—like raffia.
With a Freudian sense of fun we felt
remorse for our most aggressive howdies.
But given fire the discovery
of water was inevitable

Clouds amass like the glaze on clay
buttery birds collect in glossy sky
the fat moon coming our way looms out
and slides. Anarchies sleep
in this overabundance

of time like inert technicalities.
A nameless crowd (I wonder whose) reminds me
of unmortared masonry. Tomorrow is the same
day in my experience. But sleep
can only give us the pleasure of pleasure

generous if we're awake.

2.

Nostalgia is the elixir drained
from guilt . . . I've been writing . . .
with the fingers of my non-writing hand
I patted the dashboard. "Hi, car."
It responded "Hello Mommy."

The city is uncarlike. She who had lived
all her life in the city and absorbed
all its laws in her blood . . . madness, really
. . . she waited for the light
to change and stepped into the traffic

on red. Objects always flicker.
Rain threatens but what can it do.
Knocking, buzzing, sloshing . . .

somewhere between empty and full . . .
the excitement is mental, internal

as they remain urgently still.
We have stayed in the city
over which it really is raining.
Reflections water the gardens.
The fields that pressed in the passing

landscapes were immobilized by trees.
Uneven individual glowing.
The photograph craves history.
The automobile drove to the photograph.
It faces me as I awake.

3.

The sun is just appearing.
The first bulky
clogged, distorted moment was dairy
yellow—an instant magnificent
with claustrophobia. How could one contemplate

"paradise" without thinking about love?
Rushing out into the open, I
believing it to be . . .
sometimes it takes just such
a motivated coincidence. Gold

from a petrified honeycomb lies
under the ironlike utility poles.
My merchant horse wickers.
My dog yaps in the park, always lamenting:
"Marvelous! Perfect!"

She sees her subjects
in an incomplete benevolent focus.
Meanwhile a great music forms
in the driveway—a band
of finches. It seems

as if everything might be somewhere
in that mass of sound
where bound together with the lyricism of wasps
and spiders they appear
to crave their own innate activity. And going

by the usual criteria for knowledge
I vowed not to laugh
but to scatter things. In the bowl
of my left palm I placed my right
forefinger, to signify a) Feeding

b) A batch, c) The Appraisal, d) Too much consolation
is like a forgetfully boundless vow.

4.

Imagine observing ones fear
of death metaphorically by falling
in love. And then today
become tomorrow as one steps out
of the bathtub into the pond—

aloof!—and down over the ditch.
The water splits, opal in the sunlight
—a moment when one, two, five—my words
are the terminus of a long train
of thought—and the sand dries.

The romantic intellect (the word
is unavoidable) takes in the excellence
of life on the whole. Thinking drops
(our daylight is like a ball)
and then leaps back. Lights

come on in the water
(because daylight is domesticity's underline)
and the pace of the movements
lit by them is altered
but inconsistently; some things go faster

others slower, and thus my flailing
arms altogether miss the sluggish sleeve
of my coat, and my mind has arrived
at the park long before my legs
slowly carry me to my front door.

Thus grotesquely elongated
with longing, two courses of experience
meet—how capably! A bouquet
adds weight. A dog
chases the rolling orange, the orange

opens and something is removed
—a telephone. A man is ringing
and he's divided horizontally.
He has in tow the stillness
of a barge, which takes on

the burden of the excellence
of happiness, that nameless reliving
spent in life.
Commitment? that sort of autobiography.
Confession? that sort of misunderstanding

—like infidelity to an impossible task.
What can take it over? It is as moral
for night to fall.

5.

"Angels, it seems, don't always know
they are moving." Spring
is not my "instruction" . . . mildly prime
. . . the remnants of a tremendous example.
The tree set upright to give

more room jiggles in the wind.
I've a complicated sense of injustice
. . . solitude unused . . . while vibrating
to music I draw on my napkin
in a small sufficient apartment.

In a time of brain and desire
patience is the mental equivalent of running.

*

ROBERT GRENIER

Prewar Late October Sea Breeze

for Ken Irby

reflections yet related light orange white to boom-boom
aster said amended sanded stable object courier tan bag loups to
fire angel tankard some warmth bangs in the afternoon sun
    blue waves
and some heat left in the fall moonlight a tomb military
to wrest away any reflected snowy tankward areas in Lebanon

from the page & dream & matter *every* wastrel songstress
    embassy
patience & strife piano onlooker's personal strip of rat-monk
    affection clangs
for cannon 'guns' some livid retching queasy yellow greasy
    seedy sore
intelligent matted bearded generally sunny fellow seeks abroad
    asylum to find but carrier
frequency canvasbacks & hunters—sallow virginal pools in
    windy amber watercolor

*

Wrath to Sadness

for Anselm Hollo

reproachful eyes'
beauty but the

face downcast in
Irish Russian Jewess'

Portuguese green eyes
furious beauty bottom smoldering

from proprietary Injury white
cheeked stung Insight & Pride red

downcast and burning American
with Right & Conviction suddenly

as if after an immense journey of thinking
suddenly as if out of nowhere

with forethought & malice spontaneously
looks up into my eyes

and the 'archaic smile' opens
again finally

to recite my doom

*

For Windows

for Kit (from D.H. Lawrence)

there's a great divinity
in man that doesn't get
to come out its
attempts are often
excruciatingly well
realized not
only artful but
songlike too and
beloved
often lively and
realistic often
rhythm
relaxing but *seer*
having undertaken this said
spiritual journey as
yet fundamentally
diamond-backed

✽

Prayer for Boom

for Robert Creeley

breast snoring saxophone *soddenly in place* are so palpable
eventide evocative of manifest narrative reservoirs of mental
means me that *in his place* those heavy fleshed flanked &
fleshy congested lungs of his immaterial contours that heavy
dogs hairy heave upward through their noses by breathing in
sleep I felt the Bronx mutually through a nostril *mine* and jaw

political subdivision suffused with teeth & bone pink & grey
green gains gums with animal animadvertent brown fluid
naturally that stands for/streams from *corpus delicti* us vs. all
suffering gibberant satisfactory though lyrical magical looks on
earth & *affirms* why asleep at least with the model monkey all
mere effort of breathing aura in & out options bastions
corporations ideas geophysics iron poets teaching in extant
universities *so forth is as dreaming sounds* our ears both *ever
and anon* falls dusk palms dog here ah fellow Boom, listening,
as human & man, to dawn's birds; your snores, greenery, *both*
my friends, *our* dual existence equally love fostered thus subject
to death unknown by heart attack in time

✳

JAMES SHERRY

Disinterment

Producify by exclusioness
give by subvert
replumb or dismake shiftment
submonition to Thursday

Dismorphology   Unheraldrate
rememberment   deassurify

Ok to refriend (stamp)
depertinent takeability
unmongst
rephrasatory unfemalization

Disregard, recoriate pairitude
comparement of sculpturority;   defile (side) vs.
unremergement as selfification
safed to suspiciate, not reever, simplicon of nonfinement

uncontinued deferral of reselfizationicity
cat-meow yellowize
unregenerate redigressivity
unlistening, hand descention from wrist
prechandelierizement digiticity
deconnoiter hydromarinertudinousness
foppitude respite feminotropicity
desophisticate identizoid—African sculptines

*

CHARLES BERNSTEIN

Of Time and the Line

George Burns likes to insist that he always
takes the straight lines; the cigar in his mouth
is a way of leaving space between the
lines for a laugh. He weaves lines together
by means of a picaresque narrative;
not so Hennie Youngman, whose lines are strict-
ly paratactic. My father pushed a
line of ladies' dresses—not down the street
in a pushcart but upstairs in a fact'ry
office. My mother has been more concerned
with her hemline. Chairman Mao put forward
Maoist lines, but that's been abandoned (most-
ly) for the East West line of malarkey
so popular in these parts. The prestige
of the iambic line has recently
suffered decline, since it's no longer so
clear who "I" am, much less who *you* are. When
making a line, better be double sure
what you're lining in & what you're lining
out & which side of the line you're on; the
world is made up so (Adam didn't so much
name as delineate). Every poem's got
a prosodic lining, some of which will
unzip for summer wear. The lines of an
imaginary are inscribed on the
social flesh by the knifepoint of history.
Nowadays, you can often spot a work
of poetry by whether it's in lines
or no; if it's in prose, there's a good chance

it's a poem. While there is no lesson in
the line more useful than that of the pick-
et line, the line that has caused the most ad-
versity is the bloodline. In Russia
everyone is worried about long lines;
back in the USA, it's strictly soup-
lines. "Take a chisel to write", but for an
actor a line's got to be cued. Or, as
they say in math, it takes two lines to make
an angle but only one lime to make
a Margarita.

*

The Harbor of Illusion

At midnight's scrawl, the fog has
lost its bone and puffs of
pall are loamed at
tidal edge. No more to count
than density arrows its
petulance at crevice laced
with dock, not hour's
solstice nor brimmed detour—
over the haunch of lock and
tress the vein pours sweetly
and Devil's door knows no
more than pester and undone—
the seering moors where I
refrain of lot and camphor.
Only this, a ripple
against a blind of shore that sands
us smooth and mistless: let
he who has not stunned make
sound, cacophany of

nearing, having fell, of
pouring, having stalled. Though
free to bore and load, let
rail retail conclusion, finicky jejubes
at waste of moor, or lord these
tower, tour the template, thoroughfare
of noon's atoll.

✳

The Kiwi Bird in the Kiwi Tree

I want no paradise only to be
drenched in the downpour of words, fecund
with tropicality. Fundament be-
yond relation, less 'real' than made, as arms
surround a baby's gurgling: encir-
cling mesh pronounces its promise (not bars
that pinion, notes that ply). The tailor tells
of other tolls, the seam that binds, the trim,
the waste, & having spelled these names, move on
to toys or talcoms, skates & scores. Only
the imaginary is real—not trumps
beclouding the mind's acrobatic ver-
sions. The first fact is the social body,
one from another, nor needs no other.

✳

Live Acts

Impossible outside you want always the other. A continual
recapitulation, & capture all that, against which our redaction
of sundry, promise, another person, fills all the

conversion of that into, which intersects a continual
revulsion of, against, concepts, encounter,
in which I hold you, a passion made of cups, amidst
frowns. Crayons of immaculate warmth ensnare our
somnambulance to this purpose alone.
The closer we look, the greater the distance from which
we look back. Essentially a hypnotic referral, like
I can't get with you on that, buzzes by real fast, shoots
up from some one or other aquafloral hideaway,
emerging into air. Or what we can't, the gentleman who
prefers a Soviet flag, floats, pigeoning the
answer which never owns what it's really about.
Gum sole shoes. The one that's there all the
time. An arbitrary policy, filled with noise, & yet
believable all the same. These projects alone contain
the person, binding up in an unlimited way what
otherwise goes unexpressed.

*

The Voyage of Life

*Over the remote hills, which seem to intercept the
stream, and turn in from its hitherto direct course,
a path is dimly seen, tending directly toward that
cloudy Fabric which is the object and desire of the
Voyager.—Thomas Cole*

Resistance marries faith, not faith persist-
Ence. Which is to say, little to import
Or little brewed from told and anxious
Ground: an alternating round of this or
That, some outline that strikes the looking back,
That gives the Punch and Judy to our show.
If it be temperate, it is temper-

Ance that make us hard; by strength of purpose
Turn Pinocchio into ox or gore
Melons with pickaxes, which the fighting
Back in turn proposes slugged advantage,
Slumped discomfit: rashes of ash, as
On a scape to ripple industry with
Hurls, the helter finds in shrubbing stuns. We
Carve and so are carved in twofold swiftness
Of manifold: the simple act of speak-
Ing, having heard, of crossing, having creased.
Sow not, lest reap, and choke on blooming things:
Innovation is Satan's toy, a train
That rails to semblance, place of memory's
Loss. Or tossed in tune, emboss with gloss in-
Signias of air.

＊

Special Pleading

Somewhere she was certain, but the sensation
was tenuous, unsteady, carved with an aimlessness
of irregular proportion and indistinct
features. Alarm bells ring & the camera pans
the dissolve, shot of graded rotation around
a cutting edge, burning to black
as tempted coordinate, padded with felt
& bravado. *"What are you—waiting
for the light?"* Succession and distracting
as mattering, melting. I really
kept thinking what is "spent light"—meaning
light that has vanished down the hallways
of what is already forgiven, a forgetfulness
formed, ideas as always locked
in place writ as conduct and traded as

colored. Now I can remember. Finally,
one type of stymied grace to invert
onto an exterior as holding,
tiling of an horizon made flesh.
The tin to the top. . . : life stolen from
or played against, that envelopes
even the shadows of a pause, cutting
left as half-torn turn of a fleeting
contour, moves it elsewhere, as if you
break loss from the "icon of loss".
As it happens, sliding and then arrested—
where the buildings are people or the people
are the project of their configurations:
A social tune that we can never hear but
play out, as the earth its own organ and
the blacktop of the road a vision of
Paradise. No more to mourn, the straw
shepherd guards his straw sheep & the chorus
sighs in silence. Such heat neither absolves
nor furnishes: we are plied in the mid-
day, smoked in the afternoon, & with night
fused into beings we never were & will
no longer be. Monsters are made of these sweetened
intentions & ferment in the fellowship
of good times. But the tide need not
go out at next evening's call. The impossible
is a bell worn round the neck to let
the misters know we wander—such
cackle as girls & boys will make
discomfit to their less demonstrative
fold.

*

STEPHEN RODEFER

Pretext

Then I stand up on my hassock and say sing that.
It is not the business of POETRY to be anything.
When one day at last they come to storm your deluxe cubicle,
Only your pumice stone will remain. The left trapezius for now
Is a little out of joint. Little did they know you came with it.
When nature has entirely disappeared, we will find ourselves in
    Stuttgart.
Till then we're on the way. The only way not to leave is to go.
The gods and scientists heap their shit on Buffalo and we're out
    there,
Scavenging plastic trees. When nature has entirely disappeared,
We'll find ourselves in the steam garden. Evening's metonym for
    another
Beady-eyed engineer with sexual ideas, who grew up eating
    animals.
Do you like the twelve tones of the western scale? I prefer
    ninety.
I may work in a factory but I slide to the music of the spheres.
My job is quality control in the language lab, explaining what
    went
Wrong in Northampton after the Great Awakening. So much
    was history.

My father is a sphinx and my mother's a nut. I reject the glass.
But I've been shown the sheets of sentences and what he was
Really like remains more of a riddle than in the case of most
    humans.

So again I say rejoice, the man we're looking for
Is gone. The past will continue, the surest way to advance,
But you still have to run to keep fear in the other side.
There is a little door at the back of the mouth fond of long
    names
Called the juvjula. The pidgeon means business. It carries
Messages. The faces on the character parts are excellent.
In fact I'm having lunch with her next week. Felix nupsit.
Why should it be so difficult to see the end if when it comes
It should be irrefutable. Cabin life is incomplete.
But the waterbugs's mittens SHADOW the bright rocks below.
He has a resemblance in the upper face to the man who robbed
    you.
I am pleased to be here. To my left is Philippa, who will be
    signing for me.

*

Codex

That is the glebe and this is the glissando. The future is
    nothing
But a flying wing. You must make your case either with names
    or with an unfolding.
A position or a disclosure, a microbus. The corridor, the
    cascade, what stuck.
Glacier notes over the tops of hills. To be close again, as it was
    in the leanto.
Lengthen the line and increase the leading. These are the
    helloes of progress.
At the kitchen table the books are pored over, much as a
    neighbor will burn a cigaret.
The bungalow, radioed and occupied, has no other path to
    follow but the venture,
The undeniable yielding turmoil mapped out for us for life.

Somebody might ought cook someone a square meal. Life in
   our adulthood
Is mistaken for wanting completion. What it longs to do is
   continue being.
The BEES are sleeping beneath the pergola. At the end of each
   lesson is the vocabulary.
If one opening clouds, another will clear, so long as you both
   will breathe.
Where's a shovel or something, I say, what can dig, or a trowel?
   Language pointed
To its content. A crowd of people at the beach screaming
   "Tuna! tuna!" The evening
Breeze, trembling trees, the night, the stars. And there you are,
   in a manner of speaking.

So at sunset the clouds went nuts. They thought they were a
   text.
This language of the general o'erflows the measure, but my
   brother and I liked it alot.
I think I'll just pause long enough here to call God a bitter
   name.
Ripeness is all right but the lip is a couplet and nobody knows
   fuck-all about it.
The THREAD has always been bias. There are alternatives to
   purchasing goods
To recruit admirers. Right, but is it what Verdi would have
   wanted?
Nor is it enough to be seen by your youngers as having carried
   the tradition
To a good place. Given disasters everywhere, don't drink from
   the tap.
And for what reason make anything that is not for flight?
There are treatments to keep your retina from becoming
   detached but for what—
To see this? Why, there are things about Israel not dreamed of
   in the Bible.

How could I miss you when my aim is dead. The goal is sea
    sounds not yet writ.
All right. Enjoy the heads of your beaches. I'm not going in
    order
To get tied up on spec, but I wanted you to meet your fellow
    brains. Thank you,
People of destiny, for your brilliant corners. I like your voice.
    Look where it's come from.

*

Biographies (in alphabetical order)

KEITH ABBOTT was born in Tacoma, Washington in 1944, grew up in the Northwest, and now lives in Albany, California. He edited BLUE SUEDE SHOES, a poetry magazine in the 70s. With Pat Nolan, Steve Carey, Sean Lazarchuk and Victoria Rathbun, he formed a loosely associated group of writers whose esthetics were strongly influenced by ancient Chinese and Japanese poetry, as well as California Zen, Ted Berrigan, and French Surrealism. These days he writes mostly fiction. His latest novel is SOMEONE'S ANGEL CHILD (1987). Among his many poetry collections are GOOD NEWS BAD NEWS (1984) and ERASE WORDS (1977).

SAM ABRAMS was born in 1935. He was, with Paul Blackburn, Joel Oppenheimer and Carol Berge, one of the founders of the St. Marks' Poetry Project, just before the Ted Berrigan/Anne Waldman era. Among his works are a number of pseudonymous erotic novels he wrote for Olympia Press. He is a Professor of Classical Literature at the Rochester Institute of Technology.

MICHAEL ANDRE was born in Quebec in 1946. Now based in New York City, he edits UNMUZZLED OX, one of the most interesting magazines in America for its mixture of avantgarde poetry, art, practical jokes and philosophical insouciance. Andre's books include STUDYING THE GROUND FOR HOLES (1978) and LETTERS HOME (1979).

DAVID ANTIN was born in 1932 and teaches in the Visual Arts Department of the University of California in San Diego. He has expanded the territory of recent American poetry with his experiments in "talk," a way of making brilliant, oral poetry. His books include TALKING AT THE BOUNDARIES and TUNING.

WILL BENNETT was born in 1952 in Dunmore, Pennsylvania. He was co-editor (with George-Thérèse Dickenson) of ASSASSIN

(1975–1980), a Surrealist magazine. He lives in New York. His latest books are SUN, MOON AND STARS (1987) and ZERO (1984).

BILL BERKSON was born in New York City in 1939. He was a close friend of Frank O'Hara, who dedicated many poems to him. He is a noted art and dance critic and a frequent contributor to ART IN AMERICA. Among his many books is LUSH LIFE (1985), a selection of poems. He lives in Bolinas, California.

ALAN BERNHEIMER was born a New Yorker in 1948. He has lived in San Francisco and its environs since 1977, where he now heads ComputerLand, a corporation. Active in the "language" group, he studied with Ted Berrigan and Clark Coolidge at Yale, where he also met Kit Robinson and Rodger Kamenetz. His books are: CAFE ISOTOPE (1980), STATE LOUNGE (1981) and THE HAMLET OF THE BEES (1981).

CHARLES BERNSTEIN was born in New York in 1950. He is the leading figure of the New York "language" group that includes Bruce Andrews, James Sherry and George-Thérèse Dickenson. As editor of L-A-N-G-U-A-G-E (with Andrews) he is the principal theoretician of the movement. The current attraction of young academic critics to "language" writing stems in part from Bernstein's definitions of the terms of the discourse. His criticism is collected in CONTENT'S DREAM: ESSAYS 1975–1984 (1986). His latest poetry books are THE SOPHIST (1987), RESISTANCE (1987), and ISLETS/IRRITATIONS (1983).

TED BERRIGAN (1934–1983) said, "I invented the New York School of poetry." In many ways he did. The leading figure of the second generation of New York School poets was born in Providence, Rhode Island. After moving to New York in the early sixties and meeting Frank O'Hara, Berrigan developed a poetry based on talk, "found poetry," collage and Surrealism. He was the "eminence grise" of the early days of the St. Marks Poetry Project, and the enthusiastic ideologue of "The World" magazine published by Anne Waldman. His own magazine, "C" was a short-lived but potent journal in the late 1960s. Berrigan's influence extended way past New York. He excited and formed young poets wherever he taught: at Yale, in Iowa City, in Chicago, and in Brooklyn. He has written prose: CLEAR THE RANGE (a novel, 1977); has published collaborations, BEAN SPASMS (with Ron Padgett and Joe Brainard, 1968); and has recorded many hours of talk on poetry and art. His many poetry books include: THE SONNETS (1964, 1967 and 1982), NOTHING FOR YOU (1977) and SO GOING AROUND CITIES: NEW AND SELECTED POEMS 1958–1979 (1980).

KAY BOYLE, born in St. Paul, Minnesota in 1902, is the muse of this book. The author of THE UNDERGROUND WOMAN (1975) and THIS IS NOT A LETTER (1985) is our link with the spirit of previous avantgardes. She is an embodiment of courage, from the 1920s into our own muddled age. Her journey from the Paris of exiles (recalled in BEING GENIUSES TOGETHER, with Robert McAlmon), through the sixties when she emerged as a symbol of resistance against the Vietnam War, has been an unbroken affirmation. The exhortation of her "Poem" sounds clear and tough to us.

SUMMER BRENNER was born in 1945 and lives in Berkeley, California. She has affinities with a number of other women writers, including Laura Chester, Gloria Frym, and Janet Hamill, all of whom use erotic motifs in their work. Among her books are EVERYONE CAME DRESSED AS WATER, FROM THE HEART TO THE CENTER, and her most recent, THE SOFT ROOM (1983).

JIM BRODEY was born in 1942 and is one of the chief experimentalists of the New York School. His work is influenced by music, and he has written a great deal of music criticism. He traveled widely in the 1970s, before returning to New York where he now manages a hotel in midtown Manhattan. His latest book is JUDYISM (1980).

MICHAEL BROWNSTEIN was born in 1943 in Philadelphia, and now lives in New York City. He is a poet, novelist and translator. He has published COUNTRY COUSINS (a novel) and translations of Max Jacob, as well as a number of poetry books, including: HIGHWAY TO THE SKY (Winner of the Frank O'Hara Award, 1969), and ORACLE NIGHT (1982).

JANINE CANAN was born in Los Angeles in 1942. She is a practicing psychiatrist in Berkeley, California. She has published five books of poetry, the latest of which is HER MAGNIFICENT BODY: NEW AND SELECTED POEMS (1986).

SANDIE CASTLE was born in 1954 in Baltimore, where she lives. Her electric performances have earned her the title of "guerrilla duchess of Baltimore." She has dazzled audiences in her native town and elsewhere for seven years. Her collection is THE CATHOLICS ARE COMING (1984 & 1985).

MAXINE CHERNOFF was born in 1952 in Chicago where she still lives. With Paul Hoover, her husband, she edits NEW AMERICAN WRITING (formerly OINK!), and is an important promoter of poetry in Chicago. Her genuinely Surrealist sympathies are evident in many of her innovative prose poems. She received the Carl Sandburg Award for poetry in 1985. Her books are THE LAST AUROCHS (1976), A VEGETABLE EMERGENCY (1977), UTOPIA TV STORE (1979), NEW FACES OF 1952 (1985) and BOP (1986).

LAURA CHESTER was born in Cambridge, Massachusetts in 1949. She edited RISING TIDES: 20TH CENTURY AMERICAN WOMEN POETS, and is one of the founders of The Figures, an important publisher of avantgarde writing. She is now working on a collection of sensual writing for women. Her strongly erotic, feminist work is published in several collections, including MY PLEASURE (1980), LUPUS NOVICE (1987) and FREE REIN (1988).

TOM CLARK was born in Chicago in 1941. For ten years in the 60s and 70s he served as poetry editor of THE PARIS REVIEW, of which he remains an advisory editor. His acute critical acumen and polemical skill have helped define the current climate of the American poetry scene. He has been vehemently opposed to the formalist tendencies of the "language" group. Presently at work on a biography of the poet Charles Olson, he has also written biographies of Ted Berrigan, Jack Kerouac and Damon Runyon. He has written a novel, THE EXILE OF CELINE (1987). Among his many poetry books are AIR (1969), STONES (1970), WHEN THINGS GET TOUGH ON EASY STREET (1978), PARADISE REVISITED (1984) and DISORDERED IDEAS (1987).

ANDREI CODRESCU was born in 1946 in Sibiu, Romania, and came to the U.S. in 1966. He is a poet, autobiographer, essayist and translator. He is a regular commentator on National Public Radio, and the editor of EXQUISITE CORPSE: A MONTHLY OF BOOKS & IDEAS. Among his many books are two autobiographies, THE LIFE AND TIMES OF AN INVOLUNTARY GENIUS (1976) and IN AMERICA'S SHOES (1983); a volume of essays, A CRAVING FOR SWAN (1986); and many poetry collections including LICENSE TO CARRY A GUN (Big Table Award, 1970), THE HISTORY OF THE GROWTH OF HEAVEN (1973), GRAMMAR & MONEY (1973), NECROCORRIDA (1978), and SELECTED POEMS: 1970–1980 (1984). He is the editor of this anthology.

JACK COLLOM was born in Chicago in 1932. He studied forestry, and worked in factories for 20 years before getting a Late English MA on the GI Bill. Now a poet-in-the-schools in Boulder, Colorado, he has written MOVING WINDOWS: EVALUATING THE POETRY CHILDREN WRITE (1985). The latest of his several collections of poetry is THE FOX (1981).

CLARK COOLIDGE was born in Providence, Rhode Island in 1939. He lives in Western Massachusetts. Chief experimentalist, jazz connoisseur, he has brought poetry and music closer than anyone since Gertrude Stein. He is on the Poetics Faculty at the Naropa Institute in Boulder, Colorado. Among his books are FLAG FLUTTER AND U.S. ELECTRIC (1966), CLARK COOLIDGE (1967), ING (1968), SPACE (1970), POLAROID (1975), QUARTZ HEARTS (1978), A GEOLOGY (1981), THE CRYSTAL TEXT (1986) and MELENCOLIA (1987).

DENNIS COOPER was born in 1953 in Pasadena, California. He is one of the important members of the Los Angeles "new wave" poetry circle. He is now living in Amsterdam. His books are SAFE (1984), HE CRIED (1984), THE TENDERNESS OF WOLVES (1982), IDOLS (1979) and TIGER BEAT (1978).

JOEL DAILEY was born in Johnson City, New York in 1953. He edits FELL SWOOP in New Orleans, where he lives with his poet wife Elizabeth Thomas. He collaborated with the poet/performer David Franks on a number of projects in New Orleans. His latest books are ANGRY RED BLUES (1986) and CURRENT (1982).

TOM DENT was born in New Orleans in 1932. After living in New York, where he was part of the "Umbra" group (Ishmael Reed, David Henderson, et al), he returned to his native New Orleans in 1965 where he helped found the FREE SOUTHERN THEATRE, an important civil rights forum. Among his books are THE FREE SOUTHERN THEATRE BY THE SOUTHERN THEATRE (with Gilbert Moses and Richard Schechner, 1970), MAGNOLIA STREET (1976), and BLUE LIGHTS AND RIVER SONGS (1982).

GEORGE-THÉRÈSE DICKENSON was born in 1946 and is the director of Incision Arts, a prison arts organization. She co-edited ASSASSIN (1975–1980) with Will Bennett, and now edits INCISIONS: PRISON WARD POETRY and BLACK ROSE: A JOURNAL OF CONTEMPORARY ANARCHIST THEORY. She performs occasionally with musicians. Her latest collection is TRANSDUCING (1985).

ELAINE EQUI was born in Chicago in 1953 where she teaches at Columbia College. A natural Surrealist, and a terrific performer of poetry, she is part of an active Chicago poetry scene that includes Jerome Sala, Al Simmons, Henry Kanabus and others. Her books are FEDERAL WOMAN (1978), SHREWCRAZY (1981), and THE CORNERS OF THE MOUTH (1986).

HARRISON FISHER was born in New York in 1954. He lives in Albany, New York. An American Surrealist, his latest books are THE GRAVITY (1977) and THE ROMANTIC ABSTRACT OF THE PHYSICAL AGON (1977).

GLORIA FRYM was born in Brooklyn in 1947, grew up in Southern California, and lived in New Mexico for many years. She now lives in Berkeley, California, where she works with prison inmates. Her books are BACK TO FORTH (1982), IMPOSSIBLE AFFECTION (1979) and SECOND STORIES (1979).

DICK GALLUP was born in Greenfield, Massachusetts in 1941. He was a close collaborator of Ted Berrigan's in the late 60s and early 70s and an influence on many younger poets. His intense lyrical verse is deliberately understated and quiet. Among his books, the best known is WHERE I HANG MY HAT (Winner of the Frank O'Hara Award for poetry, 1971). He now lives in San Francisco where he drives a taxicab at night.

AMY GERSTLER was born in San Diego in 1956, and is now a resident of Los Angeles. Among her collections are WHITE MARRIAGE/RECOVERY (1984), EARLY HEAVEN (1984), MARTINE'S MOUTH (1985) and THE TRUE BRIDE (1986).

JOHN GIORNO was born in New York City in 1936. He is the foremost performing poet today, whose long poems and sound experiments have attracted immense audiences both in the United States and Europe. He has toured with William Burroughs for extended periods. Giorno Poetry Systems, the audio and video company has has founded, produces work by the best avantgardists working in those mediums today, including Philip Glass, Laurie Anderson, Patti Smith, Jim Carroll, Anne Waldman, and Husker Du. Giorno has starred in movies, notably Warhol's SLEEP (he was the man sleeping), and he invented Dial-a-Poem, the innovative poetry phone program that was widely imitated. His books include DRINKING THE BLOOD OF EVERY WOMAN'S PERIOD (1967), CANCER IN MY LEFT BALL (1973) and IT'S A MISTAKE TO THINK YOU'RE SPECIAL (1984).

JOHN GODFREY was born in Massena, New York in 1945. After graduating from Princeton in 1967, he moved to the Lower East Side of New York. He is an important New York School poet, included in many New York anthologies and magazines. His recent work has been moving in the direction of prose poetry. His books include 26 POEMS (1971), MUSIC OF THE CURBS (1976), DABBLE: POEMS 1966–1980 (1982), WHERE THE WEATHER SUITS MY CLOTHES (1984) and MIDNIGHT ON YOUR LEFT (1987).

JUDY GRAHN was born in Chicago in 1940. A radical feminist, she is a powerful performer of her work and has a large following in the U.S. and abroad. She lives in California and is active in the gay/lesbian movement there. Her newest work is THE QUEEN OF SWORDS. Among her books are EDWARD THE DYKE, THE COMMON WOMAN POEMS, A WOMAN IS TALKING TO DEATH, SHE WHO, and THE QUEEN OF WANDS.

DARRELL GRAY (1945–1986) was born in Sacramento and grew up in Kansas. In Iowa City in the early 1970s he founded the Actualist Movement with Allan Kornblum, George Mattingly, Dave Morice, Joyce Holland and others. The Actualists held a number of conventions that were well-attended multi-media events, both in Iowa and in Berkeley. A number of Actualist magazines and book publishers, including Blue Wind (Iowa & Berkeley), Toothpaste (Iowa & Minneapolis), Matchbook (Iowa) helped define the movement. Gray's own intentions for Actualism were, paraphrasing Guillevic, "to do to things what light does to them." A fine polemicist and essayist as well as poet, he published a number of books including THE BEAUTIES OF TRAVEL, SOMETHING SWIMS OUT and RUBY PORT: THE FOOD POEMS OF PHILIPPE MIGNON, TRANSLATED BY DARRELL GRAY. He died in a rooming house in Oakland, California. The landlord threw out Gray's personal effects, including diaries, photographs, and the complete manuscript of an unpublished novel.

ROBERT GRENIER was born in Minneapolis, Minnesota in 1941. After graduating from Harvard, he lived and taught in Iowa City, Berkeley, and San Francisco. He is a noted critic, editor and translator, as well as a prolific poet. His criticism includes ATTENTION (essay on narrative, 1985). He has edited SELECTED POEMS BY ROBERT CREELEY (1976) and WATERS/PLACES/A TIME BY LARRY EIGNER (1983). He translated SELECTED POEMS: GEORG TRAKL with Christopher Middleton (1968). His latest poetry books are A DAY AT THE BEACH (1985) and PHANTOM ANTHEMS (1986). He is active in the San Francisco "language" group.

JIM GUSTAFSON was born in Detroit in 1949, where he now lives, making a living as a feature writer for the DETROIT NEWS. He lived briefly (and tumultously) in San Francisco, Chicago, Austin and New York. He was the editor of Jeffrey Miller's posthumous book, THE FIRST ONE'S FREE. In the late 1970s he stopped publishing, "due to a general disgust with the state of what is alleged to be American writing." His books are: TALES OF VIRTUE AND TRANSFORMATION (1975), BRIGHT EYES TALKS CRAZY TO REMBRANDT (1978), and SHAMELESS (1979).

JESSICA HAGEDORN was born in Manila, Philippines in 1949. She is interested in the correspondences between poetry and music, and has often worked with jazz musicians. Her first book was DANGEROUS MUSIC (1975), followed by PETFOOD AND TROPICAL APPARITIONS (1981), a collection of poetry and short prose that makes poignant social comments. She is part of a loosely knit group of third world women poets that includes Ntosake Shange, Thulani Davis, Pat Jones, and Cyn. Zarco. She is the Program Coordinator of the St. Marks Poetry Project in New York City.

JANET HAMILL was born in Jersey City in 1945, and now lives in New York City, after brief stays in Mexico, Europe and Africa. Her books are TROUBLANTE (1975) and THE TEMPLE (1980).

WILLIAM HATHAWAY was born in Madison, Wisconsin in 1944. Lives currently in Saratoga Springs, New York, after several years in Louisiana. His books are TRUE CONFESSIONS & FALSE ROMANCES (1972) A WILDERNESS OF MONKEYS (1975), THE GYMNAST OF INERTIA (1982) and FISH, FLESH & FOWL (1985).

LYN HEJINIAN was born in 1941 and is the publisher of TUUMBA, one of the language group's most important publication, along with THE FIGURES, and ROOF BOOKS. Her own work is musical, erotic, and philosophical. One of her most notable new books is REDO (1984). She lives in Berkeley, California.

VICTOR HERNANDEZ CRUZ was born in Aguas Buenas, Puerto Rico in 1949, and was raised in New York City. He pioneered the hip New York Spanish-infused lingo that became a trademark of the Nuyorican poetry scene. His books include SNAPS (1969), MAINLAND (1973), TROPICALIZATION (1976) and BY LINGUAL WHOLES (1982). He lives in San Francisco.

DAVID HILTON was born in Oakland, California in 1938. He was one of the original members of the Actualist movement, founded in Iowa City in 1970 by Darrell Gray. He lives in Baltimore. His books are HOOLADANCE (1976) and THE CANDLE FLAME (1976).

ANSELM HOLLO was born in Helsinki, Finland in 1934. He settled permanently in the U.S. in 1966, and has been an important American poet ever since. He is also a translator (from Finnish, Swedish, German, French and Russian), a journalist and teacher. He lives in Salt Lake City with the painter Jane Dalrymple. Hollo's poetry, originally influenced by Ezra Pound, Charles Olson, and Robert Creeley, has inspired many younger poets, including members of the "language" group (many of whom were his students in Iowa City in the early 1970s), younger New York School poets, and the Baltimore group. The most recent of his twenty-seven collections of poetry are HEAVY JARS (1977), FINITE CONTINUED (1980), NO COMPLAINTS (1983), and PICK UP THE HOUSE (1986). Among his thirty-one translated books, the most recent are: POEMS 1958–1980 by Pentti Saarkisoski (1983) and AUGUST STRINDBERG by Olof Lagercrantz (1984).

BOB HOLMAN was born in LaFollette, Tennessee in 1948. Now living in New York City, he has directed many poets' theatre productions, and hosts "The Double Talk Show," on cable TV, with Pedro Pietri and Vito Ricci. His books are BICENTENNIAL SUICIDE (1976), TEAR TO OPEN (1979), 8 CHINESE POEMS (1981) and SWEAT&SEX&POLITICS (1984).

PAUL HOOVER, born in Harrisonburg, Virginia, in 1946, now lives in Chicago where he is poet-in-residence at Columbia College. He was the co-editor (with Maxine Chernoff) of the important magazine OINK!, now renamed NEW AMERICAN WRITING. His books are LETTER TO EINSTEIN BEGINNING DEAR ALBERT (1979), SOMEBODY TALKS A LOT (1982), NERVOUS SONGS (1986) and IDEA (1987).

FANNY HOWE was born in 1940. She lives in Boston and teaches at MIT. She writes fiction as well as poetry. She is a poet of extreme precision, concerned with the formal elements of verse, but

also a fine lyricist. Some of her books are EGGS, THE AMERIN-
DIAN COASTLINE POEM, POEM FROM A SINGLE PALLET,
ALSACE LORRAINE, FOR ERATO: THE MEANING OF LIFE,
and her latest, ROBESON STREET (1985).

SUSAN HOWE was born in Boston in 1937. She is one of the
foremost experimentalists working today, claimed equally by fem-
inists and the language group. Her critical study of Emily Dick-
inson, MY EMILY DICKINSON (1986) has changed the
traditional view of the poet, and won the Before Columbus Foun-
dation's American Book Award. Her poetry books include DEFEN-
ESTRATION OF PRAGUE (1983), and THE EUROPE OF
TRUSTS: SELECTED POEMS (1987).

RODGER KAMENETZ was born in Baltimore in 1950. He has
explored the sense of displacement in his Jewish-American iden-
tity in THE MISSING JEW (1979). He is loosely affiliated with a
number of Baltimore poets, including Kraft Rompf and David
Hilton, who have also felt the need for a sense of belonging within
the imprecise outlines of the late 20th Century. His other books
are: NYMPHOLEPSY (1985) and TERRA INFIRMA (1985).

HENRY KANABUS was born in Amberg, Germany in 1949. He
makes his home in Chicago, where he studied with Ted Berrigan
in the mid-70s. He was active in Chicago Surrealist circles, part of
the STONEWIND and BODY POLITIC/ YELLOW PRESS groups.
Has published five books of poetry, the latest of which are THE
WAR MAGICIAN (1986) and REPTILES IN CONFINEMENT
(1986).

FAYE KICKNOSWAY was born in 1936 and grew up in Los An-
geles and Detroit. Her tough, urban Surrealism and hard-edged
feminist vision have become increasingly elaborate from book to
book. These include SHE WEARS HIM FANCY IN HER
NIGHTBRAID (1979) and now ALL THESE VOICES: SELECTED
POEMS (1986). She lives in Honolulu where she teaches at the
University of Hawaii.

MARILYN KITCHELL, born in New Rochelle, New York in 1951,
now lives in rural Mississippi, where she farms, raises goats,

prints and publishes. She is co-editor, with husband Tom Bridwell, of Salt-works Press. Her work is strongly allied with that of the language poets, though she connects also to some other strains of experiment, particularly the work of Ted Enslin. Her books are TOUCAN (with Tom Bridwell, 1978), 4, THE ROAD (1980), WEEDS, WOOD, STONE & METTLE (1980).

STEVE KOWIT was born in 1938 in New York. He is a California resident, Buddhist animal rights activist and poet/teacher. His books are HEART IN UTTER CONFUSION (1982), CUTTING OUR LOSSES (1982), LURID CONFESSIONS (1983), PASSION-ATE JOURNEY (1984) and INCITEMENT TO NIXONICIDE (Neruda translations, 1979).

ROCHELLE KRAUT was born in Germany in 1952. Her poetry books are CIRCUS BABIES and ART IN AMERICA. She also writes and directs plays in New York City.

ALEX KUO was born in Boston in 1939. He now lives in Idaho where he is working on the satellite optical interpretation of en-dangered species and transcribing it into narrative text. His book is CHANGING THE RIVER (1987).

MIRA TERU KURKA was born in New York in 1952, where she lives and works as a newsmaker at Time, Inc. She is doing gradu-ate work in invertebrate paleontology. FRUIT AND GOVERN-MENT (1980) is her only poetry collection.

BILL KUSHNER was born in 1931 in New York where he lives. He is the author of a play, A NIGHT FOR GHOSTS (1968), and two intensely erotic, gay poetry collections, NIGHT FISHING (1976) and HEAD (1986).

JOANNE KYGER was born in 1934 and lives in Bolinas, Califor-nia. She has lived in Japan where she became interested in Zen Buddhism. Her work is often fragmentary, part of a long journal-poem. She is on the faculty of the Poetics School at the Naropa Institute. Among her many books is ALL THIS EVERY DAY (1975).

PHILIP LAMANTIA, born in 1927, was "discovered" by André Breton at a tender age. Since then he has become the chief elder of American Surrealism. Originally associated with the poets of the San Francisco Renaissance, he has not published or spoken publicly for a number of years. Very recently he emerged from his isolation to begin a new phase of his career. His new work, using Surrealist techniques, is passionately environmentalist, taking for its focus the California Coast and its Native American people. Lamantia's work influenced many younger poets, notably Ivan Argüelles and Jim Brook. Among his many books are EROTIC POEMS, EKSTASIS, NARCOTICA, and the recent BECOMING VISIBLE (1981) and MEADOWLARK WEST (1986).

ART LANGE was born in 1952 and lives in Chicago. He is a music critic, and associate editor of Down Beat magazine. He was editor of Brilliant Corners: A Magazine of the Arts (1975–1979). His poetry books include EVIDENCE (1981) and NEEDLES AT MID-NIGHT (1986).

STEVEN LAVOIE was born in Madison, Minnesota in 1953, but grew up in a Northern California vineyard. He is a librarian in East Oakland, active on the Bay Area poetry scene since the mid-70s. With Pat Nolan, Darrell Gray, and Keith Abbott, part of a Surrealist-leaning group that publishes LIFE OF CRIME, a polemical newsletter. His latest books, PLASTIC RULERS (1985) and LIPSYNCH (1986) seem to mark a change of style closer to "language" writing.

GARY LENHART was born in Newark, Ohio in 1947, and grew up in Albany, New York. He now lives in New York City with his wife, the painter Louise Hamlin. He is one of the editors of MAG CITY, an important publication among the new generation of Lower East Side magazines. His books include DRUNKARD'S DREAM, BULB IN SOCKET and ONE AT A TIME (1983).

STEVEN LEVINE was born in 1953 and lives in New York City, where he emigrated from Chicago in the midseventies, under the influence of Ted Berrigan. His latest book is PURE NOTATIONS (1981).

LEWIS MAC ADAMS, a Texas native, was Water Commissioner of Bolinas, California, in the mid-70s. Later he became editor of WET: THE MAGAZINE OF GOURMET BATHING in Los Angeles. Former Director of the San Francisco Poetry Center, he recently wrote and directed a documentary on the life of Jack Kerouac. He now writes for the movies and lives in Los Angeles. His latest books are LIVE AT THE CHURCH (1977) and AFRICA AND THE MARRIAGE OF WALT WHITMAN AND MARILYN MONROE (1982).

CLARENCE MAJOR was born in 1936 and lives in Boulder, Colorado. He has edited the influential anthology THE NEW BLACK POETRY (1969), and has published the DICTIONARY OF AFRO-AMERICAN SLANG (1970), an important scholarly work. His erotic, comic, and meditative poetry appears in several volumes, including THE SYNCOPATED CAKEWALK (1974), and INSIDE DIAMETER: THE FRANCE POEMS (1985).

JACK MARSHALL was born in 1937 in Brooklyn. He traveled in Europe, Africa and Mexico, and now resides in San Francisco. The latest of his seven collections of poetry are ARABIAN NIGHTS (1986) and ARRIVING ON THE PLAYING FIELDS OF PARADISE (1983).

BERNADETTE MAYER was born in 1945. A prodigious experimentalist and prolific poet, she has published numerous collections. She lives in New York City where she was Program Director of the St. Marks Poetry Project for a number of years. Among her works are the book-length MEMORY, a poem-fleuve of thoughts recovered in meditation, THE GOLDEN BOOK OF WORDS, STUDYING HUNGER, ERUDITIO EX MEMORIA (another grand mnemonic attempt at recalling all the books of her life), MIDWINTER DAY, MOVING and STORY. Her recent work is political and directly involved with community issues in the Lower East Side where she lives.

JEFFREY MILLER (1948–1977) was born in Flint, Michigan. He was part of the Monte Rio, California poetry group that included, variously, Andrei Codrescu, Pat Nolan, Bruce Cheney and Hunce Voelcker. Prodigiously talented, he emerged as an astounding performer of poetry as well during the mid-70s. He was to have read in the First International Punk Poetry Festival in San Francisco, an event attended by thousands of people, but he was killed in a car accident shortly before, on his 29th birthday. His book THE FIRST ONE'S FREE, was edited posthumously first by Andrei Codrescu, then in its final form by Jim Gustafson. A new collection of his poetry will be published soon by EXQUISITE CORPSE.

EILEEN MYLES was born in Cambridge, Massachusetts in 1949. She was artistic director of the St. Marks Poetry Project in New York City from 1984 to 1986. An important "younger" New York School poet, she edited DODGEMS (1977–78) with Susie Timmons, and LADIES MUSEUMS with Susie Timmons and Rochelle Kraut, an anthology of "downtown women poets," (1977). Her latest books are THE IRONY OF THE LEASH (1978), and POLAR ODE (in collaboration with Anne Waldman, 1979).

ELINOR NAUEN was born in Sioux Falls, South Dakota in 1952. She has a passion for baseball and cars. Among her books is CARS (1980), which contains a long paean to the automobiles in her life. She is fiction editor of WOMAN'S WORLD. She lives in New York City.

PAT NOLAN was born in 1943 in Montreal. He now lives in Monte Rio, California where he runs the Black Bart Poetry Society, which publishes LIFE OF CRIME, the newsletter of a group strongly influenced by New York School, Surrealist, and Oriental poetries. This is, strictly speaking, the "California School," because its members, which have included at various times, Keith Abbott, Steven La Voie, Steve Carey, Hunce Voelcker, Jeffrey Miller, Victoria Rathbun and Andrei Codrescu, have all been connected by an active sense of place in the mid-70s. Pat Nolan's latest books are THE GREAT PRETENDERER (1984) and FUNDAMENTAL (1982). His translations from the French are included in THE RANDOM HOUSE BOOK OF TWENTIETH CENTURY FRENCH POETRY.

ALICE NOTLEY was born in Needles, California in 1945. She was married to Ted Berrigan until the poet's death in 1983. She is raising her two children, Anselm and Edmund, in New York City.

Her poetry is strongly influenced by the California desert where she was born. She has a painterly sense of color. She is a prolific writer, and has written complex longer poems, notably SONGS FOR THE UNBORN SECOND BABY (1979). Among her other books are MARGARET & DUSTY (1985), SORRENTO (1984), WALTZING MATILDA (1981) and WHEN I WAS ALIVE (1980).

MAUREEN OWEN was born in Graceville, Minnesota in 1943. Her interest in Zen led her to Japan where she lived for two and a half years and where her two oldest children were born. She began editing TELEPHONE BOOKS and TELEPHONE MAGAZINE in New York City in 1969, and has over 30 titles and 19 issues of the magazine to date. She was director of the St. Marks Poetry Project (1976–77), and an enthusiastic teacher of various Project workshops. Her exuberant style and tremendous energy shine in her strongly feminist works, which include COUNTRY RUSH (1973), NO TRAVELS JOURNAL (1975), HEARTS IN SPACE (1980) and AE (AMELIA EARHART) (1984).

RON PADGETT is, with Ted Berrigan and Dick Gallup, part of the original triumvirate of second generation New York School poets. He was born in 1942 in Tulsa, Oklahoma, and moved to New York in the early sixties. He has been an innovative and prolific poet who pioneered group collaborations and teaching poetry to children. As one of the best American translators from the French, he introduced younger poets to seminal works of avantgarde literature, including: THE POET ASSASSINATED by Guillaume Apollinaire (1968) and KODAK by Blaise Cendrars (1976). He has co-edited (with David Shapiro), AN ANTHOLOGY OF NEW YORK POETS (1970) and THE COMPLETE POEMS OF EDWIN DENBY (1986). His own poetry books include HOW TO BE A WOODPECKER (1983) and TRIANGLES IN THE AFTER-NOON (1979).

MICHAEL PALMER was born in New York City in 1943. He studied philosophy at Harvard, and studied for a time at the University of Florence. The philosophical bias of his work is evident in his deep concern with language, music and dance. He has worked as a choreographer with the Margaret Jenkins Dance Company. His books include: PLAN FOR THE CITY OF O,

BLAKE'S NEWTON, THE CIRCULAR GATES, WITHOUT MU-
SIC, TRANSPARENCY OF THE MIRROR, ALOGON, NOTES
FROM ECHO LAKE and FIRST FIGURE. He lives in San Fran-
cisco.

FRANK POLITE was born in Youngstown, Ohio in 1934. He is a
world traveler who has gone for extended stays to the Middle and
Far East. His whereabouts are presently unknown, according to
his publisher at City Miner books. The selection included here is
from LETTERS OF TRANSIT (1979 & 1980).

JANINE POMMY-VEGA was born in Jersey City in 1942. She has
lived in Jerusalem, Paris, Amsterdam, London, Spain, Ireland,
South America and Hawaii. Magic, language and the feminine are
her chief themes. Her recent books are HERE AT THE DOOR
(1978), JOURNAL OF A HERMIT (1979), THE BARD OWL (1980)
and APEX OF THE EARTH'S WAY (1984).

ISHMAEL REED was born in Chattanooga, Tennessee in 1938. He
is a man of letters in the grand tradition: poet, novelist, editor,
anthologist, polemicist, professor. Co-founder of THE EAST VIL-
LAGE OTHER, one of the chief underground newspapers of the
60s, he has since edited many literary collections. His political
and poetic vision of America is best described by the name of the
BEFORE COLUMBUS FOUNDATION, a literary and philosophi-
cal society Reed chairs. His own publishing company, I. REED
BOOKS, publishes Y'BIRD, a magazine of Third World writing.
His novels include YELLOW BACK RADIO BROKE-DOWN
(1969), MUMBO JUMBO (1972), and THE LAST DAYS OF LOUI-
SIANA RED (1974). Among his poetry books are CONJURE: SE-
LECTED POEMS 1963–1970 (1972), CHATTANOOGA (1973),
and SECRETARY TO THE SPIRITS (1977).

ALBERTO RIOS was born in 1952 in Nogales, Arizona. He
teaches at Arizona State University. His books are WHISPERING
TO FOOL THE WIND (1982, winner of the Walt Whitman
Award), THE IGUANA KILLER (1984) and FIVE INDISCRE-
TIONS (1985).

KIT ROBINSON was born in Evanston, Illinois in 1949, and now lives and works in Berkeley, California. He is active in the "language" group, whose chief anthology, IN THE AMERICAN TREE, takes its title from one of his poems. He has worked with California Poets in Schools, Tenderloin Writers' Workshop, Poets Theater, and KPFA Radio. His books are ICE CUBES (1987), DAY OFF (1985), WINDOWS (1985), RIDDLE ROAD (1982), TRIBUTE TO NERVOUS (1980), DOWN AND BACK (1978), THE DOLCH STANZAS (1976), CHINATOWN OF CHEYENNE (1974) and INDIVIDUALS (with Lyn Hejinian) (1987).

STEPHEN RODEFER was born in 1940 in Bellaire, Ohio. He now lives in San Francisco. His translations of Francois Villon's poetry are, like Paul Blackburn's translations of Provencal poets, classic recreations in the American idiom. His own poetry also points the way to a bridging of differences between various modalities of contemporary poetries, from the freedom of Surrealist invention to the discourse of "language" writing. His books of poetry include THE KNIFE (1965), ONE OR TWO LOVE POEMS FROM THE WHITE WORLD (1976), THE BELL CLERK'S TEARS KEEP FLOWING (1978), PLANE DEBRIS (1981) and FOUR LECTURES (1982).

BOB ROSENTHAL was born in Chicago in 1950. He is one of the founders of the Yellow Press, Chicago's foremost poetry publisher. He lives with his wife Rochelle Kraut in New York City, where he is involved in dramatic productions, and edits Frontward Books. He wrote RUDE AWAKENINGS (1982).

JEROME SALA was born in 1951 in Chicago where he grew up. He is an electrifying performer of his own work, and was the source (with Elaine Equi and others) of Chicago's brief vogue for poetry performance in the late 70s. His books are SPAZ ATTACK (1980), and I AM NOT A JUVENILE DELINQUENT (1985).

ED SANDERS is a poet, rocker, inventor, journalist, and environmental activist. Born in St. Louis in 1939, now a resident of Woodstock, New York, Sanders is the lead singer and founder of The Fugs, a visionary poetry-rock group, whose latest album is NO MORE SLAVERY (1986). In the 1960s Sanders owned and operated

The Peace Eye Bookstore, a focal meeting point for politico-mystical outsiders and the publishing headquarters of "Fuck You: A Magazine of the Arts," one of the most influential journals of the time. In the late 1960s he followed and covered the Charles Manson case and trial and wrote THE FAMILY (1969). He writes long poems in which his satirical genius and his penchant for inventing neologisms have free rein. Notable among these is SAPPHO ON EAST SEVENTH STREET (1985). His most recent book is HYMN TO MAPLE SYRUP AND OTHER POEMS (1986), and COFFEE HOUSE PRESS is bringing out his collected poems in 1987.

CHRISTY SHEFFIELD SANFORD was born in Atlanta, Georgia and now lives in Gainesville, Florida in a "pink Spanish-Mediterranean house." She collaborates with jazz musicians on poetry performance and has strong affinities with the San Francisco erotic feminists and the Los Angeles new wave poets.

LESLIE SCALAPINO was born in 1948 and lives in Berkeley, California. Her intensely erotic poetry with its hypnotic repetitions has fascinated many readers. Her books are THE WOMAN WHO COULD READ THE MINDS OF DOGS (1976), INSTEAD OF AN ANIMAL (1978), THIS EATING AND WALKING ALL THE TIME IS ASSOCIATED ALL RIGHT (1979), CONSIDERING HOW EXAGGERATED MUSIC IS (1983) and THAT THEY WERE AT THE BEACH (1985).

SIMON SCHUCHAT was born in 1954 in Washington, D.C. He has lived in Chicago, New York, Shanghai, New Haven, Cambridge and Guangzhou (Canton). He is a scholar and a diplomat, presently awaiting appointment as a vice consul to Tokyo. He has written on 13th Century Chinese poetry, which has influenced his work, but he remains essentially a New York School poet whose early work was influenced by Ted Berrigan. His books are SVELTE (1972), BLUE SKIES (1974), and LIGHT AND SHADOW (1978).

DAVID SHAPIRO was born in 1947, and lives in New York City. He was a professional violinist, and is an art critic as well as a poet. His books include A MAN HOLDING AN ACOUSTIC PANEL (1971), LATENESS (1977) and TO AN IDEA (1983).

JAMES SHERRY was born in 1946 and is the publisher of ROOF BOOKS, one of the influential publishers of the "language" group. He is also the founder the Segue Company, distributor of avantgarde literature. He lives in New York City.

JACK SKELLEY was born in 1956 in Los Angeles where he lives. He is a poet, song writer and guitar player. Was editor of BARNEY: THE MODERN STONE AGE MAGAZINE (1981–84), an important publication for the Los Angeles new wave poets of the early eighties. His books are MONSTERS (1982) and FEAR OF KATHY ACKER (1984). He has recorded an album titled BEYOND BARBEQUE with Lawndale, a rock group (1986).

MICHAEL STEPHENS was born in Washington, D.C., in 1946, and grew up in Brooklyn and Long Island. He now lives in New York City and teaches at Columbia University. He is a poet, novelist, playwright, and essayist. Among his many books are THE DRAMATURGY OF STYLE, 1986 (essays), SEASON AT COOLE, 1985 (novel), TRANSLATIONS, 1984 (poetry), CIRCLES END, 1982 (poetry), STILL LIFE, 1978 (stories), TANGUN LEGEND, 1978 (poetry), and PARAGRAPHS, 1974 (stories).

LORENZO THOMAS was born in 1944 and teaches at the University of Houston, where he lives. One of the most influential black poets of the 70s, his work has a quiet visionary intelligence and great lyrical force. His books are CHANCES ARE FEW (1979) and THE BATHERS (1981).

DAVID TRINIDAD was born in 1953 in Los Angeles where he lives. He is part of the Beyond Baroque group, which includes, among many others, Dennis Cooper, Amy Gerstler and Jack Skelley. Strongly influenced by pop culture and new wave, these poets infused the current American poetry scene with a new romantic sense. Trinidad's latest books are LIVING DOLL (1986) and NOVEMBER (1987).

PAUL VIOLI was born in 1944 in New York. He is a splendid urban Surrealist in the manner made famous by Frank O'Hara and Kenneth Koch. He teaches occasionally at the St. Marks Poetry

Project and at New York University. His latest books are SPLURGE (1981), AMERICAN EXPRESS (1982) and LIKEWISE (1988).

CHUCK WACHTEL was born in 1950 and lives in New York City. He is a novelist, JOE THE ENGINEER (1983), and a fine poet in the New York realist manner pioneered by Paul Blackburn and Joel Oppenheimer. Among his poetry books are SONGS TO HELP BRING ABOUT THE REDISTRIBUTION OF AMERICA'S GREAT FORTUNES (1979), THE NEWS (1982) and THE COR-IOLIS EFFECT (1985).

ANNE WALDMAN was born in New York in 1945. She is well known both in the U.S. and in Europe. Justly famous for her performances, she has recorded her work in English and French. She was editor of "The World" magazine in the late sixties and early seventies, and Director of the St. Marks Poetry Project in New York City during that time. She is co-founder (with Allen Ginsberg) of the Jack Kerouac School of Disembodied Poetics at the Naropa Institute in Boulder, Colorado, where she lives. She has edited a number of anthologies, and is the author of many poetry books including FAST SPEAKING WOMAN (1975 & 1978), SHAMAN (1978), CABIN (1981 & 1984), FIRST BABY PO-EMS (1982 & 1983), MAKEUP ON EMPTY SPACE (1984), IN-VENTION (1985) and SKIN MEAT BONES (1985).

ROSMARIE WALDROP was born in 1935 in Germany. She lives in Providence, Rhode Island where she runs Burning Deck Press with Keith Waldrop. Her latest books of poetry are STREETS ENOUGH TO WELCOME SNOW (1986) and DIFFERENCES FOR FOUR HANDS (1984). She has written a novel, THE HANKY OF PIPPIN'S DAUGHTER (1987). An experimental writer of note, her books include criticism, AGAINST LAN-GUAGE? (1971), and translations of Paul Celan and Edmond Jabes.

LEWIS WARSH was born in New York City in 1944. He is a central figure, both as poet and publisher (United Artists Books) of the New York School, and is the author of two novels, AGNES

& SALLY (1984) and A FREE MAN (1987); two volumes of autobiographical writing, PART OF MY HISTORY (1972) and THE MAHARAJAH'S SON (1977), and numerous books of poems including DREAMING AS ONE (1971), BLUE HEAVEN (1978), and INFORMATION FROM THE SURFACE OF VENUS (1987).

MARJORIE WELISH was born in New York City in 1944. She is an art critic whose work appears in ARTFORUM. Her major collection to date is HANDWRITTEN (1977).

TERENCE WINCH was born in 1945 in New York City. He now lives in Washington, D.C. where he plays in a traditional Irish band, Celtic Thunder. He won the Before Columbus Foundation's American Book Award in 1986 for IRISH MUSICIANS/AMERICAN FRIENDS, published that year. He has also written LUNCHEONETTE JEALOUSY (1975), NUNS (1976), THE ATTACHMENT SONNETS (1978), and TOTAL STRANGERS (1982).

JEFF WRIGHT was born in 1951 in West Virginia. He lives in New York City where he edits COVER: THE ARTS, a weekly newspaper. He is a performer, collagist, graffitist, art critic, and impresario of the "New Romanticism." His latest book is ALL IN ALL (1986).

JOHN YAU was born in 1950 in Lynn, Massachusetts. He is an art critic as well as a poet, a frequent contributor to Artforum, and ART NEWS. His most recent book, CORPSE & MIRROR, was John Ashbery's Choice for the National Poetry Series (1983). His latest work is CENOTAPH (with Archie Rand, 1987).

GEOFFREY YOUNG was born in Los Angeles in 1944. Since 1982 he has lived in Great Barrington, Massachusetts, where he edits The Figures, a press he founded in California. The Figures is one of the principal publishers of "language" writing. His own books include ELEGIES (1985) and ROCKS AND DEALS (1987).

CYN. ZARCO was born in Manila, Philippines in 1950. She is a poet and journalist, and a member of the circle affiliated with

Ishmael Reed in California, that includes many Third World and Black poets. Her book CIR'CUM.NAV'I.GA'TION won the Before Columbus Foundation's American Book Award in 1986.

BILL ZAVATSKY was born in 1943 in Bridgeport, Connecticut. He lives in New York City where he edits Sun Books, and SUN, a magazine of avantgard poetry and translations. He translated THE POEMS OF A.O. BARNABOOTH by Valery Larbaud from the French (with Ron Padgett), and edited THE WHOLE WORD CATALOGUE, an important resource book for teaching poetry to children. He is an expansive American Surrealist, combining some of Blaise Cendrars' narrative drive with Majakovsky's grand gesturing. His books include THEORIES, OF RAIN (1975), and POEMS FOR STEVE ROYAL (1984).